TOXIC SUBSTANCES CONTROLS Guide

Second Edition

TOXIC SUBSTANCES CONTROLS
Guide

Federal Regulation of Chemicals
in the Environment

Second Edition

———◆———

Mary Devine Worobec
Cheryl Hogue

The Bureau of National Affairs, Inc., Washington, D.C.

Library of Congress Cataloging-in-Publication Data

Worobec, Mary Devine.
   Toxic substances controls guide : federal regulation of chemicals
in the environment / Mary Devine Worobec, Cheryl Hogue.—2nd ed.
   p.   cm
   ISBN 0-87179-752-6 (softcover)
   1. Chemicals—Law and legislation—United States.   2. Hazardous
substances—Law and legislation—United States.   3. Hazardous
wastes—Law and legislation—United States.   4. Environmental law—
United States.   I. Hogue, Cheryl.   II. Title.
KF3958.W67   1992
344.73'0424—dc20   92-17102
[347.304424]   CIP

Published by BNA Books
1250 23rd St., NW, Washington, D.C. 20037

Printed in the United States of America
International Standard Book Number: 0-87179-752-6

This book is a newly revised edition of the *Toxic Substances Controls Guide*, first written as a *Primer* by Mary Devine Worobec in 1984 and updated in 1986. That publication was revised and retitled as a *Guide* to toxic substances controls in 1989.

The *Guide* recounts the extension of federal authority to regulate chemicals in the environment. To a chemist, engineer, or company administrator, the subject is not one that usually is covered in academic training, which, naturally enough, concentrates on the technical or business aspects of using chemicals.

However, anyone in chemical management should be aware of the legislation that has been put on the books since the National Environmental Policy Act set up the Environmental Protection Agency in 1970. Different laws were enacted with different purposes in mind—to protect the environment, to ensure workplace health and safety, or to monitor consumer products. Succeeding laws were intended to plug regulatory loopholes, and by the time the Toxic Substances Control Act was passed in 1976, regulation of chemical safety was recognized as a public health measure. Regulation of chemicals is authorized if they present any long-term threat to public health or the environment, regardless of their origin, use, or disposal.

This book explains the provisions of major laws affecting the chemical lifecycle and covers statutes dealing with chemicals in the environment, in the workplace, and during their transport and disposal. Its goal is to show the interrelationships between these laws.

The Bureau of National Affairs, Inc. (BNA) is in a particularly good position to assess these legislative developments. BNA publishes a number of news and information services covering administrative and regulatory activity carried out by the Environmental Protection Agency, the Occupational Safety and Health Administration, the Department of Transportation, and the Consumer Product Safety Commission.

Mary Devine Worobec, author of the original *Primer* and its first revision, followed chemical regulatory developments closely, first as managing editor of BNA's *Chemical Regulation Reporter* and then as managing editor of *Occupational Safety & Health Reporter*. The 1989 revision as a *Guide* was edited by Dr. Girard Ordway, senior scientific editor of BNA's Environment and Safety Services, and also former managing editor of *Chemical Regulation Reporter*.

The lead editor for this current revision was Cheryl Hogue, senior editor of Environment and Safety Services. Part I was prepared by Janey Cohen, an editor on *Occupational Safety & Health Reporter*; Parts II and III by Susan Bruninga, an editor on BNA's *Daily Environment Report*; and Parts IV and V by Amy Porter, an editor on *Chemical Regulation Reporter*.

The body of chemical regulation and environmental legislation continues to grow. By the time the 1989 edition of this book was issued, Congress had made extensive amendments to the Clean Water Act, requiring states to identify toxic "hot spots" of water not expected to meet water quality standards. The Federal Insecticide, Fungicide, and Rodenticide Act has been amended in an effort to clear the backlog of pending reregistrations. Important amendments to the Comprehensive Environmental Response, Compensation, and Liability Act were made in the Superfund Amendments and Reauthorization Act of 1986, and a self-contained title of that act—the Emergency Planning and Community Right-to-Know Act of 1986—required advance planning and access to information on chemicals used and produced, in case of plant disasters.

Material in this latest edition is current through September 1992, and includes information on the sweeping Clean Air Act amendments of 1990; the Hazardous Materials Transportation Uniform Safety Act of 1990, which amends and reauthorizes the Hazardous Materials Transportation Act; and the pending reauthorization of the Resource Conservation and Recovery Act.

Patricia R. Westlein
Associate Editor
Environment and Safety Services

CONTENTS

Introduction

Part I   Chemical Use and Assessment Laws

Toxic Substances Control Act (TSCA)

Federal Insecticide, Fungicide, and Rodenticide Act (FIFRA)

Federal Food, Drug, and Cosmetic Act (FFDCA)

Occupational Safety and Health Act (OSH Act)

Part II   Chemical By-Product Laws

Clean Air Act (CAA)

Contents

Clean Water Act (CWA)

Safe Drinking Water Act (SDWA)

Part III   Chemical Waste and Disposal Laws

Resource Conservation and Recovery Act (RCRA)

Comprehensive Environmental Response, Compensation, and Liability Act (CERCLA)

Part IV   Chemical Transport Laws

Hazardous Materials Transportation Act (HMTA)

Part V   Other Laws Affecting Chemicals

Consumer Product Safety Act (CPSA)

Federal Hazardous Substances Act (FHSA)

Flammable Fabrics Act (FFA)

Poison Prevention Packaging Act (PPPA)

Ports and Waterways Safety Act (PWSA)

Natural Gas Pipeline Safety Act (NGPSA) and Hazardous Liquid Pipeline Safety Act (HLPSA)

THE ENVIRONMENTAL DECADE

Efforts to regulate chemicals in the United States started more than a century ago. Those first efforts were aimed at protecting human health, at removing narcotics and poisons from patent medicines, and at avoiding explosions during transportation.

Although there were some early attempts at federal protection of the environment, it was not until the 1970s that cleaning up the air, water, and land became a national priority. Much of the regulatory activity in the initial years of that decade was of a general nature, aimed at controlling the volume of waste products that U.S. industry emptied into the air, waterways, landfills, and open dumps. In the years since, numerous refinements to the early environmental laws have evolved into statutes that regulate a myriad of chemicals.

In 1970 alone, Congress revised the Clean Air Act to create national standards for air quality, passed the Occupational Safety and Health Act to protect workers from health hazards, and enacted the Resource Recovery Act to encourage refuse recycling and better waste management. Additional legislation followed:

- In 1972, Congress tackled water pollution with passage of the Federal Water Pollution Control Act, with its goal that all waters in the U.S. be made safe for swimming by 1983.
- In 1974, Congress attacked groundwater pollution with passage of the Safe Drinking Water Act.
- In 1972, regulation of pesticides under the Federal Insecticide, Fungicide, and Rodenticide Act was strengthened.
- In 1976, the Resource Conservation and Recovery Act was enacted to encourage recycling and hazardous waste control.
- In 1976, Congress enacted the Toxic Substances Control Act to authorize evaluation and regulation of both new and exist-

1

ing chemicals that could not be regulated under other environmental laws.

- In 1977, and again in 1990, the Clean Air Act was changed to further expand control of toxic substances and other pollutants in the air, including those that damage the earth's protective ozone layer.
- In 1980, the superfund law—the Comprehensive Environmental Response, Compensation, and Liability Act—was passed to clean up abandoned and uncontrolled hazardous waste sites and repair other damage to the environment.
- In 1988, the Federal Insecticide, Fungicide, and Rodenticide Act was amended to speed up the review and reregistration process for older pesticides.
- In 1990, Congress passed the Hazardous Materials Uniform Safety Act, which adopted new safety standards for the movement of chemicals and other hazardous goods.

These new laws, along with others aimed at protecting or regulating land use, parks, ocean dumping, beaches, wetlands, marine animals, noise, and energy production, created a new arena in which U.S. industry would have to operate. Not only the chemical, steel, auto, and other heavy industries were affected; virtually every other facet of the U.S. economy, from farming and mining to fishing and building construction, was affected as well.

Although many of these laws were not envisioned as chemical control laws when initially enacted, implementation of them over the years has become very chemically oriented. Much of this is because experience has shown that synthetic or artificially concentrated substances are more apt to damage health and the environment.

The Regulatory Framework

In practice, many of the laws enacted to protect health and the environment are chemical control laws, at least in part. These laws break down roughly into four broad areas: chemical use and assessment laws, statutes affecting chemicals as by-products of processes, laws involving cleanup and intentional disposal of chemicals, and laws on transporting chemicals and hazardous substances. Each of these categories contains a number of primary statutes that directly regulate how chemicals must be handled.

In the following chapters, these categories will be examined in the order in which they affect chemical substances—from discovery through use, cleanup, and ultimate disposal, and during transport between the various stages. None of the categories, however, can be examined without looking either forward to or backward from other sections of the book. The web of chemical control laws creates an interweaving of complex requirements that touch on almost everything manufactured or imported for use in the United States.

Practical Aspects of Regulation

Categorizing chemical control laws might give the impression that each is a specific entity, with no effect on those operating outside its domain. As any member of the regulated community knows, this is not true.

A law intended to protect the air may mean that entire production processes must be changed. And in doing so, a producer may discover the changes that now protect the air could later be found to pollute water.

Purchasers of products may find that what is available to them is changed because of an environmental or health requirement imposed on some far-removed or unknown firm. For example, regulations establishing procedures concerning safe usage of a substance, issued after evaluation of the substance as part of procedures mandated under a given law, may end up costing a coffee or soft-drink manufacturer millions of dollars, even though the manufacturer's use of the substance is limited. Examples of substances for which this has been the case include chemicals used to decaffeinate coffee, lubricate hydraulic equipment, or package a finished product.

Similarly, a cosmetic manufacturer may be forced to reformulate its products when the government bans a major pesticide that is coincidentally used to retard bacterial growth in cosmetics. Or a small business may be forced to file for bankruptcy when a raw material used to make its product is banned.

In other instances, situations such as the following may occur:

- A firm may suffer financially when it must install expensive equipment to control the emission of wastes from a minor but necessary process in its operation.
- Waste disposed of in a landfill years ago may later leak from the site. By law, all firms that disposed of hazardous wastes in the site can be held liable for expensive cleanup operations.
- A truck carrying a hazardous substance may be involved in an accident, leaving both the carrier and the shipper liable for penalties and subject to requirements under several laws.
- A firm may purchase a chemical only to discover later that worker exposure may be difficult to control.

Chemical control thus is a balancing act that involves many federal laws and many federal, state, and, often, local government agencies. While the safety of a new substance will be assessed by one government agency, use of the new substance may fall under the jurisdiction of several others, simply because a single chemical usually has a number of uses. The tangle grows as uses of the substance multiply, when it has to be shipped, and when it must be disposed of or cleaned up.

For the regulated community this means looking at several layers of legislation and regulation to get a true picture of the breadth of the regulatory framework covering its operations.

Old Versus New Chemicals

About 70,000 chemicals are known to be in use in the United States. Each year another 1,000 industrial chemicals, 200 pesticides, 80 food additives, and 200 drugs are developed as totally new chemical entities.

Under the web of U.S. laws affecting chemicals, each new substance will be examined before use or manufacture is approved to make sure it meets various health and safety criteria. Does it kill fish, harm crops, make workers or consumers ill, cause cancer or birth defects, destroy the stratospheric ozone layer, or last so long that it might cause damage to the environment in later years?

If the answer is yes to any of these questions, production of the substance may be barred. More likely, however, production will begin but with controls imposed under various laws to minimize adverse impacts associated with the new chemical.

There is a different scenario for existing chemicals, many of which have been in use for scores of years. In many cases, these substances were marketed with no evaluation of their safety. Some have been found to be environmental and health nightmares, but only after the damage has been done. Two prime examples are asbestos, which is an excellent insulator but causes profound respiratory damage and cancer years after exposure, and polychlorinated biphenyls, which after years of use in virtually every piece of heavy electrical equipment is putrefying major bodies of water and is suspected of having a number of serious negative effects on human health.

As more of these older chemicals are evaluated, and as the technology is developed to associate their use with later effects, controls imposed on them are likely to parallel those being imposed on some new substances.

Even now, virtually every chemical and substance used in the United States is subject to some type of control. During manufacture, workers who are exposed must be monitored. During use, by-products are created that must be treated in specified ways, and when use of a substance is completed, the wastes that remain must be disposed of in approved ways. And at each juncture, the chemical must be transported to the site of the next stage in the proper manner. This is the cycle of what one U.S. government official called "cradle-to-grave" regulation of chemicals.

Specific Laws Discussed

The U.S. government assesses the safety of chemicals under three basic laws: the Toxic Substances Control Act; the Federal Insecticide, Fungicide, and Rodenticide Act; and the Food, Drug, and Cosmetic Act. In addition, once a chemical is manufactured, the Occupational Safety and Health Act may be used to regulate worker exposure to the substance.

During each phase of use, by-products and wastes are created. The Clean Air Act regulates chemical by-products emitted into the air. The Clean Water Act and the Safe Drinking Water Act are intended to perform the same function for by-products that enter water.

The Resource Conservation and Recovery Act regulates the intentional disposal on land of wastes listed as hazardous, estimated by the federal government to be in excess of 240 million tons per year. Cleanup of wastes disposed of in the past is conducted under the Comprehensive Environmental Response, Compensation, and Liability Act.

All of these products of an industrial society must be moved from one place to another. With most of the chemicals and wastes considered hazardous, still another law, the Hazardous Materials Transportation Act, regulates transport of the four billion tons of hazardous materials that travel in more than one million vehicles in the United States each year.

These 10 laws make up the basic framework of U.S. regulatory efforts aimed at controlling chemicals. The history, intent, and requirements of each are explained in the chapters that follow. In addition, 7 other federal laws with chemical control provisions are described in brief. Together these 17 laws make up the bulk of chemical regulation in the United States.

In the chapters following, specific regulatory citations to the Code of Federal Regulations (CFR) are provided as the laws are discussed, where this could be done with brevity. The CFR citations for the regulations issued under a given law are always given on the applicable *At a Glance* page.

Many of the regulations promulgated under these laws are published and kept up-to-date in BNA reference and notification services. The applicable *At a Glance* page notes which BNA service contains the regulations and the text of the law, plus those services that report developments affecting regulations under the statute. A BNA service page number for the law is provided. No page number is given for the text of the regulations because these page numbers change frequently. Readers should consult the index of the BNA service listed on the applicable *At a Glance* page for the page number at which a specific regulation appears.

Citations to the location of the laws in the U.S. Code (USC) also are given on all *At a Glance* pages.

Citations to legal decisions mentioned in the various chapters are given both for the official court reporter (when available) and for the applicable BNA legal reporting service, i.e., Environment Reporter Cases (ER Cases) or Occupational Safety and Health

Cases (OSH Cases). Where legal decisions are published as a distinct part of a BNA service, this fact is noted on *At a Glance* pages.

Public Law numbers and enactment and amendment dates provided on *At a Glance* pages are those for the most recent substantive general change in the law. While in some cases earlier versions of the law carried the same name, it is standard practice to refer to the most recent major amendments by the name of the initial law. This procedure eliminates any need to list the dozens of laws and amendments that otherwise would have to be enumerated. Where earlier versions of a law carried a different name, or where a law has become known under a recognized but different name, this fact is mentioned in the discussion of the laws.

This second edition of *Toxic Substances Controls Guide* contains a new feature—a "Latest Developments" section for nearly every law. This new section summarizes the major changes affecting each statute since the 1989 edition of the *Guide*.

Of particular note regarding BNA's coverage of federal regulation of chemicals in the environment is the *Index to Chemical Regulation,* published as part of the *Chemical Regulation Reporter* service. The index lists every chemical regulated by the federal government and provides the Code of Federal Regulations (CFR) or *Federal Register* (FR) citation and BNA parallel citation for the full text of the rules. The index is updated monthly to include new proposed and final regulations involving chemicals. An index to chemicals by Chemical Abstracts Service Registry Number also is included.

Part I

Chemical Use and Assessment Laws

Toxic Substances Control Act
(TSCA)

Public Law Number: Pub. L. No. 94-469

U.S. Code citation: 15 USC 2601 *et seq.*

Enacted: September 28, 1976; effective date, January 1, 1977
   Amended: 1981, 1983, 1984 (reauthorization only), 1986, 1988 (see
      note), 1990

Regulations at: 40 CFR 700–799

Federal agency with jurisdiction: Environmental Protection Agency
   (EPA)

Congressional committees/subcommittees with jurisdiction:
   House of Representatives: Commerce, Transportation, and Tourism
      Subcommittee of the Energy and Commerce Committee
   Senate: Toxic Substances and Environmental Oversight Subcommit-
      tee of the Environment and Public Works Committee

BNA reporting services: *Chemical Regulation Reporter, Daily Environment
   Report, Toxics Law Reporter*
   Text of law appears in *Chemical Regulation Reporter* Reference File at
      91:0101 *et seq.*
   Text of regulations appears in *Chemical Regulation Reporter* Reference
      File

What TSCA regulates and why: The act provides the regulatory vehicle
   for controlling exposure and use of raw industrial chemicals that fall
   outside the jurisdiction of other environmental laws. Where other
   environmental laws control chemicals during use and disposal,
   TSCA was passed to assure that chemicals would be evaluated before

11

use to make sure they pose no unnecessary risk to health or the environment.

Under TSCA, chemical manufacture, use, import, or disposal may be banned, controlled, or restricted.

The act provides for listing all chemicals that must be evaluated before manufacture or use in the United States. Existing chemicals are being ranked as to their hazard potential and are subjected to toxicity testing when necessary to assure that their benefits outweigh their risks.

Note: The provisions of TSCA have remained unchanged. However, the Asbestos Hazard Emergency Response Act of 1986 (Pub. L. No. 99-519) was added as Title II of TSCA; the act requires asbestos inspections and control systems for school systems.

TSCA was also amended in 1988 (Pub. L. No. 100-551) to add a radon abatement program that authorizes grants and technical assistance to states for indoor radon control.

Latest developments: In October of 1991, the Fifth Circuit Court of Appeals overturned EPA's ban of asbestos products using the authority of TSCA section 6 (*Corrosion Proof Fittings v. EPA,* 33 ER Cases 1961 (5th Cir. 1991)). The agency had begun work in 1979, the last year of the Carter administration, to ban products made with the known human carcinogen. But EPA did not issue the ban in its final form until July 1989. When the agency finally did issue the rule, an industry group promptly challenged it in U.S. appeals court.

The appellate court ruled that the agency failed to consider less economically burdensome alternatives to a ban. However, the Fifth Circuit also said in a clarification requested by EPA that the agency can continue the ban on new uses of asbestos and asbestos-containing products that were not on the market on July 12, 1989, the day the ban took effect. According to EPA attorneys, the Justice Department refused to take an EPA appeal of the Fifth Circuit decision to the Supreme Court. Some members of Congress expressed concern about the adequacy of TSCA after the Fifth Circuit decision, but by mid-1992 there was no movement in either the Senate or House to change the law.

In the second session of the 102nd Congress, the House was considering a bill (H. 3554) to amend TSCA by adding a new title.

Toxic Substances Control Act—Contd.

The proposed addition, called the Lead Exposure Reduction Act of 1991, would:

- Ban the use of zinc-enriched industrial paints that have an incidental presence of lead that exceeds 0.19 percent. This type of paint is used on bridges and infrastructures.
- Require EPA to initiate a review of possible substitutes for lead chromate pigments. These pigments are used in paints for yellow highway lines and school buses.
- Expand the lead abatement worker training requirements.
- Require lead paint abatement contractors to be licensed by the federal government.
- Mandate creation of an advisory council, composed of labor-management working groups, to oversee EPA's implementation of the licensing and worker training provisions.

COVERAGE OF THE LAW

In 1976 Congress passed the Toxic Substances Control Act (TSCA) to set in motion a system under which all new chemical substances entering the U.S. market would be evaluated for their effects on human health, other living organisms, and the environment.

Public Law Number 94-469, passed by Congress on September 28, 1976, and signed by President Gerald Ford on October 12, also authorized the U.S. Environmental Protection Agency (EPA) to compile a list of existing substances and collect information on their use and on their health and environmental effects. This information then could be used to control or ban substances that caused harm to health or to the environment but that slipped through loopholes in other laws.

The intent of the law was to complete the chain of U.S. environmental laws that had been passed piecemeal in the previous six years. For this reason, TSCA is in many ways a "cleanup" statute. Unlike most other environmental protection laws passed during the 1970s, it regulates raw materials rather than finished products or process waste.

TSCA thus acts to fill the void left by other statutes and regulations. For example, food, drug, and pesticide chemicals are not covered by TSCA because their evaluation is authorized under other laws. Also exempted are nuclear materials, tobacco, firearms, and ammunition. Most chemical substances, however, come under the purview of the act in one way or another.

For example, a chemical substance may be used in dozens of different industrial processes, in food products, in home cleaning products, and in clothing as a dye component. Even though no one of these uses creates a problem, the combined effect of these many uses may cause health or environmental damage. Under TSCA, EPA can require that the effects of an existing chemical on health and/or the environment be evaluated through a series of toxicity tests. After reviewing the test results, the agency may decide that the substance's risks outweigh its benefits and may take action to ban or control manufacture of the raw chemical.

But even if such action is not taken, the testing ordered by the agency will be sent to government bodies that protect workers, regulate food, and evaluate the safety of consumer products, to use the example above. With scientific evidence in hand, these agencies may decide to ban the substance's use in some or all products, or may decide that the substance conveys sufficient benefits to outweigh any risks it poses. What happens under TSCA, therefore, is of interest to virtually all manufacturing firms, even those making products that are exempt from its direct reach.

DEVELOPMENT OF THE LAW

In signing TSCA, President Ford said:

> The bill closes the gap in our current array of laws to protect the health of our people and the environment. The Clean Air Act and the Water Pollution Control Act protect the air and water from toxic contaminants. The Food and Drug Act [the Food, Drug, and Cosmetic Act] and the Safe Drinking Water Act are used to protect the food we eat and the water we drink against hazardous contaminants. Other provisions of existing laws protect the health and the environment against other polluting contaminants such as pesticides and radiation. However, none of the existing statutes provide comprehensive protection.

TSCA was drafted to provide this comprehensive protection of health and the environment at a time when the environmental movement of the 1970s had exposed several serious chemical hazards that could not be attacked under existing laws. In each case, the substance in question performed its job well and was widely used by U.S. industry. Unanticipated side effects, when discovered, however, could not be remedied under any existing regulatory framework. The problems encountered with two widely used chemicals, polychlorinated biphenyls (PCBs) and chlorofluorocarbons (CFCs), were examples of this.

Lack of a Regulatory Framework

PCBs

Before the passage of TSCA, PCBs, used as heat transfer fluids in millions of electrical transformers and capacitors, and in hydraulic equipment, could not be regulated in the environment under existing laws until and unless they began to show up in drinking water. But even though heavy contamination of river and lake sediment was occurring, the highly stable PCB molecules tended to contaminate sediment rather than drinking water. Thus, even as this environmental pollution increased, there was no way under existing law to ban manufacture of PCBs or to control their use, despite an increasing list of adverse health effects associated with them. Exposure of workers to PCBs in the workplace could be controlled, the concentration of PCBs in drinking water could be limited, and emission of PCBs in air could be controlled. But exposure of the general public to the health hazards of PCBs, primarily a skin disease called chloracne and possibly increased risk of developing cancer through skin contact or eating contaminated food and fish, could not be effectively prevented. With this in mind, Congress specifically included a ban on the manufacture of PCBs in TSCA.

CFCs

Used as spray-can propellants and as refrigerants, CFCs are so stable that when released into the environment they do not react with anything until they drift up to the stratosphere 10 to 20 years after use. There they are decomposed by solar ultraviolet radiation. The free chlorine then breaks up ozone in the stratosphere, a potentially serious problem. Ozone filters the ultraviolet radiation reaching the earth; an increase in this radiation because of a reduction in the amount of ozone would affect the earth's climate and could cause an increase in skin cancer. Even though this process apparently posed some threat to health and the environment, no effective way existed to regulate CFC emissions. CFCs are not air pollutants in the usual sense and thus were not covered by the Clean Air Act. They are not poisonous and posed no risk to workers. Even though CFCs could be regulated in consumer products, no law regulated their industrial use. Passage of TSCA provided such a law, and use of CFC propellants was banned.

The controversy over lack of a regulatory framework to control such substances as PCBs and CFCs became the impetus for passage of TSCA. The controversy led to a law that not only would control substances that could not effectively be controlled by other laws, but also would control these substances before they were dispersed into the environment.

Need to Evaluate Risk

The word *toxics* as used in TSCA does not refer to poisons or any specific class of chemical, no matter how dangerous substances may be in certain situations. Instead, it is the evaluation of such situations that determines whether a substance falls under the jurisdiction of TSCA. The act allows manufacture of a dangerous substance if its conditions of use and manufacture do not pose an unreasonable risk to health or the environment. The criterion of unreasonable risk allows test data, exposure estimates, and use patterns to be taken into account when EPA decides whether to regulate a substance under the act. In addition, the act does not establish a time limit for damage or set other conditions on the definition of unreasonable risk. A chemical that is acutely and immediately toxic may be regulated under the act, as may a substance that causes chronic health or environmental damage only after decades of use. Likewise, a substance that would be highly toxic in the environment may escape regulation under the act if the substance is used in a closed system and thus does not enter the environment. Similarly, manufacture of even a small quantity of a highly toxic substance may be banned if the substance is likely to harm workers, consumers, or rivers, forests, or wildlife under its planned or current uses. It was with all of these variables in mind that legislators in 1971 sat down to draft a federal toxics law. Their task was not completed until 1976.

PROVISIONS OF THE LAW

As passed by Congress, TSCA has four major purposes:

- To screen new chemicals to see if they pose a risk (section 5)
- To require testing of chemicals identified as possible risks (section 4)
- To gather information on existing chemicals (section 8)
- To control chemicals proven to pose a risk (section 6)

The act is a risk/benefit-balancing statute. While it gives EPA broad authority to regulate chemicals in U.S. commerce in a variety of ways, it also requires the agency to make certain risk findings before doing so. The agency may decide that a substance poses no unreasonable risk, that a substance should not be controlled because its benefits outweigh its risks, or that risks posed by a substance are too great to be acceptable. The act requires EPA in making such decisions to consider the benefits of a substance to society's economic and social well-being, the risks posed by alternative substances, and possible health or economic problems that could result from regulation of a substance.

The act also gives the agency may avenues for controlling a chemical, including hazard warning labels; bans on manufacture, use, or import; requirements for specific controls during use or manufacture; or court action to protect the public health or the environment.

A major thrust of the act is to make industry responsible for the chemicals it manufactures and distributes. To this end, EPA may require industry to test existing chemicals that are suspect and to submit unpublished health and safety test results. Any time a company becomes aware that a chemical poses a substantial risk, the firm must notify EPA of the situation within 15 days.

Section 5: New Chemical Screening (PMN)

In looking at TSCA in any detail, it makes sense to start with the premanufacture notification (PMN) program under which EPA assesses the safety of new chemicals before manufacture (40 CFR 720–723). The agency receives nearly 2,000 such new chemical notifications each year from manufacturers wishing to make or import a chemical new to the U.S. market. Most are approved easily under the 90-day review timetable provided for in the law.

Coverage and Exemptions

With few exceptions, all new chemicals must undergo PMN review before manufacture. Only existing chemicals, chemicals used solely for research and development, and chemicals regulated under other laws, such as pesticides and drugs, are exempt from this review.

The act also allows the agency to take specific action to exempt from PMN requirements new chemicals that it determines do not present an unreasonable risk. Using this criterion, the agency in June 1982 issued rules to exempt chemicals used in certain instant photographic film products from premanufacture review.

A broader exemption from PMN requirements issued in April 1985 creates a scaled-down version of premanufacture review for new chemicals made or imported in volumes of less than 1,000 kilograms per year. The provision requires companies to provide certain identification and test data on the chemicals and gives the agency 21 days to review the data. Manufacturers and importers are required to notify EPA before use of the substance or its site of manufacture changes.

All nonexempt substances are considered new chemicals, and thus are subject to PMN requirements. Authorized under section 5 of the act, this program involves notifying EPA at least 90 days before importing or beginning manufacture of a new chemical substance.

Chemical Inventory

Shortly after the act was passed, EPA began to compile an inventory of all existing chemicals and asked manufacturers to submit chemicals for inclusion. Once the initial inventory was completed, all chemicals not listed were considered new chemicals and subject to premanufacture review as of July 1, 1979. The agency since has updated the inventory several times to include existing chemicals that were omitted from the initial inventory and chemicals reported by processors before December 31, 1979.

By law, a partial inventory update is required every four years. During the inventory reporting period, makers and importers of chemicals that are produced at an annual volume of 10,000 pounds or more per plant site and that are listed on the TSCA inventory must notify EPA and provide current production data. The latest update, completed in 1991, listed approximately 70,000 chemicals.

Each new chemical that completes premanufacture review and begins to be manufactured is automatically added to the inventory (40 CFR 710).

Before beginning to make a new chemical, a company must check to see if the substance is already listed on the inventory. If not, it is considered a new chemical under TSCA and a premanufacture notification must be submitted for EPA review.

Content of a PMN

Under the act, the premanufacture notice must include the following:

- The common or trade name of the substance (frequently a generic name devised by the firm as a way of maintaining confidentiality)
- The chemical identity and molecular structure
- Estimated production levels, usually for each of the first three years of manufacture
- Proposed use of the chemical
- Method of disposal
- Estimated levels of exposure in the workplace and the number of workers involved
- A description of by-products, impurities, and other related products
- Available test data on health and environmental effects related to manufacture if the data are within the manufacturer's possession and control
- A description of known or reasonably ascertainable test data

As might be noted from the foregoing, a manufacturer is not required to test the new chemical and does not have to conduct such testing solely so that it can be submitted to EPA with the premanufacture notice.

Approval of the PMN

After reviewing a premanufacture notice from a firm planning to make a new chemical, the agency publishes a notice in the

Federal Register advising that the premanufacture notice has been received and giving the date upon which the 90-day review period ends. During this 90-day period, the agency evaluates the risks posed by the chemical, often by searching chemical literature and by checking on known effects of chemicals with similar composition. If the review indicates there is no cause for concern, the manufacturer is notified and production may begin. At this time the substance will be added to the inventory of existing chemicals.

Problems With the PMN

If the agency has questions about a substance submitted for premanufacture review, it has several avenues open to it, as discussed below.

Negotiation

The agency may extend the review period for 90 more days. In practice, the agency frequently contacts the manufacturer and asks for more information on the chemical. If the information is available, the chemical usually can be evaluated within either the 90-day or 180-day time limits.

In some cases, the agency and the manufacturer agree that more than 180 days will be needed to gather the additional data sought. In such cases, the manufacturer may ask EPA to suspend the review period while the data or information is collected. When the data are available, the review period would begin to run again from the point where it was stopped.

Regulatory Action

The agency also has two authorities to prevent manufacture of a new chemical that may pose a risk to health or the environment. It may seek an order banning manufacture pending receipt of more information on the chemical, or seek a court order banning manufacture until a formal ban is imposed through rulemaking by EPA.

For example, the agency may have enough concern about the new substance to prohibit manufacture until it acquires still more information. In such cases, the agency may decide, at least 45 days before the end of the 180-day review period, to issue an order under section 5(e) of the act to prohibit or limit manufacture until enough information is submitted to allow EPA to make a reasoned judgment, an action the manufacturer may protest to the agency administrator. The agency also has authority to seek a court injunction to bar manufacture or use until sufficient data are received to evaluate the substance's risks.

Rather than issuing orders under section 5(e), however, the agency frequently develops consent agreements with the manufacturer. Under these agreements, the potential manufacturer agrees to restrict the new chemical's production, use, disposal, or exposure. Because these agreements apply only to the original manufacturer, the agency routinely follows up such an action by issuing a *significant new use rule* to extend the restrictions to all subsequent manufacturers or importers.

In addition, the agency may propose to ban manufacture under section 6(a) of the act on the ground that the substance would pose an unreasonable risk. Since such a rule could take several years to complete, the agency may, under section 5(f) of the act, propose an order or seek an injunction to ban manufacture until the rulemaking is completed.

New Chemical Follow-up

The agency also has several options for following new chemicals once they begin to be manufactured and technically become existing chemicals, as illustrated in the following examples:

- In one case, a new chemical submitted for review is approved for production because it poses little threat under proposed conditions of use. If the use were to change, however, EPA would want to be notified so that it could take another look at the substance.
- In another case, the agency may want to keep track of a chemical during use to make sure no harmful effects occur from the use.

Significant New Use Rule

In the first case just mentioned, to monitor the actual conditions of use, the agency can propose a significant new use rule (SNUR) for the new chemical under section 5(a)(2) of TSCA. Under such a rule, production volume, worker exposure, or certain uses of a chemical could be restricted. This type of rule might be used, for example, to prevent use of a new industrial chemical in consumer products or to require workers to wear gloves and other protective equipment (40 CFR 721).

EPA issued a *generic SNUR* rule in 1989 to close a loophole in this regulation. Initially, EPA enforced SNURs by issuing consent orders under section 5(e) of TSCA. However, each order applied only to the company submitting the premanufacture notice. Once the firm began manufacturing the chemical and it was added to the TSCA inventory, any business could make the compound for any use without informing the agency and without observing requirements for controls. With the generic SNUR, EPA can either limit the use of the chemical or extend the restrictions placed on the initial manufacturer to all makers of the substance.

The generic SNUR rule also established a workplace hazard communication program. The program includes listing environmental hazards on labels and material safety data sheets. Since the promulgation of the generic SNUR, EPA has instituted abbreviated procedures for issuing significant new use rules for new chemical substances.

Reporting Rule

In the second case mentioned earlier, the agency also may approve a new chemical but may want to monitor to make sure it causes no ill effects. In such cases, the agency may add it to one of the lists of existing substances on which reporting of data and effects is required, or to a list requiring maintenance of records on exposure, use, or production under the act's reporting and record-keeping provisions.

Section 4: Testing Requirements

A second major authority under TSCA is the ability of EPA to require industry to test chemical substances already on the market or about to be produced.

When Can Testing Be Required?

Under section 4 of the act, testing can be required in either of the following circumstances:

(a) If a chemical may pose an unreasonable risk to health or the environment and there are insufficient test data on the substance to evaluate its effects

(b) If a chemical produced in large volumes could enter the environment in substantial quantities or be in contact with humans in significant amounts and there are insufficient test data on the substance to evaluate its effects

In such cases, the EPA administrator can propose a rule to require the manufacturer of the chemical or mixture to conduct testing that would show whether the substance poses health or environmental hazards. But before proposing such a rule, the agency must show that existing test data on the substance are insufficient to evaluate its risk and that testing is necessary to develop the needed data.

Types of Testing

Under the act, the testing required must be specific with respect to the type of effects being evaluated. It may include evaluation of persistence, environmental fate, or ecological effects. Or EPA may specify testing for various acute or chronic health effects, including the substance's ability to cause cancer, gene mutations, birth defects, or behavioral changes.

The agency must specify the chemical to be tested, the standards to be used in conducting the tests, and the time period for submitting test results to EPA. In addition, the agency must consider relative costs of each of the types of tests that could be used to answer the concerns about the chemical and also whether laboratories and personnel are available to do the testing.

Testing Guidelines

Testing under section 4 must be done using specific testing guidelines developed by the agency. The agency's original plan was to put these testing protocols in the form of regulatory documents developed through formal rulemaking, and in fact several testing standards were proposed in 1979.

In an attempt to increase its flexibility and avoid use of formal rulemaking, however, the agency issued toxic substances testing guidelines in the fall of 1982. Rather than making them part of the Code of Federal Regulations, EPA published a notice saying that the guidelines were available for a fee through the National Technical Information Service in Springfield, Virginia.

In another about-face, in 1985 the agency decided to go back to the strict regulatory approach. EPA then issued the guidelines as rules that must be followed when testing chemicals under TSCA, published the testing guidelines in the *Federal Register*, and made them part of the Code of Federal Regulations (40 CFR 796, 797, 798). Also issued as rules were final Good Laboratory Practice Standards under TSCA (40 CFR 792).

How Chemicals Are Chosen for Testing

Interagency Testing Committee

The primary way chemicals are chosen for testing is through a rather complicated process mandated under section 4 of the act. Under this process, an Interagency Testing Committee (ITC), formed in 1977 and composed of representatives of eight federal agencies, designates substances that in its view require testing for one of the reasons discussed earlier. Once the committee designates a chemical for testing, EPA has one year either to propose a test rule on the substance or to explain why testing of the substance is not needed.

The committee issued its first list of designated chemicals in October 1977 and issues a revised list every six months, in the spring and fall. At no time, however, can the list contain more than 50 chemicals. In other words, if the list of chemicals reaches 50, some designations must be removed before additional substances can be listed, a requirement designed to assure that the committee sets testing priorities rather than creating a catalog of suspect chemicals.

In April 1985, the committee created a new category of chemicals that it recommends for testing "with intent to designate." The new level of recommendation acts as an early warning system, allowing affected parties to comment on the chemicals the committee intends to designate for priority testing.

The names of the chemicals in the intent-to-designate category are released six months before ITC plans to designate them formally for priority testing. In this way, test data and other information on the substances can be submitted. In some cases, the data submitted under the intent-to-designate system are sufficient to resolve ITC concerns, so that the committee decides no further testing is needed and does not formally designate the substance.

A key problem with the ITC method of designating chemicals for testing was that EPA in the early years of TSCA consistently failed to meet the one-year time limit for responding to an ITC testing designation. In 1979, EPA was sued by an environmental group, the Natural Resources Defense Council, to force it to respond to the backlog of testing recommendations. Subsequently the court held EPA had failed to comply with the testing requirements of section 4 (*Natural Resources Defense Council v. Costle,* 14 ER Cases 1858 (S.D.N.Y. 1980)). In January 1981 a timetable for answering the recommendations was made part of the court order in the case to force the agency to clear up the backlog of testing recommendations within three years.

In an effort to comply with the court order, the agency stressed voluntary industry testing of chemicals. Voluntary testing also allowed EPA to avoid the lengthy delays that accompany requiring testing by formal regulatory rulemaking. The Reagan administration made voluntary testing a favored goal and was able to clear up the backlog of recommended chemicals considerably by threatening to require testing unless industry volunteered to do the testing EPA deemed necessary.

Voluntary Testing Illegal

EPA's reliance on voluntary testing agreements with the chemical industry was abruptly halted in August 1984. At that time, the U.S. District Court for the Southern District of New York ruled that such agreements are illegal because they are unenforceable and are not specifically authorized under TSCA. The ruling, in response to a lawsuit by the Natural Resources Defense Council, said the voluntary testing plan "subverted the statutory scheme" of the act (*Natural Resources Defense Council v. Environmental Protection Agency*, 21 ER Cases 1625, 21 ER Cases 1919 (S.D.N.Y. 1983)).

After this decision, the environmental group and the chemical industry met to work out some way of speeding testing. In August 1985, they created and submitted to EPA for consideration a new vehicle designed to obtain testing quickly while incorporating some of the enforcement and regulatory standards that TSCA requires. The new enforceable testing consent agreement would impose deadlines for the chemical industry to develop voluntary testing plans, and would require companies to comply with export notification requirements.

In an interim rule issued June 30, 1986, EPA authorized consent testing agreements negotiated under section 4 of TSCA. EPA estimated that the formal test rule procedure could take two years but that a consent order could reduce the time period by half. Several consent agreements were reached; the agency said the process seems to work better for environmental testing than for health effects studies.

Petitions, Other Methods

Testing of specific chemicals also can be requested by private citizens through use of the petition provisions contained in section 21 of TSCA. The agency must respond to such a petition within 90 days. If it grants the petition for regulation, rulemaking must begin immediately. If the petition is denied, the agency must explain the denial in a *Federal Register* notice.

The agency, as a result of data obtained through its use of the data collection authorities granted to it by the act or through its receipt of information from other government agencies, may single out a chemical for testing because it believes the chemical may pose a risk to health or the environment. EPA also produces Chemical Hazard Information Profiles of suspect chemicals. These profiles assess exposure, use, toxicity, and other factors that would contribute to risk. The agency may propose a test rule if it decides additional testing is needed to complete assessment of the profiled chemical.

Other Testing Provisions

Cost Sharing

Section 4 of the act also contains several other requirements that relate to testing of chemicals. One of the major requirements covers cost sharing for testing that is required under a test rule (40 CFR 791). When the agency requires a chemical to be tested, all manufacturers and processors of the substance must take part in the testing, with only minor exceptions. Since only one set of tests of a substance usually is needed, the manufacturers and processors may agree with the agency to have one firm or an independent laboratory perform the tests. In such cases, the manufacturers and processors would share the cost of the testing.

Under certain circumstances, a manufacturer or processor may ask to be excluded from taking part in such testing. This must be done by formal petition to the EPA administrator.

Firms planning to make a new chemical also may petition the administrator to ask that the agency specify what testing should be done on the new substance. This provision has never been used and is unlikely to be.

Immediate Rulemaking Requirements

Section 4(f) of TSCA requires regulatory action if the agency receives information indicating a chemical presents or will present "a significant risk of serious or widespread harm to human beings from cancer, gene mutations, or birth defects." In such cases, EPA must, within 180 days of receiving the information, begin rule-making action to control the risk under the "new chemical," "un-reasonable risk," or "imminent hazard" provisions of the act, or it must explain in the *Federal Register* why the risk is not unreasona-ble. The agency may extend the 180-day deadline by 90 more days with sufficient cause, but again must explain this extension in the *Federal Register*. Any such action by EPA, be it to begin rulemaking on the substance or to decide that no control of the substance is needed, is subject to review by federal courts.

The "significant risk" provision has been triggered several times: for 4,4′-methylenedianiline in 1983, formaldehyde in 1984, and methylene chloride in 1985.

Section 8: Gathering Information on Chemicals

Section 8 of TSCA gives EPA authority to require chemical manufacturers and processors to collect, record, or submit certain information on chemicals. The rationale behind this section is that reasoned judgments on the safety or hazards of chemicals cannot be made unless information on chemicals is freely available to EPA. This section, therefore, does not allow regulation of chemical hazards but merely authorizes collection of a variety of data so that the need for regulation can be assessed. To this end, industry must maintain, collect, submit, and/or allow inspection of various types of information that EPA needs to evaluate the safety of listed chemicals. Among the types of information involved are data on chemical production, use, exposure, and disposal; records of allegations of significant adverse reactions to health or the environment; unpublished health and safety studies; and notification of previously unknown risks.

The chemical inventory described earlier under "Section 5: New Chemical Screening (PMN)" also is authorized by section 8 of the act, as are exemptions for small firms that may be economically damaged if forced to collect and submit the requested data.

Data must be collected, recorded, or reported to EPA under the following four parts of section 8:

- Section 8(a): general reporting
- Section 8(c): allegations of adverse reactions
- Section 8(d): health and safety studies
- Section 8(e): "substantial risk"

Lists are published only under sections 8(a) and 8(d).

Failure to submit requested information is either a civil or a criminal offense, and may subject violators to fines and/or jail sentences.

Section 8(a): General Data Collection

Section 8(a) of the act authorizes the agency to require submission of a multitude of general information on chemicals that EPA is considering regulating because it suspects they may be hazardous. After the agency evaluates this information, more specific information may be sought by moving the chemical to a reporting list that requires submission of more data. For example, a wide variety of general data might be required for a large number of chemicals. From that group, a smaller number would be singled out for submission of more detailed data. As the data collected by the agency become more complete, the chemical may become subject to testing or other regulatory action under one of the other sections of TSCA.

Current use of section 8(a) is to require chemical manufacturers and importers and some processors to submit data on production, use, by-products, and human exposure for hundreds of listed chemicals (40 CFR 712). EPA requires this type of information for all chemicals recommended for testing by the Interagency Testing Committee because they are suspected of posing hazards to health or the environment.

Procedure for Listing

Chemicals are included on the section 8(a) general reporting list through formal rulemaking. EPA proposes a list of chemicals for inclusion on the list but the data need not be reported until after the rule becomes final. The chemicals on the list may change between proposal and promulgation of the final rule. For example, in 1980 when EPA proposed the first list of chemicals under section 8(a), 2,300 chemicals were proposed for data collection. In a reflection of Reagan administration efforts at deregulation of industry, the final reporting rule, promulgated under section 8(a) in June 1982, listed only 250. By the end of 1991, the list had grown to approximately 700, which included both specific chemicals and chemicals listed as part of categories.

Chemicals proposed solely because of high production volume were dropped from the final reporting requirements, and some chemicals on which the agency had received reports of substantial risk were added. Also deleted were chemicals for which sufficient data to evaluate effects were available. This action was in line with the section's requirement that data demanded may not be duplicative or unnecessary.

Section 8(c): Allegations of Adverse Reactions

Section 8(c) of TSCA authorizes EPA to require chemical manufacturers, processors, and distributors to keep records of allegations of significant adverse reactions to health or the environment. Under the law, health reactions to chemicals reported by employees must be recorded and maintained for 30 years, while records of other reported reactions must be kept for 5 years (40 CFR 717).

Types of Records

Among the types of records that must be kept are reports of consumer allegations of personal injury or adverse health effects, reports of occupational disease or injury, and reports of damage to the environment. The aim of this section is to collect enough data to allow EPA or industry to spot any pattern that may suggest exposure to a specific substance is causing health or environmental problems. If such a trend were noted, the agency could act to protect against the problem before it became widespread.

The records need not be submitted to EPA automatically, but the regulation authorizes the agency to require submission of the records if needed.

This section has been particularly controversial in the chemical industry since EPA outlined broad plans to implement it in 1977. In 1980, the agency issued a proposed rule that would require manufacturers, processors, and distributors in a wide variety of industries to collect and submit data on health or environmental hazard allegations. When this proposal defined an allegation as a "statement made without formal proof or regard for evidence," those affected by the regulation complained loudly that roomfuls of records would have to be kept. Their chief complaint was that every time an employee sneezed or got a headache, the employee could allege some workplace exposure caused it and thus force the employer to keep a record of that sneeze or headache for 30 years.

Since that time, EPA has eased the number and types of allegations that must be recorded by limiting reportable effects to those that are unknown and reported in writing. The definition of adverse effect also was revised to include only effects that substantially impair activity, are long-lasting, or are irreversible. Accidental spills or other releases to the environment that are reported under other environmental statutes do not need to be recorded.

Section 8(d): Unpublished Health and Safety Studies

Section 8(d) of the act requires chemical manufacturers and processors to report unpublished health and safety studies on listed chemicals. EPA adds all chemicals recommended by ITC to the automatic reporting provisions of its rules under section 8(a) and (d). Manufacturers and processors need not submit research and development studies to EPA, nor must they submit certain monitoring data or nonconfidential studies to another federal agency. As with section 8(a), these limitations are to prevent duplicative and unnecessary reporting.

Section 8(e): "Substantial Risk" Notification

The final requirement imposed by section 8 requires chemical manufacturers, processors, and distributors to report substantial risks associated with chemicals. Section 8(e) gives firms 15 working days to notify EPA whenever a study or event indicates that a chemical may cause a health or environmental problem.

Types of Reports

Among the data reported under this section are toxicology test results or results of animal studies that indicate a chemical may have a mutagenic effect or may have other adverse health effects. Many firms also report adverse health effects posed by accidents or spills, especially if the effects were not previously known.

In July 1991, EPA instituted the TSCA section 8(e) Compliance Audit Program (CAP), which dramatically increased the number of substantial risk notification reports. CAP is an enforcement program that provides incentive for manufacturers voluntarily to report risks by reducing penalties and by placing a $1 million limit on the overall penalty that can be imposed. In early 1984, some 500 section 8(e) reports had been submitted to EPA; by early 1992, that number had jumped to more than 2,000. After receiving a section 8(e) report, EPA evaluates it to see if some type of control action is needed to protect against the risk.

Use of Reports

Some of the substances on which such notices are received will be added to the section 8(a) reporting list described earlier. This assures the agency has production and exposure data on the substances and allows it to decide whether further controls under other sections of TSCA are needed.

Section 6: Control of Chemicals Posing Unreasonable Risks

TSCA also contains provisions for controlling or banning specific chemicals that EPA finds pose or will pose an unreasonable risk to health or the environment. Under section 6 of the act, the agency may prohibit or limit manufacture, processing, distribution in commerce, use, or disposal of a chemical that poses an unreasonable risk. Action against a specific substance under this section may range from something as simple as requiring a warning label to something as serious as imposing a complete ban on production, import, and use in the United States. Restrictions on substances also may encompass public warnings, notification to the agency before the substance is handled in a certain way, recordkeeping requirements, or any combination of such actions.

Procedures for Regulation

Formal Regulation

Under section 6, the agency must formally propose regulations outlining the least burdensome restrictions it believes necessary to control the risk. The agency must list the substance's effects and the effects of exposure to it both on humans and on the environment, the benefits of use and availability of substitutes, and the economic consequences of EPA's proposed action on the economy, small business, and technical innovation.

Immediate Regulation

Even though formal rulemaking procedures apply to actions taken under section 6, EPA may make such a rule effective at the time it is proposed if this is necessary to control the risks associated with the chemical. In addition, the agency may couple its authorities under this section with the "imminent hazard" provisions of section 7 of the act. In such cases, the agency could seek a court order to seize, halt manufacture, recall, publicly warn of, or in other ways control a chemical that poses "an imminent and unreasonable risk of serious or widespread injury to health or the environment." This "imminent hazard" provision is geared to protecting health and/or the environment until a final rule under section 6 can control the hazard.

Types of Regulation

The wide breadth of control mechanisms possible under section 6 of TSCA is apparent from the actions taken thus far. As of mid-1992, only polychlorinated biphenyls (PCBs), chlorofluorocarbons (CFCs) used as aerosol propellants, friable (crumbling) asbestos in schools, and disposal of 2,3,7,8-tetrachlorodibenzo-p-dioxin (TCDD) wastes were regulated under section 6. Each of these substances, however, was regulated differently.

PCBs

In drafting the toxics law, Congress mandated that PCB manufacture be banned and that existing uses be phased out. In addition, the law required EPA to promulgate regulations on labeling and disposal of PCBs. Although the agency was late in complying with this mandate, it did put PCB regulations into effect in 1979. However, in 1980, exemptions in the rules that permitted continued use of totally enclosed PCBs and PCBs in concentrations lower than 50 parts per million were overturned by a federal court.

In that lawsuit, filed by the Environmental Defense Fund, the court ruled the agency had no scientific basis or justification to support continued use of PCBs in totally enclosed electrical equipment and placed the agency on a timetable for issuing new rules. (*Environmental Defense Fund v. EPA*, 636 F.2d 1267, 15 ER Cases 1081 (D.C. Cir. 1980)). Although the labeling, recordkeeping, and disposal portions of the rules and the provisions slowly phasing out nonenclosed uses were upheld, the court accepted the environmental group's argument that the exemptions in the final rules would allow continued use of 99.3 percent of all PCBs in use.

The agency put an interim PCB inspection and maintenance program into effect shortly after the court decision and began rewriting the stricken portions of the rules. In late 1982 it promulgated two parts of the new final rules but told the court it would take at least until the end of 1984 to address the question of regulating PCBs as uncontrolled by-products created in manufacturing other substances. The first two rulemakings set specific percentage cutoff points (in parts per million) below which enclosed and controlled PCBs would be exempt from regulation, required phasing out of electrical equipment containing PCBs in food and feed manufacturing and handling facilities, and set up an inspection and restricted-access program for certain electrical equipment containing PCBs.

Late in 1984, EPA issued a rule defining PCBs inadvertently generated during manufacturing processes and set limits on the amount of PCBs that would be exempt from regulation in such cases. Subsequently, EPA issued a final rule phasing out use of higher secondary voltage transformers containing PCBs in or near commercial buildings and banning new installations after October 1, 1985. The rule also set a variety of requirements aimed at reducing PCB fires. It set dates by which transformers containing PCBs had to have additional protections installed, by which fire departments had to be notified about the location of PCB transformers, and by which such equipment had to be labeled (40 CFR 761).

In response to a criticism by the General Accounting Office that EPA's failure to identify facilities that contain PCBs impedes efforts to inspect for violations of the PCB rules, EPA proposed in September 1988 to institute a tracking and manifesting system similar to that set up under the Resource Conservation and Recovery Act. The rule, which became final in December 1989, requires those dealing with PCBs to obtain an identification number from EPA and to provide reports on receipts and storage of quantities of PCBs.

Enforcement actions by the agency are being rigorously pursued. In June 1988 EPA assessed a $15 million fine against a pipeline company for leakage and spillage in violation of the PCB regulations. The agency estimated that the required cleanup would cost the company $400 million.

The PCB rules illustrate the wide variety of actions EPA can take under TSCA to control use of a chemical.

CFCs

In March 1978, EPA, the Food and Drug Administration (FDA), and the Consumer Product Safety Commission (CPSC) acted together to prohibit use of CFCs in aerosol products. While FDA and CPSC acted to ban products delivered in aerosol cans propelled with CFCs, EPA enacted a ban on manufacture and processing of fully halogenated chlorofluoroalkanes for use as aerosol propellants. This combined rulemaking, undertaken because propellant uses of CFCs were believed to deplete the ozone layer of the stratosphere, is a good example of the use of TSCA to control chemical hazards where other laws cannot.

EPA used the authorities contained in section 6 of TSCA to ban manufacture for aerosol propellant uses, to require annual reports from manufacturers and processors on CFCs for propellant uses, and to issue exemptions from the ban for certain essential propellant uses that could not be discontinued or converted to use of a non-CFC propellant (40 CFR 762). The action basically outlawed most aerosol uses of CFC propellants, but allowed a few uses such as in pharmaceutical tablet press lubricants and fingerprinting systems.

The agency in 1980 also began investigating the possibility of regulation of CFC uses in refrigeration and cooling and in urethane foam, but dropped these plans in early 1983 after deciding the hazard to the ozone layer was not as great as was once thought. But this assessment was revised when a seasonal hole in the ozone layer became more pronounced in Antarctica during 1984. By October 1987, stratospheric ozone concentrations above the southernmost continent dropped by 50 percent during the period when depletion takes place—the southern hemisphere's spring.

When first observed, the ozone hole appeared to be bigger in odd-numbered years and smaller in even-numbered ones, a pattern scientists attributed to a biennial movement of air. But researchers began to reexamine this theory after severe Antarctic ozone depletion occurred in 1989, 1990, and 1991. In February 1992, the National Aeronautic and Space Administration (NASA) reported that substantial ozone depletion is likely to occur over the Arctic as well and spread to parts of the northern hemisphere before 2000.

Detailed measurement and analysis have shown that oxides of chlorine participate in the reactions that destroy the ozone layer. Studies also have revealed that the chlorine originates largely from chlorofluorocarbons.

An EPA report said that all uses of fully halogenated CFCs and halons (analogous bromine-containing compounds) and methyl chloroform would have to be stopped now to stabilize concentrations within the next 100 years. Even if chlorine emissions are eliminated now, stratospheric chlorine levels will continue to grow for 6 to 8 years, the report said.

Another environmental concern intensified when it was found that CFCs are also "greenhouse effect" gases. Unless solar radiation striking the earth is reradiated into space, the earth will warm up. Some substances interfere with this process by absorbing the reradiated energy. Although the principal worry has been about the increasing levels of carbon dioxide resulting from industrialization, it has been recognized since 1975 that CFCs also are effective greenhouse gases and that their presence in the atmosphere contributes to the warming trend. However, a United Nations report released in October 1991 found that the loss of ozone created a cooling effect, so scientists are uncertain how important a role CFCs play in possible global climate change.

The concerns about the warming trend prompted international action, and in 1987, 47 nations reached an accord through the Montreal Protocol on Substances that Deplete the Ozone Layer. The United States ratified the protocol in October 1988.

The treaty, which went into effect January 1, 1989, provided for a freeze in CFC production at 1986 levels and a subsequent reduction in production. The European Community and 24 nations that signed the protocol agreed to review the document—especially in respect to hydrochlorofluorocarbons—in 1992.

In 1990 amendments to the Montreal Protocol, signatories agreed to cut in half the manufacture and use of five chlorofluorocarbons by 1995, with an 85-percent cut by 1997. Developing countries were given a 10-year grace period. The newest amendments to the protocol also call for a 70-percent cut in methyl chloroform (1,1,1-trichloroethane) by 2000, and a phaseout by 2005. Halon production must be cut in half by 1996 and phased out by 2000. There are exemptions to the halon reductions for certain limited uses, such as firefighting systems in aircraft and computer rooms.

In February 1992, President George Bush announced that the United States will halt production of CFCs by December 31, 1995. The decision followed reports from the National Aeronautics and Space Administration that CFCs are depleting the earth's protective ozone layer much faster than earlier predictions indicated.

Although one of the principal reasons leading to the passage of TSCA was to provide a means of controlling CFCs, EPA has decided that limitation of CFCs will be regulated under the Clean Air Act rather than TSCA because the emissions are into the air.

Asbestos

When a voluntary program to inspect schools for friable asbestos failed, the agency issued a rule requiring such inspections of public and private school buildings to determine whether students were being exposed to airborne asbestos fibers (40 CFR 763). As part of this rule, adopted in May 1982, school systems had to inspect their facilities; post the results of the inspections and report the results to EPA, school employees, and parents; and keep records of the inspections and the results, indicating where any friable asbestos is located. This effort was only partly successful, and in 1984 EPA began fining many school districts for noncompliance.

In 1989, EPA issued an asbestos ban and phaseout rule designed to prohibit the manufacture and distribution in commerce of products accounting for 94 percent of the asbestos used in the United States. But in October 1991, the U.S. Court of Appeals for the Fifth Circuit overturned the rule on the grounds that during the rulemaking process the agency rejected alternatives that could be less burdensome to industry (*Corrosion Proof Fittings v. EPA*, 33 ER Cases 1961 (5th Cir. 1991)).

In November 1991, EPA challenged the appellate decision, arguing that allowing controlled use of asbestos was deemed ineffective to curb health risks. But later that month, the appeals court denied EPA's petition for a rehearing—an action that confirmed that the agency cannot ban asbestos use under its current rule. In early 1992, EPA attorneys said the Justice Department chose not to appeal the Fifth Circuit's decision to the Supreme Court.

Also in November 1991, EPA announced that it will follow OSHA's lead in addressing the need to promulgate any new regulations requiring inspection of commercial buildings, such as office buildings, for friable asbestos. The agency also set a final rule that applied the regulations of OSHA for workers exposed to asbestos to persons engaged in asbestos removal or cleanup if those persons would not ordinarily come under OSHA rules.

TCDD

A 1980 rule on TCDD illustrates the authority granted EPA by the act to take emergency action when an imminent hazard exists. In this case, the rule took effect immediately upon proposal in March 1980, even though a comment period and a hearing kept the final rule from publication until May 1980 (40 CFR 775).

The specific reason for the rule was discovery of the dioxin TCDD in waste generated during manufacture of the herbicide 2,4,5-trichlorophenol and its relatives 2,4,5-T and Silvex. The agency, fearful that a large amount of waste from a pesticide production facility in Jacksonville, Arkansas, would be disposed of improperly, proposed the rule to require that EPA be notified 60 days before disposal of such waste. This allowed the agency to investigate and approve of the disposal method to be used in discarding the highly toxic waste material.

Although the regulation mentioned the Arkansas facility by name, it also applied to any firm planning to dispose of wastes containing TCDD and required that the content of the wastes be analyzed. The agency justified the rule by saying that disposal of the highly toxic wastes in ordinary landfills or incinerators could create a serious and imminent health problem. Since that time, EPA has taken action to bring disposal of dioxins under the Resource Conservation and Recovery Act.

In June 1987 EPA promulgated a rule that requires the testing of 12 specific organic chemicals for contamination with dioxins and furans. The rule also requests that any information on adverse effects of the 12 chemicals be submitted.

Genetic Engineering

An extension of the authority of TSCA assumed by the agency is the regulation of the development and production of genetically engineered microorganisms. Premanufacture notification has been submitted to the agency to cover the development of a number of genetically engineered microorganisms. As of mid-1992, EPA had yet to issue a regulation under its TSCA authority specifically addressing genetically altered microbes.

Other Provisions

As a comprehensive chemical control and assessment law, TSCA contains a variety of other hazard-control provisions, including the following:

- *Referral.* Under section 9 of TSCA, EPA is authorized to refer regulation of a chemical to another government agency if EPA "has reasonable basis to conclude" that an unreasonable risk caused by the substance "may be prevented or reduced to a sufficient extent" by action under another federal statute. The provision was used for the first time in 1985, when EPA referred regulation of the chemical 4,4'-methylenedianiline to OSHA. Referrals are made after EPA makes a finding of unreasonable risk and passes this information on to the other agency or agencies in question. Since the first referral, controversy has arisen over whether EPA must refer a chemical for regulation or whether the referral is discretionary. At issue is the question of overlapping regulatory jurisdictions. For instance, a residual risk might remain if the receiving agency regulates the substance but is unable to regulate all uses and/or exposures. As of early 1992, EPA interpreted the section as allowing EPA to regulate the substance if the receiving agency agrees there is a risk but declines to regulate it. This interpretation and other questions surrounding use of section 9 are in flux.

- *Import/Export.* Imports or exports of chemicals that may pose a hazard during manufacture, use, or disposal either in the United States or other countries can be banned or controlled under TSCA (regulations at 40 CFR 707).
- *Citizens' Suits and Petitions.* Citizens or public interest groups may file suit in federal court alleging that EPA is in violation of the act or attempting to force it to take action to control a chemical hazard. Citizens also may petition the agency to issue, amend, or repeal a rule regulating a chemical. Such petitions, filed under section 21 of the act, must be answered by the agency within 90 days.
- *Enforcement.* Enforcement actions by EPA, including inspections, imposition of penalties, and seizure of substances manufactured in violation of the act, are authorized under TSCA. In April 1988, EPA reached a consent agreement with a chemical importer for a fine of $1.28 million as a penalty for importing 11 chemicals without submitting premanufacture notification. The original penalty proposed was $4.5 million. Several other failures to submit premanufacture notification have resulted in million-dollar fines.
- *Testing Protocols.* Development and evaluation of protocols (testing methods) for evaluating and analyzing chemicals is authorized.
- *Confidentiality of Data.* Protection from public access of certain data claimed to be confidential by the firm or group submitting the data to EPA is authorized by TSCA (regulations at 40 CFR 2). This provision is intended to allow industry to submit information to the agency without concern that its release may aid competitors.

Federal Insecticide, Fungicide, and Rodenticide Act

(FIFRA)

AT A GLANCE

Public Law Number: Pub. L. No. 92-516

U.S. Code citation: 7 USC 136 *et seq.*

Enacted: October 21, 1972
Amended: 1975, 1978, 1980, 1983, 1984, 1988 (major amendments,
Pub. L. No. 100-532), 1990

Regulations at: 40 CFR 162–180

Federal agency with jurisdiction: Environmental Protection Agency
(EPA)

Congressional committees/subcommittees with jurisdiction:
House of Representatives: Department Operations, Research, and Foreign Agriculture Subcommittee of the Agriculture Committee
Senate: Agricultural Research and General Legislation Subcommittee
of the Agriculture Committee

BNA reporting services: *Chemical Regulation Reporter, Daily Environment
Report, Toxics Law Reporter*
Text of law appears in *Chemical Regulation Reporter* Reference File at
91:0201 *et seq.*
Text of regulations appears in *Chemical Regulation Reporter* Reference
File

What FIFRA regulates and why: The act provides regulatory authority
for registration and use of pesticides and similar products intended
to kill or control insects, rodents, weeds, and other living organisms.
Key to the definition of "pesticides" is the concept of intended use,

Federal Insecticide, Fungicide, and Rodenticide Act—Contd.

which allows a broad range of regulatory authority over chemicals and devices that function as pest control agents, regardless of their original purpose of manufacture. Under the law, if a product is represented in such a way as to result in use as a pesticide, the product is considered to be a pesticide under section 2 of FIFRA.

A manufacturer wishing to make a new pesticide must register it with EPA. This procedure includes submission of test data, proposed uses, and suggested labeling. If the product is to be used on agricultural crops, EPA must establish tolerances for residues of the substance before use of the crop for food is permitted. The manufacturer requests EPA to set a tolerance but the agency makes the final decision.

Under FIFRA, pesticide manufacture, use, import, or disposal may be banned, controlled, or restricted. Regulations under the act allow EPA to establish safety standards for pesticide products and to remove from the market, restrict use of, or refuse registration for products that do not meet those standards.

Amendments passed in 1988 provided for a process to speed up reregistration and modified indemnification and storage and disposal provisions for banned pesticides.

Latest developments: Amendments to the 1990 Farm Bill (Pub. L. No. 101-624) permitted EPA to waive fees for manufacturers of pesticides for minor uses. These amendments also established a 90-day period after a firm cancels a registration for a registration to be transferred to another manufacturer.

A June 1991 Supreme Court decision upheld the authority of cities and towns to control and even ban the use of pesticides by ruling that FIFRA does not preempt local regulations dealing with pesticide use (*Wisconsin Public Intervenor v. Mortier,* 111 Sup. Ct. 2476, 33 ER Cases 1265 (1991)). A bill (HR 3850) introduced in Congress in November 1991—the Federal State Pesticide Regulation Partnership Act—would reverse the high court's decision. In July 1992, a federal appeals court ruled that EPA could not allow the use of carcinogenic pesticides that can concentrate in processed foods even if the agency determines that the chemicals pose a minimal risk.

COVERAGE OF THE LAW

The first federal legislation concerned with control of chemical pesticides was the Federal Insecticide Act of 1910, a bare-bones law that was replaced in 1947 with the first version of the Federal Insecticide, Fungicide, and Rodenticide Act. The 1947 act's initial mandate was registration and labeling of pesticides to protect consumers from ineffective products.

Jurisdiction for the act first was placed with the Department of Agriculture (USDA), but was passed to EPA in 1970. Congress has amended the law several times—in 1964, 1972, 1975, 1978, 1980, and 1988—with the 1972 amendments (entitled the Federal Environmental Pesticide Control Act of 1972, Pub. L. No. 92-516) providing the format for pesticide regulation as it exists today. The version of the law established by the 1972 amendments is commonly referred to as FIFRA.

FIFRA provides the regulatory vehicle for controlling the use and safety of the one billion pounds of pesticide products produced and used in the United States each year. Of the $6 billion worth of such products produced each year, 70 percent are herbicides and agricultural products. There are about 23,000 different pesticide products registered for use in the United States, but these products contain only about 600 groups of active ingredients.

FIFRA authorizes EPA to regulate "pesticides," a term which, under the act, includes almost anything intended to be used to kill, repel, or control any nonhuman form of life, from viruses and fungi to coyotes and oak trees. Key to this definition is the concept of intended use, which allows a broad range of regulatory authority over chemicals and devices that function as pest control agents, regardless of their original purpose of manufacture. Under the law, if a product is represented in such a way as to result in use as a pesticide, the product is a pesticide under section 2 of FIFRA.

In addition to insecticides and rodenticides, products to control plants, trees, weeds, fungi, algae, bacteria, viruses, nematodes, and other life forms are considered to be pesticides. Also included are herbicide products used to stop plant growth or defoliate crop plants.

Disinfectants used to kill bacteria in homes and hospitals and chemicals used to retard growth of unwanted bacteria, fungi, or other living organisms in leather, cloth, wood, and other materials are also among the products regulated by EPA under the act.

In addition to chemical pesticides, the agency regulates products that regulate plant growth; biological products, such as pheromones (sex attractants) and juvenile growth hormones (substances that keep insects from maturing and reproducing); and even bacteria and parasites if used as pesticides. In 1984, EPA included in this category new organisms derived through recombinant-DNA technology for use as pesticides. In some cases, the agency may decide not to regulate a pesticidal agent (e.g., an insect predator) if it is adequately regulated by another agency, usually USDA.

Pesticidal devices (e.g., traps for mice and other animals) also are covered by FIFRA, but are not subject to the full registration requirements imposed on chemical products.

Only microorganisms or drugs that affect humans or animals are excluded from regulation under FIFRA, chiefly because these are regulated as vaccines or drugs by the Food and Drug Administration (FDA). (See chapter on FFDCA.) Examples of such excluded items are vaccine products and products for killing lice on humans or parasites on animals.

DEVELOPMENT OF THE LAW

The original 1910 pesticide law was mainly a labeling law which made it unlawful to manufacture insecticides or fungicides that were adulterated or misbranded. This permitted the federal government to set standards and then to inspect and remove from the market any products that did not meet those standards. The

1910 act did not establish safety criteria, but rather was aimed at protecting consumers from dishonest advertising, a primary focus of regulatory activity that did not begin to change until 1947.

This authority was broadened somewhat in 1947 when Congress passed the original version of FIFRA. This new law covered more types of products but still was primarily a labeling statute. It required that pesticides carry adequate warning labels and precautionary instructions, and that the products be registered with USDA before interstate or foreign shipment.

A major loophole, however, nullified most safety features of this registration requirement: If USDA refused to register a product, the manufacturer could market it anyway after filing a protest with the agency. In such cases, USDA could only prevent marketing by seizing the product and proving that it was mislabeled or adulterated.

The U.S. pesticide regulatory scheme grew in 1954 when FDA was given authority under the Federal Food, Drug, and Cosmetic Act to establish pesticide residue tolerances (allowable limits for pesticide residues on food and animal feed). (See chapter on FFDCA.) The authority to set such tolerances now is carried out through a complicated cooperative plan whereby FDA sets pesticide residue limits for processed foods; USDA sets limits for edible portions of meat; and EPA, since it collects safety data on pesticides, sets limits for raw (unprocessed) meat and agricultural products. FDA enforces most of the limits, although USDA enforces some limits under its meat inspection program.

In 1964, Congress amended FIFRA to eliminate the loophole that allowed marketing of unregistered products and introduced the first glimmer of safety concerns in the pesticide regulatory scheme by allowing USDA to deny or suspend registrations. Even at this point, however, the act's major aim was protection of consumers from ineffective products.

Risk Evaluation

Some of the concerns that later spawned the environmental movement of the 1970s were beginning to surface during the late 1960s. After Congress passed legislation to control air and water pollution in 1970, it began to look at the question of pesticide safety. In that same year, the pesticide regulatory staffs of both USDA and FDA were consolidated and incorporated into the newly created Environmental Protection Agency.

During the next few years, the new agency, in response to rising public pressure from environmental activists, canceled the registrations of several pesticide chemicals (DDD and, for most uses, DDT) because they had adverse effects on the environment that were unreasonably severe, given the alternative methods of control available.

Congress shared in this increasing concern for the environment and in 1972 passed major amendments to FIFRA which established the basic form of the present federal pesticide regulatory structure. This new law was intended to ensure that the beneficial effects of chemical substances used to control insects, fungi, and rodents would not be outweighed by the environmental harm they caused.

FIFRA's chief thrust is prevention of unreasonable adverse effects on the environment, which under the law includes water, air, land, all plants, humans and other animals, and the interrelationships among them. The law requires that all pesticides be registered with EPA before shipment, delivery, or sale in the United States. As part of this registration procedure, EPA must evaluate the risks to the environment from use of the product. Pesticides manufactured before the 1972 amendments must be reexamined (reregistered) to make sure they meet current safety standards, a process that is still going on. Products that fail to meet these standards, or that pose unreasonable adverse effects, must be denied registration or be canceled.

Amendments in 1975 tempered some of these provisions by requiring EPA to submit proposed cancellations to a scientific review panel and to the Secretary of Agriculture. The agency also must weigh the impact of its decision to cancel a pesticide against the effect of the cancellation on food production and prices.

Further amendments passed in 1978 addressed problems EPA was encountering in reregistering thousands of pesticide products, allowing the agency to group the pesticides by active ingredients and register them on a generic rather than individual product basis.

The basic framework set out in 1972, however, still stands while Congress continues to struggle with the difficult economic, scientific, and environmental issues involved in pesticide regulation.

PROVISIONS OF THE LAW

As passed by Congress, FIFRA has four main thrusts:

- To evaluate the risks posed by pesticides using a system of registration with EPA (section 3)
- To classify and certify pesticides for specific uses and thus control exposure (section 3)
- To suspend, cancel, or restrict pesticides that pose a risk to the environment (section 6)
- To enforce these requirements through inspections, labeling notices, and regulation by state authorities (sections 12, 14, and 16)

Under the act, a pesticide cannot be legally shipped or sold in the United States unless it is registered by EPA. The agency can refuse to register a pesticide judged unduly hazardous. To obtain registration, manufacturers must agree to conditions or restrictions specified by EPA to control or reduce any hazard. For example, the agency may allow registration of a toxic or carcinogenic pesticide under the condition that it be used only against certain pests, on certain crops, in certain areas, or only by specially trained and certified applicators wearing protective equipment and following specific application methods and procedures.

The agency also has the authority to require manufacturers to submit test data needed for EPA to decide whether to register a pesticide. These data may include test results from studies concerning toxicity, carcinogenicity, mutagenicity, reproductive effects, effects on metabolism, environmental fate, and results of exposure to the substance, as well as results from other studies used to assess the human and environmental risks posed by a product. Such testing for a new active ingredient can cost millions of dollars.

Pesticide labels provide the agency with another way to regulate the activities of pesticide users. It is a violation of FIFRA to sell a pesticide with a label that does not meet EPA standards and it is a violation to use a pesticide "in a manner inconsistent with its labeling." Thus, the agency can make it illegal to spray a particular pesticide near lakes and streams simply by requiring the manufacturer to prohibit such spraying on the registered label.

FIFRA is unusual among federal environmental laws in requiring EPA to consider not only the risks posed by a pesticide, but also its economic, social, health, and environmental benefits. The agency may, for example, have to decide whether to allow continued use of a pesticide that poses a significant risk to human health or the environment but that is the only available defense against a particular pest on a particular crop. In such cases, EPA may decide to allow continued use of the pesticide against that pest on that single crop but to ban all other uses. In doing so, the agency would be applying the risk/benefit requirements of the act by deciding that the risk posed by the pesticide is outweighed by the economic and social benefit the crop provides.

Section 3: Pesticide Registration

Registration of all pesticide products sold or distributed in the United States is required by section 3 of the pesticide law. When a firm wants to manufacture, formulate, import, or distribute a pesticide product, it must apply to EPA for registration (regulations at 40 CFR 152, 158, 162). This requirement applies not only to newly discovered chemicals, but also to new combinations or mixtures of already registered pesticides and to new pesticide brands, even if identical in composition to existing products. Registration also is required for a new use of an already registered product.

Before it will register a product, EPA requires evidence to show:

- The product will not cause unreasonable harm to humans, crops, livestock, wildlife, or the environment when used in accordance with label directions.
- The product will perform its intended function without adverse effects. (In weighing this evidence, the agency looks not only at whether the substance will kill the target pest, but also whether it will kill nontarget organisms, livestock, wildlife, or beneficial insects or organisms. The law allows the agency to

waive the requirement for data showing that the pesticide is effective except in the case of products such as disinfectants that combat pests that endanger human health. The agency has used this waiver procedure in some cases.)

- The product will not result in harmful residues on food or feed. (The agency uses this residue data to establish tolerances, as described below. Pesticide labels must provide specific use directions to ensure that the pesticide does not leave residues exceeding the approved tolerance. Such labeling generally includes precise mixing and application directions and specifies how often and at what point in the crop cycle the product may be applied.)

Content of Registration Application

A registration application must include:

- Copies of the proposed labeling for the product
- Supporting test data concerning the substance's general and environmental chemical characteristics and hazards
- A statement of the product's composition, including the name and percentage by weight of each active and inert ingredient
- A proposed classification indicating whether the product should be licensed for general use or for restricted use (i.e., for use only by trained and certified applicators)

Reregistration

The new and more stringent health and safety testing requirements established by EPA since 1972 created a double standard under which older pesticide chemicals—previously registered by USDA—could continue to be marketed even though test data available to demonstrate their safety did not meet current standards, while new chemicals could not be registered and marketed until the manufacturer did the extensive testing now required.

To eliminate this double standard, Congress in 1978 directed the agency to review and reregister all older pesticides as quickly as possible so that all pesticide products would be subject to the health and safety testing requirements imposed on new products. At the level of funding and effort being expended on this program, the General Accounting Office estimated that it would not be completed until 2024.

In 1988, FIFRA was amended with a provision to speed up the reregistration process, requiring EPA to assess within about nine years the health and environmental effects of approximately 400 active pesticide ingredients that have not been fully tested according to current scientific standards. To help pay for this, manufacturers of each active ingredient will share a fee of up to $150,000, and each registrant will pay a "maintenance fee" of up to $425 each of the nine years of the reregistration program. The maintenance fee may be increased by EPA if it finds it cannot raise $14 million every year. In May 1992 EPA officials said they expect complete reregistration by 2002, five years later than anticipated.

In 1991, steps were taken to make technical corrections to the 1990 Farm Bill (Pub. L. No. 101-624) to raise fees chemical firms pay to support pesticide reregistration. But Congress had failed to pass legislation on the issue as of early 1992.

Under the 1988 amendments it is the responsibility of the registrants, rather than EPA, to determine what data must still be supplied. EPA will issue a registration standard, and companies must decide within 90 days whether they will conduct the necessary testing to support the registration. Because a given active ingredient is typically used in a number of pesticide formulations, considerable cooperation between manufacturers will be needed.

Registration Standards

To accomplish the reregistration of existing products, the agency developed a generic registration (registration by ingredient) approach through the establishment of registration standards. Under this system, a registration standard will be developed for each of the roughly 600 groups of active ingredients used in registered pesticides. Each registration-standard document will establish agency regulatory policy for products containing the chemical covered by the standard, and will spell out the test data and safety, use, and labeling criteria imposed on products containing that ingredient.

When a standard for an ingredient is completed, all products containing that ingredient and used for similar purposes will be subject to that standard. The agency will compare the products with the registration standard as a means of quickly reregistering a large number of formulated products that contain the same active ingredient.

Development of the registration standards, however, has been slow. Only 42 standards were issued in the four years after Congress directed the reregistration to begin, and the first reregistrations took place in late 1982. By 1986, the number of standards issued reached 125; by early 1992 a total of 194 standards had been issued.

The agency has a priority list giving the order in which standards will be developed for currently registered active ingredients. The list calls for simultaneous development of standards for groups of products registered for similar uses (e.g., all chemicals registered for use on corn or in swimming pools). This procedure is intended to simplify the standard writing process by allowing EPA to review all alternative products while assessing the economic benefits provided by each one. It also reduces the chances that one product will suffer in the marketplace because it is subject to new regulatory requirements before competing products.

Label Improvement Program

Related to the reregistration of existing pesticides is review of pesticide labels. Pesticide labeling is a key regulatory tool under FIFRA, because use of a pesticide in ways other than those specified on the label is a violation of the law.

Because the reregistration process is likely to continue until the turn of the century, EPA in 1980 began a program of issuing Label Improvement Notices to pesticide registrants. These notices, sent by certified mail to firms with registrations of affected products, state the changes that must be made in existing labeling and give a date for compliance. If a registrant fails to comply with the notice, the agency may begin cancellation proceedings. Among the notices issued since 1980 are notices to upgrade termiticide labeling, to clarify storage and disposal information, and to expand the farmworker safety information on labels for pesticides applied by hand.

Data Use and Trade Secrets

Generating and submitting pesticide test data is a major cost in developing and marketing a new pesticide, often reaching several million dollars. As a way of minimizing this cost, the pesticide law in certain cases allows EPA to use test data supplied by one manufacturer to register a product of another manufacturer if the new product contains all or some of the same ingredients. In such cases, the later registrant compensates the earlier producer for use of the data. Other provisions of the act allow release of some of this data to the public.

Understandably, this system has been controversial and hotly contested by the pesticide industry, with the question of how EPA may use or publicly release data a major issue in litigation over the pesticide regulatory process. In fact, in 1983 a U.S. district court declared the data-use provisions of FIFRA unconstitutional (*Monsanto v. Acting Administrator, EPA,* 18 ER Cases 2081 (E.D. Mo. 1983)). The ruling virtually halted all pesticide registration activity, leaving the agency able to register only those products for which a firm provided all of its own testing and registration data. In June 1984 the Supreme Court overturned the lower court ruling (*Ruckelshaus v. Monsanto Co.,* 104 Sup. Ct. 2862, ER Cases 1062 (1984)).

Data-Use Compensation

Congress has tried to find a solution to the data-use problem in the form of repeated amendments to FIFRA. At present, the act gives a company exclusive use, for 10 years, of data submitted to support registration of a new active ingredient. Some older data may be used by the agency to register products of other firms, if the firms offer to compensate the original data submitter. Certain categories of data, including data submitted before 1970, may be used by the agency without regard to compensation.

When compensation is required, the amount is fixed by binding arbitration. Disagreements over the appropriate amount of compensation have proved so troublesome that industry representatives have pressed Congress to extend the exclusive-use period to 15 years, after which no compensation would be required.

Public Access

Pesticide firms also have contested a 1978 amendment to FIFRA that grants public access to health and safety studies submitted by registration applicants. FIFRA data-use restrictions, the companies note, do not prevent a foreign pesticide firm from obtaining such studies and using them to register pesticides in countries that do not restrict use of data to those who pay for it. Industry has not so far been able to get Congress to put stricter controls on the release of such data, but industry lawsuits delayed the release of any data for four years after the amendments were passed.

At present, the data are safeguarded to some extent by a FIFRA requirement that members of the public, to get access to the data, must sign a statement that they will not disclose the data to any foreign or multinational pesticide firm. The agency warns data requesters of possible criminal penalties if they fail to maintain the confidentiality of the data in the studies or if they publish more than brief extracts or summaries of the data.

Special Pesticide Registrations

In addition to the standard registration process, FIFRA provides for the distribution and use of pesticides under a variety of limited registration or exemption mechanisms. These limited approvals include conditional registrations, state registrations for special local needs, emergency uses for a specific pest problem, and experimental-use permits.

Conditional Registration

While waiting for reregistration of all pesticide products to eliminate the difference between the testing required on old pesticides and that required on new ones, the agency has used conditional registration as a way of minimizing the impact on new registrations. Amendments to FIFRA in 1978 provided a temporary means of reducing the regulatory advantage enjoyed by older products by allowing EPA conditionally to register a new product without a full registration review, provided that the product is substantially similar in ingredients and proposed use to an already registered pesticide. The agency need not require the submission of the full set of test data until it demands the data from registrants of older products under the reregistration program.

Conditional registration also may be used to register a new use of an already registered product without the full set of data ordinarily required for such an amendment. Again, the "condition" of the registration is that the registrant submit the data when such data are required for reregistration of similar products.

The most controversial form of conditional registration applies to products containing new active ingredients, when the registration applicant has not had time to complete the long-term toxicological studies required by the agency. EPA may register such a product on the condition that the registrant complete the testing and submit the data within a reasonable period.

"Special Local Need" Registration

FIFRA also allows state governments to permit under a "special local need" registration additional uses of federally registered pesticides to combat a pest that is limited to a specific area or crop. A state registration is only valid for distribution and use of a product within the issuing state and is subject to veto by EPA. States, however, are barred from registering a product for use on food or feed crops unless a federal tolerance is in effect establishing an allowable level of residues of that pesticide on that crop.

As of mid-1991, there were 3,026 active special local need registrations. EPA charges an annual maintenance fee for maintaining these products. In addition, states may set time limits for these registrations. Consequently, this number may change over time as new special local need registrations are issued or as old ones expire or are canceled when the maintenance fee is not paid.

EPA regulations also allow a number of older pesticides to be sold and used in intrastate commerce without federal registration. These are pesticides registered by individual states in the years before FIFRA preempted state registration authority. Provided that such a product is distributed only within one state and the state registrant applied for federal registration before October 4, 1975, EPA rules allow continued intrastate sale until the agency acts on the federal application.

Emergency Registration Exemptions

Another class of registration is encompassed in EPA's authority to exempt federal or state agencies for any provision of FIFRA
to meet emergencies. Under regulations issued by the agency, this
provision is used to grant temporary exemptions allowing application of pesticides for unregistered uses. Such exemptions are
granted when no good alternative means are available to control a
serious outbreak of a pest or to prevent the introduction or spread
of a foreign pest, such as the imported fire ant. In 1991, EPA
approved 237 emergency exemptions.

Emergency exemptions and special local need registrations
are most heavily used by states, such as California and Oregon,
where many specialty crops are grown.

Experimental-Use Permits

The agency also has authority to permit experimental use of
pesticides by any person to develop data needed for registration of a
new product or a new use of a product. The agency also may issue
experimental-use permits to public or private agricultural research
agencies or educational institutions for more general research.

States also may issue experimental-use permits, subject to EPA
regulations. The agency's rules allow limited experimental use of
pesticides (on less than 10 acres for purely experimental purposes)
without a specific permit.

Pesticide Tolerances

A major function of EPA's pesticide regulation program is the
establishment of tolerances for residues of pesticides on food or
animal feed (40 CFR 180). Under the FFDCA, all detectable pesticide residues resulting from application of pesticides to food or
feed crops are considered unsafe, unless a tolerance level has been
established or an exemption from the requirement that a tolerance
be established is granted (see chapter on FFDCA). Tolerances or
exemptions are required for residues in or on animal products such
as meat, milk, or eggs, as well as on food or feed crops such as
apples, corn, or wheat.

Obtaining a tolerance is a necessary step in registering a pesticide for use on food or feed crops. Applicants for tolerances must provide evidence showing the level of residues likely to result from use of the pesticide and sufficient toxicological data to establish safe residue levels. Applicants also must identify a reliable analytical method that can be used to measure residues of the pesticide for enforcement purposes.

A temporary tolerance or exemption is issued with any experimental-use permit likely to result in pesticide residues on food or feed. Applicants can avoid the tolerance requirement by certifying that the experimentally treated crop will be destroyed or fed to experimental animals for testing purposes. FDA and USDA enforce the tolerances by inspecting to see that residues in processed foods or edible meats do not exceed EPA tolerances. This is done through use of a system of "action levels" above which meats or foods are considered adulterated.

In a precedent-setting case (*Les v. EPA*, No. 91-70234 (9th Cir. July 1992)), the court ruled recently that carcinogenic pesticides are prohibited from concentrating in processed foods under the FFDCA. The court set aside a final EPA order that permitted the use of four pesticides found to cause cancer. Using its 1988 risk policy, the agency had ruled that the four chemicals posed a de minimis risk. The court said EPA's actions were contrary to FFDCA. An EPA official said after the ruling that about 35 chemicals would be affected by the decision. The Department of Justice is seeking a rehearing in the case.

Section 3: Classification and Certification

In registering a pesticide use, EPA under section 3 of the act may classify the pesticide as being either for general use or restricted use (use by or in the presence of specially trained applicators), based on toxicity and potential for causing harm to nontarget organisms (regulations at 40 CFR 162, 171). The criteria for classification vary, depending on whether the product is intended for domestic (residence), nondomestic, indoor, or outdoor use, or for a combination of these.

FIFRA specifically provides for the establishment of federal and state programs to train and certify pesticide applicators. EPA monitors state certification programs and provides some funding assistance. The agency also conducts a federal certification program in a few states that do not have approved state programs.

The agency is given considerable leeway in classifying products because some may pose a risk even though they meet all the criteria for classification for general use. The agency can thus control environmental and health risks by regulating the uses and authorized applicators of a product.

General Use

Most pesticides registered by EPA receive a general-use classification, which means the product may be sold with no restrictions on who may use it. The criteria for a general-use classification are met when tests on a pesticide show it falls within certain toxicity parameters that are derived from animal tests on the substance. Among the criteria are potential for skin and eye irritation; acute, chronic, and delayed toxicity; potential for leaving residues in nontarget animals when used outdoors; and no more than minor adverse effects on nontarget organisms.

In general, the criteria for a general-use classification are more stringent for pesticides intended for domestic use than for pesticides intended for nondomestic uses.

Restricted Use

Pesticides are classified for restricted use if they are unusually toxic or for some other reason present a special hazard to human health or the environment. The specific requirements that apply to such products are established by agency regulations, which so far have been limited to the requirement that restricted products may only be used under the supervision of certified applicators. Other types of use restrictions are imposed by EPA through its authority to control pesticide labeling; it is a violation of FIFRA to use a product in ways that are not in accordance with its label.

Unclassified Pesticides

Many pesticides that were registered before the classification process was established are now unclassified but will be designated for restricted or general use when they are reregistered. The agency established criteria for classification and placed several dozen of the older active ingredients used in pesticides in the restricted category. Some registrants have protested such reclassification, complaining that the restricted-use label brands a pesticide as unduly hazardous.

Section 6: Suspension and Cancellation

Section 6 of FIFRA authorizes EPA to suspend, cancel, or restrict an existing pesticide registration to prevent an unreasonable risk to humans or to the environment.

The suspension authority is an emergency procedure that allows the agency to suspend registration of a pesticide while cancellation proceedings, which may take years, take place. In all but a few instances, the agency must announce its intent to cancel a pesticide registration at the same time it takes a suspension action. EPA has used its emergency suspension authority to ban a few pesticides, such as dibromochloropropane, deemed to pose an imminent hazard.

Because of the adversarial nature of the cancellation process, which often results in years of agency administrative hearings and court hearings, this process is used infrequently. DDT; aldrin/dieldrin; 2,4,5-T/Silvex; Kepone; mirex; ethylene dibromide; and Compound 1080 (when used for control of predators) are among those pesticides for which the cancellation process has been used.

More commonly the agency deals with potentially hazardous pesticides through an extended review process. This sometimes ends in cancellation of some or all registered uses or in other regulatory restrictions, including reclassification.

Special Reviews

The criteria and process for beginning a special review of a pesticide are set out in the EPA regulations governing cancellation procedures (40 CFR 162.11). Under those regulations, when the agency finds that a pesticide exceeds certain hazard criteria it notifies the registrants of its intention to begin a special review. The registrants then have 30 days in which they can dispute the agency's evidence of unreasonable risk. After 30 days, EPA announces its proposed determination of whether it will actually begin the special review. At that point, the agency goes through a public and internal review process in which EPA representatives may meet face-to-face with interested parties to discuss the agency's concerns about the pesticides and various options to reduce the risk. Following a final public review period, the agency announces its final decision.

This procedure, which EPA formally adopted in 1985, replaced the procedure involving a "rebuttable presumption against registration" (RPAR). The RPAR process cast the agency in an adversarial relationship with registrants and resulted in expensive and time-consuming administrative and legal disputes.

Reagan administration officials emphasized that the special review system reduces confrontation with the pesticide industry by fostering quick, negotiated solutions to reduce pesticide hazards. While the process may still result in formal cancellation proceedings, the more likely result of a special review is adoption of agreed-upon restrictions that may encompass changes in classification or use patterns, protective clothing requirements, or voluntary cancellation of registrations by the registrant for certain uses.

The effect of the nonadversarial approach is evident in the results of reviews concluded in the last few years. In some cases, the agency concluded that further review was not justified and returned the pesticide to the normal registration process. In other cases, registrants agreed to risk-reduction measures, such as cancellation of some registered uses or the adoption of new labeling prescribing the use of protective clothing and other new safety precautions. In the case of other pesticides, such as toxaphene, the agency imposed cancellation of major uses and other new regulatory restrictions, but did not use the formal proposal and comment procedures employed by previous administrations.

Reporting Adverse Effects

EPA promulgated a rule in 1985 requiring pesticide registrants to report to the agency information showing adverse effects on the environment from their products any time after a registration is granted. EPA requires that the information be submitted whenever it becomes available to the registrant, and the requirement continues as long as a pesticide is registered.

In August 1991, however, EPA announced that data indicating adverse health or environmental effects from as many as 18 pesticides under reregistration had not been fully reviewed by the agency. The disclosure came in the wake of a July 1991 accident in which 15,000 gallons of the chemical metam sodium spilled into the Sacramento River after a train derailed. California officials subsequently discovered information on the pesticide linking it to birth defects.

In January 1992, EPA said it would propose a rule in 1992 to codify and modify adverse effects reporting requirements for pesticide manufacturers under FIFRA. The proposed regulation, which would modify the 1985 rule, would require clear identification of information submitted by manufacturers to EPA under FIFRA section 6(a)(2), and identification of subsequent information that is related to the original report. When it announced plans for the rule in a pesticide registration notice (PR 92-1), EPA said it intended "to enforce aggressively" the section 6(a)(2) submission obligation and the identification requirement under the 1985 rule.

Sections 12, 14, 16: Enforcement and Penalties

FIFRA prohibits sale of unregistered, adulterated, or misbranded pesticides; use of any registered pesticide in a manner inconsistent with its labeling; and production of a pesticide in an unregistered establishment. Other infractions include refusing to keep required records or to file required reports, disclosing confidential data, violating suspension or cancellation orders, and falsifying data submitted to the agency.

To enforce the law, FIFRA allows EPA to:

- Require registration of facilities manufacturing, formulating, or distributing pesticide products
- Inspect production facilities and examine and test pesticides offered for sale
- Impose fines or criminal penalties for violations
- Stop sales of, seize, or recall products offered in violation of the law or request a court to enjoin sales of such products

EPA's enforcement resources are severely limited in comparison to the size of the industries that use or produce pesticides. In practice, most enforcement is carried out by state agencies, in most cases by a branch of the state agriculture department. FIFRA requires EPA to give state governments primary authority to enforce federal pesticide laws and regulations, provided that the states adopt adequate laws and enforcement procedures. The act also authorizes the agency to provide funding assistance to state enforcement programs.

Nearly all states have assumed primary enforcement responsibility. If a state fails to enforce the law adequately, EPA may intervene in individual cases to take direct enforcement action. The agency may also rescind the enforcement authority of a state, but to date it has never done so.

The law provides civil fines of up to $5,000 for each violation of FIFRA, and criminal penalties of up to $25,000 and one year in jail for willful violations.

Section 15: Indemnities

FIFRA provides that if the registration of a pesticide product is suspended or canceled to prevent an imminent hazard, the EPA shall indemnify persons suffering losses as a result. The 1988 amendments limit indemnity payments to "end users," a term that includes farmers and distributors.

The 1988 amendments also change provisions for the storage and disposal of banned pesticides. Formerly EPA paid these costs; the cost of storage is now shared between pesticide manufacturers and EPA. Chemical makers will be responsible for disposal.

State Authority

FIFRA preempts state regulatory authority to a great extent as far as establishment of requirements is concerned, although enforcement of the federal requirements is primarily carried out by the states. States may not permit any sale or use of pesticides prohibited under FIFRA or impose any labeling or packaging requirements different from those established by EPA.

States may, however, ban or limit use of specific pesticides and may require companies to submit test data to obtain state registration of their products. Industry has asked for legislative changes to set deadlines for state action on registration requests and to limit state authority to require data beyond that demanded by EPA.

As discussed earlier, FIFRA generally allows states to do the following:

- Administer pesticide applicator certification programs
- Issue experimental-use permits
- Register pesticides to meet special local needs
- Enforce federal pesticide laws and regulations
- Regulate pesticides in ways not specifically prohibited by the act

In June 1991, the Supreme Court ruled that the federal pesticides statute does not preempt local regulations dealing with use of pesticides in *Wisconsin Public Intervenor v. Mortier* (111 Sup. Ct. 2476, 33 ER Cases 1265 (1991). The ruling upheld the authority of cities and towns to control and even ban the use of pesticides through permitting schemes, licensing, notification, and other usage requirements. Industry argued that the decision could create the potential for inconsistent regulations nationwide, as well as duplicative and unnecessary regulations on the local level. It claimed the ruling would place a burden on both small companies and national lawn-care companies. But environmental groups hailed the high court's decision, saying it created an opportunity for pesticide safety to be improved greatly because actions on the federal level are too slow. They maintained that people can protect themselves best on the local and state levels.

In November 1991, a bill (HR 3850) was introduced in Congress that would reverse the Supreme Court decision. The Federal State Pesticide Regulation Partnership Act, sponsored by 30 House members, was backed by more than 160 groups representing the chemical industry, agriculture, commercial pesticide applicators, the food industry, and state agriculture officials.

Federal Food, Drug, and Cosmetic Act
(FFDCA)

AT A GLANCE _____

Public Law Number: Pub. L. No. 717 of 1938

U.S. Code citation: 21 USC 301 *et seq.*

Enacted: June 30, 1938; effective date, June 30, 1939
   Amended: 1941, 1945, 1951, 1953, 1954, 1958, 1960, 1962, 1976,
      1980, 1983, 1984, 1985, 1986, 1988, 1990

Regulations at: 21 CFR 1–1300

Federal agency with jurisdiction: Food and Drug Administration (FDA)
   of the Department of Health and Human Services (HHS)

Congressional committees/subcommittees with jurisdiction:
   House of Representatives: Health and the Environment Subcommittee
      of the Energy and Commerce Committee, Oversight and In-
      vestigations Subcommittee of the Energy and Commerce
      Committee
   Senate: Labor and Human Resources Committee (only full commit-
      tee has jurisdiction)

BNA reporting service: *Chemical Regulation Reporter, World Food Regulation Review*
   Citations by chemical name to CFR and *Federal Register* are published
      in Index to Government Regulations binder

What FFDCA regulates and why: The act provides regulatory authority
   to assure the safety of foods, drugs, medical devices, and cosmetics.
   Chemical provisions include regulation of human and animal drugs,
   food additives, color additives, pesticides in or on raw agricultural
   commodities, and any poisonous or deleterious substance in foods,
   drugs, medical devices, or cosmetics.

Federal Food, Drug, and Cosmetic Act—Contd.

The act's main regulatory tool is its prohibition of adulteration and/or misbranding of products under its jurisdiction. Using criteria established by regulation, the agency establishes standards that foods and drugs must meet and considers any that fail to meet these standards as being adulterated and/or misbranded. Such products are considered in violation of the law and are subject to seizure and/or criminal penalties.

Regulations promulgated under the act require approval of new drugs, certain over-the-counter drugs, medical devices, and food and color additives. Products are approved for certain uses and may not be sold for other uses without FDA approval.

Regulation of cosmetics under the act is not as strict as regulation of other substances, but relies heavily on voluntary compliance. Certain labeling procedures may be required.

Stringent export controls on drugs have been enacted, including requirements for identifying the materials and the receiving country.

Latest developments: FDA proposed rules in November 1991 that, among other things, mandated nutrition labeling for virtually all processed foods and permitted health claims for nutrients only if there is a valid relationship between the nutrients and the disease in question. Final regulations were expected in late 1992. Legislation to increase FDA enforcement activities was expected to pass in some form in 1992.

COVERAGE OF THE LAW

The third major chemical use and assessment law is the Federal Food, Drug, and Cosmetic Act (FFDCA). Like TSCA and FIFRA, this act authorizes assessment of the safety of ingredients—in foods, drugs, and related products. Through a system of evaluating the safety and effectiveness of these ingredients—a system that considers a product to be "adulterated" if it is unapproved or does not meet the basic chemical-content or contamination standards for such products—the Food and Drug Administration (FDA) uses the act to assure that regulated products are safe for use by consumers.

DEVELOPMENT OF THE LAW

The first law to regulate drugs in the United States was passed in 1848. The present Federal Food, Drug, and Cosmetic Act was passed in 1938. Beginning in 1906, early versions of the law prohibited shipment of misbranded or adulterated foods, drugs, or drinks across state lines and outlawed false therapeutic claims on labels for medicines.

All of the laws, however, had as their goals the assurance that foods and drugs sold in the United States would meet certain standards of purity and thus would not harm those who ingested them.

The 1906 Law

The need for a law to regulate foods and drugs became apparent in the late 1800s, when sanitation was poor, refrigeration consisted of keeping foods on ice, and use of addictive chemicals or drugs—including cocaine, morphine, and opium—in patent medicines was rampant and unregulated except in a piecemeal way by some states. Dr. Harvey Wiley of Purdue University began the fight to regulate ingestion of unsafe foods and drugs in 1883 when he assumed the position of chief of the Bureau of Chemistry of the U.S. Department of Agriculture. In this post, he devoted new attention to studies of food adulteration that had begun in the 1870s but that had not resulted in changes to the regulatory process.

By 1900, Wiley was much in demand as a speaker before women's clubs and business organizations as his crusade for a safer food supply captured national attention. Between 1879 and 1906 more than 100 food and drug bills were introduced in Congress. In 1906, the original Food and Drugs Act of 1906 was passed amid horror stories of dirty meat-packing plants, dangerous patent medicines, and use of poisonous additives in foods.

The Bureau of Chemistry enforced the 1906 law until 1927 when the Food, Drug, and Insecticide Administration was formed. It was renamed the Food and Drug Administration in 1931, and was transferred in 1953 from the Department of Agriculture to the Department of Health, Education and Welfare, the forerunner of the Department of Health and Human Services, the department under which FDA currently operates.

It was not until the economic hardships of the 1930s that the flaws in the 1906 law gained national attention. Among the most glaring ones were the inability of judges to find exact wording in the law by which to convict violators of the act's standards for purity of foods and to halt fraud in patent medicine sales. Although between 1933 and 1938 several efforts were made to revise the law, it was not until more than 100 people died as a result of taking a poisonous medicine that Congress passed the Federal Food, Drug, and Cosmetic Act of 1938.

The 1938 Law

A major revision of the 1906 law, the legislation enacted in 1938:

- Extended coverage of the law to cosmetics and medical devices

- Required predistribution clearance to assure the safety of new drugs
- Provided for tolerances for unavoidable poisonous substances
- Authorized standards of identity, quality, and "fill" for containers of foods
- Authorized factory inspections
- Added the remedy of court injunction to previous remedies of seizure and prosecution in cases where the act was violated

The Current Law

Later amendments added provisions to the 1938 law to create the current food and drug law. These later changes added provisions that:

- Required certification of the safety and efficacy of antibiotics and insulin
- Set up the differentiation between prescription and nonprescription drugs
- Banned the intentional addition to food of substances known to cause cancer in animals (the so-called "Delaney Clause")
- Established procedures for setting safety limits for pesticide residues on raw agricultural commodities
- Required pre-use safety assessment and approval of food additives
- Required that the safety of color additives to foods, drugs, and cosmetics be proven before use
- Required that manufacturers prove that new drugs were not only safe but also effective
- Required that medical devices be safe and effective and, in some cases, be approved by FDA prior to distribution

Responsibility for the safety of consumer products—including household cleaners and other chemical products—was transferred from FDA's Bureau of Product Safety to the newly formed Consumer Product Safety Commission in 1973 upon passage of the Consumer Product Safety Act (CPSA). At that time, the relevant provisions were removed from FFDCA and incorporated into the CPSA.

Amendments to the act in 1983, 1984, 1985, and 1988 created an "orphan drug" program to encourage development and production of drugs for which the market was small, encouraged greater competition through use of generic drugs and gave extended patent life to products to make up for time lost during regulatory review, and permitted the use of saccharin despite findings that it caused cancer in test animals.

The Nutrition Labeling and Education Act of 1990 required FDA to issue a massive series of food labeling proposals affecting more than 250,000 food labels and the way more than 80,000 types of food are marketed. In November 1991, the agency proposed rules that mandated nutrition labeling for virtually all processed foods, set standardized serving sizes for 131 food categories, established an FDA "dictionary" of nine core descriptive terms that may be used in labeling claims, and permitted health claims for nutrients only if there is a valid relationship between the nutrients and the disease in question. Final regulations were expected in late 1992, with implementation by mid-1993.

Legislation to increase FDA enforcement activities was expected to pass in some form in 1992. Proposed legislation would give FDA broader subpoena authority and would allow the agency to impose higher fines for civil violations. The Bush administration and industry opposed the legislation, arguing that it would give the agency too much enforcement authority and that the penalties would be overly punitive.

CHEMICAL CONTROL PROVISIONS OF THE LAW

The food and drug law is a chemical control law in several main areas:

- It establishes standards of chemical content for various products and considers a departure from those standards as adulteration and/or misbranding, both of which are forbidden by the law.
- It requires premarket approval of new drugs, coloring agents, and food additives to assure their safety before use.
- It specifies the levels of pesticides, chemicals, and naturally occurring poisonous substances that may be in food products.
- It regulates the safety of cosmetic products.

Adulteration and Misbranding

The key element of the FFDCA, and the source of FDA's main tools for enforcement, is its prohibition of "adulteration and misbranding." FDA interprets these words to require agency approval before a firm can market certain foods, drugs, medical devices, or other regulated products. The term "adulterated" refers to products that are defective, unsafe, filthy, or produced under unsanitary conditions. Inclusion of an unapproved ingredient in a product renders it adulterated and thus illegal. The term "misbranded" refers to false or misleading labeling statements, designs, or pictures, or to omission of required statements. This prohibition of adulteration and misbranding applies to virtually all products regulated under the law.

Premarket Approval

In a regulatory parallel to TSCA's premanufacture requirements for new chemicals and FIFRA's registration requirements for pesticides, the FFDCA requires that products regulated under the act be approved for safety prior to sale or use. For example, manufacturers of insulin and color additives must submit samples of their product to FDA laboratories for testing and the agency must certify the substance's purity, potency, and safety before it may be shipped for sale. New drugs and certain medical devices and their labeling must be approved for safety and effectiveness. Food additives must be officially listed as "generally recognized as safe" or be approved by specific FDA regulations based on scientific data. Residues of pesticides in food commodities must not exceed safety limits (tolerances) set by EPA and enforced by FDA.

These premarketing clearances are based on scientific data submitted by manufacturers, subject to review and acceptance by FDA scientists. Submission of false information is a criminal violation under the act.

Drug Safety

Under the FFDCA, substances intended for diagnosis, prevention, cure, treatment, or mitigation of disease are considered drugs and are subject to the drug requirements of the act. Since intended use determines whether a product is a drug, foods and cosmetics may be considered drugs if health claims are made for them.

Under the act, misbranding or adulteration of drugs is prohibited. New drugs must be reviewed and approved by FDA before they go on the market.

New Drugs

In the medical and legal sense, about 90 percent of the drugs marketed since 1938 are considered new drugs, for one of four reasons:

- They are actually new chemical substances.
- They use existing substances in new ways.
- They incorporate a substance not previously used in drugs.
- The drug is recognized by qualified experts to be safe and effective for its intended use but has not been used to any extent or for any material period of time for that purpose.

A new drug (as just defined) may not be commercially marketed in the United States unless it has been approved as safe and effective by FDA. This approval is based on a new drug application (NDA) that is prepared and submitted by the intended manufacturer.

In the past, this application often took years to prepare, because the manufacturer or "sponsor" had to conduct animal and human studies under the direct supervision of experts, usually physicians. But in 1991, the Bush administration announced reforms centered on accelerating FDA's review process for all new drugs, especially those to treat serious or life-threatening diseases for which there is no effective alternative therapy. The reforms included accelerated approval for new drug applications, external review of new drug applications by nongovernment scientific experts, and international harmonization of FDA's drug review standards with those of other industrialized nations.

Once an NDA is approved, the drug's formula, manufacturing process, labeling, packaging, dosage, methods of testing, etc., generally may not be changed without FDA approval. Any changes to increase safety or effectiveness, however, may be undertaken immediately, without awaiting FDA concurrence.

Over-the-Counter Drugs

Drug products sold without a prescription from a physician (over-the-counter drugs) also may be considered new drugs and thus subject to premarket approval. Manufacturers, however, may market such products without premarket clearance by FDA if the products meet certain agency standards, called *monographs.* Each monograph deals with a specific type of product, such as nose drops or cough preparations, and sets forth approved ingredients and ingredient combinations and labeling requirements.

Other Classes of Drugs

The act also provides for other types of drugs, including:

- "Not-new" drugs, which are generally presumed to be safe and effective because of their long marketing history.
- "Investigational" drugs, which are new drugs being investigated by researchers. (These may later become subjects of new-drug applications.)
- Antibiotics, which are treated as new drugs until they are approved.
- Insulin, which is subject to provisions similar to those imposed on antibiotics, including testing of samples by FDA.

All of these classifications are subject not only to the drug approval process, but also to the adulteration and misbranding provisions of the law. Applicable sections of the FDA drug regulations spell out precise labeling and warning requirements and other requirements.

Adverse-Reaction Reporting

While a drug is being marketed, any adverse effects must be recorded and reported to FDA. The agency uses these reports to track the drug, and may rescind its approval if the drug proves hazardous.

Color Additives

The FFDCA considers foods, drugs, cosmetics, and some medical devices to be adulterated, and thus in violation of the law, if they contain color additives that have not been proven to the satisfaction of FDA to be safe for a particular use. The agency's regulations, in title 21 of the Code of Federal Regulations, list permitted additives and the conditions under which they may be used. There are separate lists for foods, drugs, and cosmetics, but a specific color may appear on each list, although with different requirements for use. Unless a permitted color is specifically listed as exempt, a sample from each batch manufactured must be tested and certified by FDA before the color can be sold.

Manufacturers who want to have a new color additive listed must apply to FDA. Test data on safety is required.

Food Additives

The FFDCA defines a food additive as a substance that may through its intended use become a component of food, either directly or indirectly, or that may otherwise affect the characteristics of the food. This includes any substance intended for use in producing, manufacturing, packing, processing, preparing, treating, packaging, transporting, or holding the food, plus any source of radiation intended for any such use.

Substances on the "generally recognized as safe" list, substances approved previously by FDA ("prior-sanctioned" additives), pesticide chemicals, color additives, and new animal drugs are exempt from the food-additive requirements. The last three categories of substances, however, are subject to similar safety requirements under other sections of the law.

A substance not already approved for use as a food additive by FDA (as being either generally recognized as safe or prior-sanctioned) is subject to safety clearance from FDA. If this is necessary, testing of the substance, including studies in which the substance is fed to animals, will have to be carried out by the manufacturer in accordance with recognized scientific procedures, and the results must be submitted to FDA.

After reviewing test data and other evidence submitted by the manufacturer, FDA will approve an additive for use if agency officials decide the additive is safe. The agency does this by regulation, and may in the regulation specify conditions of use, the amount that may be in or on the food, the types of food in which the additive may be used, and any labeling that is required.

The Delaney Clause

One particularly controversial provision of the food additive requirements is the Delaney Clause, found in section 490(c)(3) of the act. This section provides that no additive may be deemed safe by FDA if it produces cancer in animals in standardized toxicological tests, or if it is shown by other appropriate tests to be a carcinogenic agent. There is an exception to allow such ingredients in animal feed if use of small amounts causes no harm to the animal and if no residues remain in the edible portions of meat reaching consumers.

In recent years, Congress has specifically permitted use of the artificial sweetener saccharin in foods despite findings that it caused cancer in test animals. The action by Congress, which has been renewed several times, allows continued use of the additive while further evidence is collected.

Migration of Packaging Constituents

Also of special interest are substances that enter a food product by migrating from the food packaging material. Such substances also must be approved as safe by the agency or the product will be considered adulterated and thus illegal. Situations in this area include chemicals migrating into foods from printing ink used on the packaging and chemicals used to make plastic bottles that enter the liquids stored in those bottles. In such cases, the substance that migrates must be tested to determine whether it is a safe food additive or a different packaging must be used. Until the safety of the substance is proven, the product is considered adulterated and must be removed from the market.

Pesticide Residues

Raw agricultural products—unprocessed fruits, grains, and vegetables—that contain residues of pesticides violate the FFDCA unless there is an exemption from a tolerance for that pesticide on that crop, or unless the amount of the pesticide residue on the crop is less than an existing tolerance. EPA, which registers pesticides before interstate distribution, sets tolerances for pesticide residues on raw agricultural crops. It does this after evaluating safety, application, and usage data provided by pesticide manufacturers (see chapter on FIFRA). These tolerances are changed frequently to set limits for use of the pesticide on additional crops or to lower or raise residue limits on crops already allowed to be treated with the pesticide.

Processed foods containing pesticide residues are considered adulterated and illegal unless the residue is due to a permitted use on a raw agricultural commodity or there is a specific food additive regulation permitting use of that pesticide on the processed food. FDA sets tolerances for processed foods under its authority to regulate food additives.

Action Levels

In a related area, FDA also sets "action levels" for chemical contaminants that occur either naturally or inadvertently. For example, fish or shellfish might be contaminated by organic chemicals, pesticides, or other residues because the water in which they live is contaminated. In such cases, FDA, in cooperation with EPA, sets levels above which contaminated fish may not be offered for sale.

Cosmetics

The safety of cosmetics is also the responsibility of FDA, but this area of regulatory activity does not receive the amount of attention devoted to the agency's food and drug activities.

As previously discussed, the FFDCA prohibits distribution of products that are misbranded or adulterated. A cosmetic is considered adulterated if it contains poisonous substances or substances that are harmful to users, if it contains a nonpermitted color, or if it is manufactured or held under unsanitary conditions. Cosmetic labels may not be false or misleading or the cosmetic will be considered misbranded.

The requirements for cosmetics, however, differ from those applied to foods and drugs in that the act does not require cosmetic firms to register manufacturing sites or formulations or to secure approval from FDA before a product is marketed. Firms are encouraged, however, to take part in voluntary programs for registration of manufacturing sites, testing, and reporting of adverse reactions.

With the exception of color additives, the regulation of which is discussed above, a cosmetic manufacturer may use essentially any ingredient or market any cosmetic until FDA proves it may be harmful to consumers. Fewer than a dozen chemical ingredients are prohibited as being harmful, but some products must bear warnings aimed at preventing a health hazard that might be associated with the product. Certain aerosol sprays and feminine hygiene deodorant sprays are two examples of products affected by this warning requirement.

Other Provisions

Other provisions of the food and drug law also regulate the following, in various degrees:

- Biological drugs, including serums, toxins, vaccines, and blood.
- Animal feeds, drugs, and grooming aids and medical devices for use on animals.
- Medical devices for use on humans, such as syringes, pacemakers, contraceptive devices, and diagnostic equipment. (Amendments to the FFDCA enacted in 1976 give the agency broad pre- and post-market authority over such products.)
- Electronic equipment such as televisions and x-ray equipment, laser products, and microwave ovens.

Anti-Drug Abuse Law

Not administered by FDA, but of interest to chemical producers, are provisions of an omnibus anti-drug abuse law (Pub. L.

No. 100-690). The measure imposes notification and recordkeeping requirements on transactions involving 20 listed chemicals often used in the manufacture of illicit drugs. Some very common solvents, such as acetone, ethyl ether, and toluene are included. The Attorney General administers the program.

Occupational Safety and Health Act
(OSH Act)

AT A GLANCE

Public Law Number: Pub. L. No. 91-596

U.S. Code citation: 29 USC 651 *et seq.*

Enacted: December 29, 1970; effective date, April 28, 1971
Amended: 1974 (reauthorization only), 1990

Regulations at: 29 CFR 1910, 1915, 1918, 1926

Federal agency with jurisdiction: Occupational Safety and Health
Administration (OSHA) of the Department of Labor

Congressional committees/subcommittees with jursidiction:
House of Representatives: Health and Safety Subcommittee of the Ed-
ucation and Labor Committee
Senate: Labor Subcommittee of the Labor and Human Resources
Committee

BNA reporting services: *Daily Labor Report, Occupational Safety & Health
Reporter*
Text of law appears in *Occupational Safety & Health Reporter* Reference
File at 71:1101 *et seq.*
Text of regulations appears in *Occupational Safety & Health Reporter*
Reference File
Legal decisions appear in Occupational Safety and Health Cases
(OSH Cases)

What the OSH Act regulates and why: The act provides the regulatory
vehicle for assuring the safety and health of workers in firms generally employing more than 10 people. Its goal is to set standards of
safety that will prevent injury and/or illness among workers. Safety,
chiefly encompassing the physical work environment, and health,

78

which concerns exposure to situations that could induce acute or chronic health effects, are covered by the act.

The regulatory program is carried out through a system of setting standards or guidelines that will provide a safe working environment. In the area of chemicals, this program includes setting standards for exposure to various chemical substances in the workplace and listing permissible exposure limits for airborne contaminants that are not subject to such standards. Informing employees of the dangers posed by substances with which they work and setting a standard policy for regulating substances that cause cancer are among the act's other regulatory goals.

Latest developments: Legislation aimed at comprehensive reform of the OSH Act was introduced in the House (HR 3160) and Senate (S 1622) during 1991, followed by hearings late that year and into 1992. The bills are considered serious attempts to bolster the worker safety and health law, which has remained unchanged for more than 20 years.

A deficit reduction bill (HR 3850) signed by President Bush in November 1990 changed the penalty structure for violations of the OSH Act, giving OSHA authority to increase civil penalties sevenfold for citations against employers violating the act.

In July 1992, a federal appeals court vacated a 1989 OSHA rule that set exposure limits on nearly 400 air contaminants. The court ruled that the agency failed to establish that a health risk existed for each substance.

COVERAGE OF THE LAW

The goal of the Occupational Safety and Health Act of 1970 (OSH Act) is "to assure safe and healthful working conditions for working men and women." The act, which in general applies to workplaces with more than 10 employees, authorizes development of standards to assure this safety. Included are both health standards, which generally are considered to be those that protect workers from exposure to harmful physical or chemical agents in the workplace, and safety standards, which are intended to protect against imminent physical "insults" such as falls, fires, cuts, construction collapse, and electrocution.

Unlike the previously discussed laws dealing with toxic substances, pesticides, and foods and drugs (TSCA, FIFRA, and the FFDCA), which assess the safety of chemicals before use, the OSH Act monitors workplace use of such substances as a way of protecting workers. This monitoring includes establishing exposure standards and guidelines aimed at keeping worker exposure to harmful agents below levels likely to have an adverse effect on health. A variety of methods, from use of protective clothing to removal of a worker from exposure to a substance after he or she reaches a certain exposure level, may be employed. Inspections and a system of penalties for noncompliance are authorized.

DEVELOPMENT OF THE LAW

The federal OSH Act was born after several years of efforts prompted by increasing public concern about workplace hazards, the effects of chemical agents on the environment, and several incidents where workers were injured by exposure to hazardous chemicals.

As part of the "Great Society" social programs of the late 1960s, President Lyndon B. Johnson in 1968 proposed a national health and safety program to protect workers. Although the 1968 measure was not successful (it died in both the House and the Senate after the House Rules Committee refused to clear it), the need for passing some type of federal occupational safety program was pointed to by voluminous testimony during hearings on the bill and on later measures. According to that testimony, state agencies and labor groups offered some protection against workplace hazards but the protection was not enough. Federal efforts were confined to certain industries such as mining, railroading, and longshoring, and were subject to varying degrees of financial and technical support.

Health and Safety Issues

Paramount among the reasons for passage of the OSH Act was the preponderance of testimony alleging that working in U.S. industry was not only hazardous but also costly in terms of time lost from work because of illness or injury. Some of the safety and health statistics offered in support of a federal law were as follows:

- Each year 14,000 workers died and 2.2 million were disabled by accidents in the workplace, according to former Labor Secretary George P. Shultz.
- Work-related deaths and injuries were causing annual losses of $1.5 billion in wages and $8 billion in the gross national product.
- About 65 percent of U.S. workers were being exposed to harmful physical agents, yet only about 25 percent of them were adequately protected.
- A total of 390,000 new cases of occupational disease were occurring each year.
- Chemical agents, including lead, mercury, asbestos, and cotton dust, were posing known health threats to workers but were not being controlled.
- A new, potentially toxic chemical was being introduced in industry every 20 minutes, according to a Public Health Service estimate.

Congressional Agreement

Although the 1968 legislative effort was unsuccessful, debate on this bill eased the way for acceptance of the concept of some kind of comprehensive federal law in this regard. When the 91st Congress was convened in 1970, it was faced with four separate bills, two considered to be pro-labor and two, sponsored by the Nixon administration, considered pro-industry.

After almost a year of debate and argument over the issue, the Senate and House finally passed separate bills on worker safety. Differences between the two measures were ironed out during five conference committee sessions, and both the House and Senate approved a compromise measure in December 1970. The new law was signed on December 30, 1970, by President Richard M. Nixon, who said, "This bill represents in its culmination the American system at its best."

The law has remained virtually unchanged during the years since. Several new regulatory programs have been added and health protection has moved into a position of greater prominence, but the basic framework of standard-setting, recordkeeping, and reporting operates much as it did when the law was enacted.

However, serious efforts to reform the OSH Act were put in motion with the introduction in 1991 of the proposed Comprehensive Occupational Safety and Health Act. The bill, offered in both the House (HR 3160) and Senate (S 1622), calls for a larger role for employees and employers in preventing safety and health hazards in the workplace through joint labor/management safety and health committees. It would speed the required time in which the Occupational Safety and Health Administration (OSHA) must respond to petitions for health and safety standards; increase OSH Act enforcement provisions; and expand coverage of the act to include federal, state, and local government employees and workers in federal nuclear facilities under the jurisdiction of the Department of Energy. The measure was pending as of mid-1992.

PROVISIONS OF THE LAW

In passing the OSH Act, Congress intended to assure safe and healthy working conditions for workers in all 50 states, the District of Columbia, Puerto Rico, and U.S. possessions. In general, the act covers workplaces with 11 or more workers. Federal employees and workplaces protected by other federal agencies are exempt, as are farms and the self-employed. The act covers both safety and health hazards, requires medical and other recordkeeping to track development and incidence of occupationally induced disease, and provides for research in the field of occupational safety and health. OSHA was established within the Labor Department to administer the new law and to carry on with earlier Labor Department efforts to regulate the mining, rail, and longshoring industries.

The main provisions of the act dealing with toxic substances are authorized by section 6, which allows OSHA to set safety and health standards. Workplaces covered by the act, in turn, are required to comply with these standards by section 5 of the act, which requires employers to furnish workplaces "free from recognized hazards that are causing or are likely to cause death or serious physical harm" to workers.

Section 8 of the act empowers OSHA to require employers to keep records of incidents in the workplace, and allows the agency or its authorized representative to inspect workplaces to assure that the mandates of the act and rules issued under it are being followed.

As drafted by Congress, the act also requires that states play a major role in enforcement. Under this provision, states may adopt occupational safety and health programs equal to the federal program and submit their program plan for OSHA approval. If the state plan is approved, the state assumes responsibility for enforcing employer compliance with the federal statute and rules. As of 1991, 23 states and U.S. territories had OSHA-approved plans covering all employees, and 2 states had plans covering public sector workers only. Occupational safety and health programs in states without OSHA-approved state plans may be preempted by OSHA, thereby giving the federal agency, rather than the state, jurisdiction over workplace safety.

As is the case with other federal agencies, standards and other requirements imposed by OSHA under the act must be promulgated after formal proposal in the *Federal Register* and collection of public comment. Rules issued by the agency are reviewable by federal courts if challenged.

The major areas where OSHA rulemaking affects toxic substances are:

- Health standards, which generally are limits on exposure to hazardous substances in the workplace
- The OSHA cancer policy, which sets forth agency action on exposure to cancer-causing substances
- The hazard communication standard, which requires chemical hazard assessment and labeling plus worker training
- Recordkeeping, inspections, and other requirements

Health Standards

In carrying out its duties under the act, OSHA is responsible for promulgating legally enforceable health and safety standards. These may require specific conditions or use of one or more work practices or processes that are reasonably necessary to protect workers. Employers must become familiar with standards applicable to their establishments and ensure that employees have and use personal protective equipment required for their safety. Even where no standard exists, employers are responsible for following the intent of the act's "general duty" clause. This requires employers to furnish "a place of employment which is free from recognized hazards that are causing or are likely to cause death or serious physical harm" to employees.

Types of Standards

The health and safety standards fall into four major categories: general industry standards, which are broadly applicable, and standards for either the maritime, construction, or agriculture sectors, which apply only to specific types of employees and work environments. The general industry standards include, for example, requirements concerning safety on working and walking surfaces, ventilation, hazardous materials handling, fire protection, electrical safety, welding and machinery safety, and toxic and hazardous substances.

It is in this last category, toxic and hazardous substances, that standards for chemicals are found. The section of regulations involved, subpart Z of 29 CFR 1910, sets specific limits and conditions for use and exposure to chemicals in the workplace. As of early 1992, 27 substances were covered by comprehensive OSHA standards. These standards set exposure limits, require monitoring, establish worker-education programs, and require medical surveillance of workers. About 400 other substances were listed as air contaminants and were subject only to specific exposure limits. However, a federal appeals court vacated this rule in July 1992, saying OSHA failed to establish that a significant health risk existed for each substance.

Standard Setting

OSHA may set a standard on its own initiative, or on request from other parties, including the Secretary of Health and Human Services, the National Institute for Occupational Safety and Health (NIOSH), state and/or local governments, employer or labor representatives, any nationally recognized standards setting body, or any other interested party. If OSHA determines that a specific standard is needed, it may call on one of several advisory groups to advise it on how best to proceed. These committees are composed of industry, labor, and government representatives.

NIOSH Recommendations

Many recommendations for setting a standard come from NIOSH, established under the act as an arm of the Department of Health and Human Services specifically authorized to conduct research on safety and health issues. NIOSH is especially active in conducting research on toxic substances and in recommending criteria for using and handling such substances in the workplace.

One of the other functions of NIOSH is that of carrying out investigations. While researching toxic substances or other hazards in the workplace, NIOSH frequently does field studies. In these cases it goes into the workplace, gathers information from workers and employers, measures exposure to chemicals being used, and generally gathers data on a suspected problem. It also may require that employers take over this duty and that workers be given medical examinations to determine if any occupationally related illness is occurring. If NIOSH requires these tests, however, the government, rather than the employer, may pay for them.

How a Standard Is Set

Section 6(b) of the OSH Act describes the process for setting a standard. A standard first must be issued as a formally proposed rule or in an even earlier version called an advance notice of proposed rulemaking. The notice, which is published in the *Federal Register,* warns that a proposed rule is being developed, outlines the terms of the proposed rule, and provides a specific period of time for the public to comment on what OSHA is planning to do. The public may request a hearing on the proposal or OSHA may schedule one. A final standard must be published 60 days after the comment period (which must last at least 30 days) ends on a proposed rule or 60 days after the conclusion of any public hearing on the proposed rule. For this reason, the notice of proposed rulemaking or advance notice of proposed rulemaking often is used to give the agency more time to gather information on the effects of any standard it is planning to propose. If a notice or advance notice of proposed rulemaking is used, the agency still must issue a proposed rule before promulgating a final rule, but it can avoid the imposition of the 60-day limit for issuance of a final standard that would apply if a proposed rule were issued initially.

After the end of either the comment period or the hearing, a final rule is published in the *Federal Register.* It includes the date the rule takes effect and explains the effect of the standard and OSHA's reason for issuing it. Parties that object to a final standard because they consider it either too lenient or too burdensome may petition a federal appeals court for review. Because the first court so petitioned usually has jurisdiction over the court case, parties objecting to a standard usually file a petition for review in what they believe will be the most favorable court within minutes after the standard is signed by the OSHA administrator. A standard still goes into effect if a petition for review is filed, however, unless the court delays implementation by issuing a stay.

Emergency Standards

Section 6(c) of the OSH Act allows OSHA to issue an emergency standard if the agency believes employees are in "grave danger" from a new workplace condition or exposure to a toxic substance. An emergency standard takes effect immediately upon publication in the *Federal Register*. At the same time, the agency must begin rulemaking to set a permanent standard, including solicitation of public comment. A final standard must be issued within six months after the emergency standard takes effect.

Legal Issues

Courts ruling on challenges to OSHA standards have given the agency several guidelines on when a standard for a toxic substance may be issued. Pursuant to the U.S. Supreme Court ruling in *Industrial Union Department, AFL-CIO v. American Petroleum Institute* (448 U.S. 607, 8 OSH Cases 1586 (1980)), OSHA must show that a "significant risk" exists before it issues a standard regulating a toxic substance. Where the agency sets a standard that tends toward "error on the side of overprotection," it must be able to cite a "body of reputable scientific thought" to support that action, the Court stated. Also, under the Supreme Court's ruling in *American Textile Manufacturers Institute, Inc. v. Donovan* (452 U.S. 490, 9 OSH Cases 1913 (1981)), a standard must be "feasible." This means that the agency must issue a standard that most adequately assures that no employee will suffer material impairment to health, limited only by the extent to which this is "capable of being done."

It was on such grounds that the Supreme Court in 1980 invalidated OSHA's standard for benzene in the first of the two cases just mentioned. Using wording in section 3(b) of the act, the Court found that the term "reasonably necessary" in the OSH Act means that a "significant risk" must exist and that OSHA in its rulemaking must show this. The phrase "significant risk," however, does not appear in the OSH Act. A revised benzene standard went into force in December 1987.

OSHA's exposure limits for almost 400 workplace air contaminants was vacated in July 1992 (*AFL-CIO v. OSHA*, No. 89-7185 (11th Cir.)). The court ruled that OSHA's "generic" rule-making for air contaminants was inappropriate and that the substances involved had little in common. It said the agency failed to establish that a significant risk of material health impairment existed for each substance, adding that nothing in the OSH Act prevents the agency from addressing multiple substances in a single rule, but each exposure limit must be able to stand alone.

The agency issued the air contaminants rule in 1989 to update exposure limits adopted in 1971. In the 1989 rule, OSHA created new exposure limits for a number of substances that previously had not been regulated.

Occupational safety and health analysts said the ruling created a serious impediment to OSHA's ability to protect workers from exposure to thousands of toxic chemicals in the workplace. OSHA is seeking rehearing in the case.

Standards for Specific Chemicals

When the OSH Act was passed in 1970, section 6(a) instructed that OSHA should quickly promulgate as health standards existing national-consensus standards and established federal standards. Section 6(b) authorized OSHA to "promulgate, modify, or revoke any occupational safety or health standard" if the agency determined that a rule should be issued in order to serve the objectives of the act.

Initial Standards Package

Under section 6(a), OSHA in 1971 promulgated a package of standards that incorporated existing federal health and safety standards that were in place under a variety of worker-protection statutes. This initial package designated about 400 substances as air contaminants and set threshold-limit values as exposure standards for them. About 380 of these substances still are subject to only the air exposure limits set out in 1971. They are found in 29 CFR 1910.1000. If the agency should decide to impose further restrictions on any of these substances or on any others, it must do so through the formal rulemaking process authorized by section 6(b).

Individual Standards

As of 1986, OSHA had designated 24 substances under section 6(b) of the act as in need of controls over and above those mandated for the original 400 air contaminant standards.

In setting standards, OSHA determines their feasibility and generally evaluates three types of health effects of the substance involved: acute or immediate health effects, chronic or long-term health effects, and carcinogenicity (ability to cause cancer). A finding of an adverse effect in any one of these categories is sufficient ground for promulgating a standard.

Each of the specific standards is slightly different in its requirements. In general, however, each stipulates specific requirements concerning the following:

- Exposure limits
- Labeling
- Protective equipment
- Control procedures
- Monitoring and measuring of employee exposure
- Medical examinations
- Access by OSHA to records of the exposure-monitoring activities

Many of the standards also include "action levels" which trigger monitoring and medical surveillance of workers who are exposed to a toxic substance at a level below the permissible exposure limit. For example, medical monitoring and surveillance might be required when workers are exposed to a specific level of a substance for a certain number of days or hours per year; the permissible exposure limit for any given exposure, however, may be much higher.

Asbestos, in 1972, was the first chemical covered by a specific final standard. In 1974, standards were set for 14 carcinogens; one was later withdrawn. Between 1974 and the end of 1991, OSHA promulgated 12 more standards:

- Vinyl chloride
- Inorganic arsenic
- Lead
- Benzene
- Coke oven emissions
- Cotton dust
- 1,2-dibromo-3-chloropropane
- Acrylonitrile
- Cotton gin dust
- Coal tar pitch volatiles

- Ethylene oxide
- Formaldehyde

In 1975, standards for toluene, beryllium, trichloroethylene, and sulfur dioxide were proposed; these have never been promulgated in final form. The cotton dust standard was overturned by the courts and although reproposed in late 1985, is still stayed. A revised asbestos standard was issued in 1986, and was scheduled to be updated in 1992.

The Cancer Policy

Another OSHA regulatory program that affects chemicals is the agency's cancer policy. Promulgated in 1980, it sets forth criteria OSHA will use to identify, classify, and regulate chemicals for which there is evidence of a carcinogenic potential as far as humans are concerned. The purpose of the policy is to improve the efficiency and specificity of rulemakings to set occupational standards for carcinogens. It also should ensure uniformity of treatment and avoid litigation over the agency's regulation of carcinogenic chemicals, OSHA has said. Codified at 29 CFR 1990, the policy describes in detail the kinds of scientific evidence that OSHA will use in determining which carcinogens to regulate, and establishes a detailed process for the writing of regulations for individual carcinogens.

Intent of Policy

The agency's announced intent in issuing the cancer policy was:

- To provide an orderly, comprehensive, consistent, and scientifically feasible system for regulatory actions to reduce or prevent worker exposure to potential carcinogens
- To permit OSHA to regulate potential carcinogens in a timely manner
- To present the factors OSHA will consider in setting priorities for the regulation of potential carcinogens
- To "carry out the intent of the [OSH] Act with respect to identification, classification, and regulation of potential occupational carcinogens"

The cancer policy is in effect except for the provisions that require OSHA to publish the candidate and priority lists, which have been stayed.

Classification Provisions

At the center of the debate over the cancer policy were its provisions for classifying carcinogens into two groups—those for which there is *substantial* evidence that a chemical is a potential human carcinogen (Category I) and those for which there is *suggestive* evidence that this may be the case (Category II). The differentiation between the two groups depends mainly on the type and number of tests that implicate the substance as a cancer-causing agent.

Priority Factors

The cancer policy also sets out a list of factors that the agency will use to evaluate which chemicals to regulate. The factors include the number of workers exposed, levels of human exposure, risk from exposure, the extent to which regulatory action could reduce the risk, whether substitutes are available, and whether other federal agencies are taking action that would control the risk.

The policy calls for development of two priority lists. A high regulatory priority list would contain about 10 chemicals drawn from those in Category I; the other list would include chemicals that meet the Category II criteria but have a lower regulatory priority. It was industry outcry over these lists that caused their withdrawal.

Rulemaking Provisions

The cancer policy also includes general provisions on use of human and animal data in evaluating the cancer-causing ability of chemicals and lists the issues the agency may consider in rulemakings on carcinogens. The policy also includes two model carcinogen standards.

Hazard Communication Standard

Late in 1983, OSHA issued a hazard communication standard that requires chemical manufacturers and importers to assess the hazards of the chemicals they make or import and to inform workers of the hazards associated with the chemicals in their work area (29 CFR 1910.1200).

Several states, labor organizations, and a group of advocacy organizations immediately challenged the standard in a federal court as being too limited to protect workers adequately and too protective of industry data, and as improperly preempting state laws that require industry to supply workers and communities with information on hazardous chemicals. In May 1985, the U.S. Court of Appeals for the Third Circuit ruled that OSHA must give employees access to trade secret information, and ordered OSHA to cover all workers unless it could prove this would be infeasible (*United Steelworkers v. Auchter,* 763 F.2d 728, OSH Cases 1337 (3d Cir. 1985)). The agency in November 1985 revised the standard to broaden access to trade secrets and issued a notice seeking information on how to broaden the standard to cover more industries and workers. Final action to broaden the standard is likely to take several years.

The court also ruled that the federal standard preempts state and local right-to-know laws in the manufacturing sector, but left open for future consideration whether the standard would preempt state laws once it is broadened.

The standard's provisions for manufacturers took effect November 25, 1985, with employee training and notification provisions becoming effective May 25, 1986. The final standard came almost three years after the agency first proposed a broad hazard communication and labeling rule that was strongly opposed by industry, chiefly because of the costs associated with compliance.

According to OSHA, the standard will reduce the incidence of chemically related occupational illness and will protect some 14 million workers. The standard has forced about 10,000 firms to develop hazard assessment data and to pass it on to purchasers and workers, who can then protect themselves better, OSHA said.

In addition to hazard assessment and worker training, the standard requires labeling of chemicals, the granting of access to safety data, and recordkeeping. The standard applies to all industries.

Hazard Determination

Under the hazard communication standard, manufacturers and importers must determine whether a hazard is posed by the substances they produce or import and must assess the nature of that hazard. The manufacturer or importer is held accountable for the hazard evaluation and must supply information on those hazards with the substances they sell. Among the hazards that must be evaluated are a chemical's physical hazards and its health hazards.

Physical Hazards

Physical hazards are dangers that are intrinsic to the substance, that generally pose hazards to property, and that are commonly recognized. These include such characteristics as flammability, reactivity, radioactivity, and explosiveness. Such hazards generally are covered by the Department of Transportation in its hazardous materials table (see chapter on HMTA).

Health Hazards

Under the standard, chemicals are presumed to pose a health hazard if they are listed under Subpart Z of the OSHA standards for hazardous and toxic substances or if they are listed as carcinogens by the National Toxicology Program (NTP) or the International Agency for Research on Cancer (IARC). This grouping alone gives a base of about 600 chemicals that are covered by the standard. Substances for which the American Conference of Governmental Industrial Hygienists have adopted threshold limit values (TLVs) also are covered by the standard.

Also considered to be health hazards are carcinogens, corrosives, irritants, and sensitizers, as well as chemicals that are toxic or highly toxic, or that exhibit target organ effects. Each of these terms is explained in the standard through the use of examples and some definitions in terms of animal tests.

In determining whether a health hazard exists, the standard says that a manufacturer must rely on animal data, human epidemiological data, evidence of cancer as outlined above (i.e., listing as a carcinogen by recognized groups such as NTP or IARC), and/or results of any studies conducted under established scientific principles that indicate a health hazard exists.

Evaluations and Communication Programs

Once a manufacturer or importer determines that a substance poses either a physical or a health hazard, this information must be supplied to purchasers of the substance. The information will be used by purchasing employers to develop the written hazard communication program required under the standard. This plan must include a list of the hazardous substances used in the workplace and a plan for informing workers and contractors of these hazards, as well as provisions for labeling containers of hazardous substances, for keeping on hand hazardous material safety data sheets provided by manufacturers/importers, and for conducting employee information and training activities.

Labeling

Manufacturers, importers, and distributors of chemicals covered under the hazard communication standard must label each chemical when it leaves their control. The labels must include the identity of the chemical, hazard warnings, and the name and address of the manufacturer or importer. According to OSHA, the labels may not conflict with Department of Transportation labeling requirements under the Hazardous Materials Transportation Act (see chapter on HMTA).

Labeling is also required of employers covered by the standard. Every container of hazardous materials in the workplace must be labeled with the name of the chemical and with hazard warnings. Various types of labeling are permitted as long as the identity of a substance is clear to those using it. The only exceptions for employers are that other labeling means, such as batch tickets, may be used on stationary-process containers and that no labeling is required on portable containers to which an employee transfers a chemical from a labeled container for his or her individual use.

Material Safety Data Sheets

As part of the hazard communication standard, OSHA requires that chemical manufacturers and importers provide a material safety data sheet with each chemical they sell. The sheet must give the identity of the chemical, the physical and chemical characteristics of the substance (such as flash point), and the physical and health hazards posed by the chemical.

Mixtures also must be labeled as such, with the characteristics of each part of the mixture in excess of 1 percent listed if the mixture has not been tested as a whole. Carcinogens, however, must be listed if they comprise more than 0.1 percent of the mixture.

The material safety data sheet also must contain a listing of health hazards from exposure, including signs of exposure, primary route of exposure, the OSHA or other exposure limit, whether the substance is a carcinogen, precautions for safe handling, and information on emergency and first aid procedures. The name and address of the manufacturer also must be included.

Employers must keep a copy of the material safety data sheet on hand for each chemical or mixture used in the workplace. The sheets must be accessible to employees at all times.

Employee Information and Training

The hazard communication standard also requires that employers train workers in hazardous materials handling and tell workers where the material safety data sheets can be found. The training must include information on the hazards of all chemicals used in their work area and on measures employees can take to protect themselves from the hazards of the substances.

Employees working when the standard took effect had to be trained by May 1986. New employees must be trained when employed or when shifting to a work area where new or different substances are used.

Trade Secrets

The hazard communication standard also provides for trade secret protection and outlines who may have access to confidential information on hazardous substances. Under the standard, chemical identity information may be omitted from the material safety data sheet under several conditions. These are that the sheet must indicate the properties and effects of the substance, that specific identity is being withheld as a trade secret, and that the trade secret claim regarding the substance can be supported.

The trade secret information, however, must be released to health professionals in a medical emergency or upon written request from a health professional who explains why the information is needed and who agrees not to release the information. If an employer refuses to release chemical-identity data, it must explain why the information is a trade secret. Such denials may be appealed to OSHA, which may issue citations for failure to honor a legitimate request. Issuance of a citation may lead to imposition of a penalty.

Trade secret information also must be released to employees or their representatives upon request. A written confidentiality agreement may be required from the employee, the representative, or the health professional.

Extension to All Workplaces

The OSHA hazard communication standard was extended to all workplaces, even to nonmanufacturing industries, on August 1, 1988, although there were court delays about its applicability to the construction industry. In general, all employers became responsible for providing warnings, training, and information on hazardous materials to their employees.

Other Provisions

Recordkeeping and Reporting

Other provisions of the OSH act require recordkeeping and reporting to OSHA of occupational safety and health problems, including illness and injuries. An annual log must be kept, but many types of serious injuries and any deaths must be reported to OSHA immediately. Such statistics must be kept on a calendar year basis. Many specific chemical standards and medical recordkeeping provisions contain additional recordkeeping and reporting requirements (e.g., to record the number of employees exposed to a certain chemical above a certain level).

Medical Records

Under 29 CFR 1910.20, employers must maintain medical and chemical exposure records for all exposed employees for at least 30 years. Employees must be permitted to see and copy those records upon written request. Access must be granted within 15 days after a request is made. In some cases, others also are guaranteed access to these records. Among them are representatives of the employee and of OSHA.

Inspections and Penalties

The OSH Act also provides for inspection of facilities that come under the jurisdiction of the act and for imposition of penalties for noncompliance. Inspections usually are performed unannounced, but the inspector must have a warrant if the employer refuses access without one.

Situations where an imminent danger is suspected are given first priority for inspection. Last priority goes to workplaces with little hazard potential or with a history of few or no OSHA violations. Certain high-hazard industries, workplaces where a fatality or major accident has occurred, and job sites where an employee complains of an OSHA violation also are given priority treatment in scheduling inspections.

The act also provides for citations and penalties. A citation is a notice from OSHA that a violation of agency regulations was found during an inspection; citations may or may not have penalties attached. Penalties of up to $70,000 per violation are authorized, with the exact amount determined by the gravity of the offense. Penalties also may be imposed for falsifying records, failing to post required OSHA notices, interfering with an OSHA inspector, or failing to correct a violation.

Part II

Chemical By-Product Laws

Clean Air Act
(CAA)

Public Law Number: Pub. L. No. 101-549

U.S. Code citation: 42 USC 7401 *et seq.*

Enacted: December 31, 1970; effective when enacted
   Amended: 1973, 1974, 1977 (major amendments, Pub. L. No. 95-95),
       1978, 1980, 1981, 1983, 1990 (major amendments, Pub. L. No.
       101-549)

Regulations at: 40 CFR 50–80

Federal agency with jurisdiction: Environmental Protection Agency
   (EPA)

Congressional committees/subcommittees with jurisdiction:
   House of Representatives: Health and the Environment Subcommittee
       of the Energy and Commerce Committee
   Senate: Environmental and Public Works Committee

BNA reporting services: *Environment Reporter, Daily Environment Report*
   Text of law appears in *Environment Reporter* Federal Laws at 71:1101
       et seq.
   Text of regulations appears in *Environment Reporter* Federal
       Regulations
   Legal decisions appear in Environment Reporter Cases (ER Cases)

What the CAA regulates and why: The act provides the regulatory vehicle
   for prevention and control of discharges into the air of substances
   that may harm public health or natural resources. Included are both
   stationary sources of pollutants (factories, etc.) and mobile sources
   (automobiles, trucks, and airplanes).

Clean Air Act—Contd.

Under the act, the EPA sets national ambient air quality standards to specify the level at which air pollutants can be safely tolerated. These are national standards which all areas in the United States must meet. More than 100 areas still failed to meet these requirements as of early 1992.

Substances entering the air from any source are regulated through a system of national emission limits and permits for individual dischargers. Both new and existing polluters are required to comply with standards under the act. The amount of discharges permitted depends on the type and age of the plant and the type of substance being released. Various types of pollution control equipment are used to bring a pollution source into compliance.

Most enforcement and issuing of permits for pollution sources is carried out by states that adopt EPA-approved State Implementation Plans for controlling air pollution.

Latest developments: The CAA was amended in 1990, providing one of the most comprehensive pieces of environmental legislation ever enacted. The new law set out to cut emissions of air pollutants by 56 billion tons per year through incorporation of market-based strategies that allow polluters to trade air pollution credits.

The primary focuses of the act are to clean up the air in urban areas, to regulate toxics more stringently, and to tackle the sensitive problem of acid rain. Instead of mandating the usual command-and-control form of regulation, the CAA sets goals and allows industries to find their own cost-effective means of meeting them.

The revised CAA was hailed as a model for other environmental legislation that will come up for reauthorization.

COVERAGE OF THE LAW

The goal of the Clean Air Act (CAA) is to prevent or control discharge into the air of substances that may harm public health or natural resources. It also intends to cut emissions of those substances that cause acid rain, deplete the stratospheric ozone layer, and contribute to global climate change.

The act contains specific plans to achieve these goals and tight deadlines for when they should be met. EPA is authorized under the act to address pollution problems caused by both existing and new stationary facilities, as well as motor vehicle sources. To do this, EPA must promulgate hundreds of rules reflecting not only health-based standards, but also standards based on current, state-of-the-art technology.

Amendments to the CAA adopted in 1977 required EPA to set national ambient air quality standards after determining at which levels air pollutants could be safely tolerated. These standards were to have been met by the end of 1987. The 1990 amendments to the act set a strategy for states to address those areas that have failed to attain the air quality standards.

Unlike chemical use and assessment laws, the CAA is a by-product control law. Its aim is to control air quality by regulating discharge into the air of substances that would change the ambient quality of the air. These substances enter the air as by-products of some activity or process. Factories create air pollution by discharging various substances and particles of ash generated during industrial processes. Automobile exhaust also causes air pollution.

The CAA as amended in 1990 embodies several progressive and creative new themes. Specifically, the new law:

- Encourages the use of market-based principles and other such innovative approaches as performance-based standards and emissions banking and trading
- Sets standards for the California pilot program, a clean-fuel vehicle plan, that can be met by the most cost-effective combination of alternative clean fuels and technology
- Establishes a program to reduce emissions of pollutants that cause acid rain by promoting the use of low-sulfur coal and natural gas as well as innovative technologies to clean high-sulfur coal
- Promotes energy conservation and creates a market for alternative fuels derived from grain and natural gas to cut oil imports by one million barrels of oil per day
- Sets maximum achievable control technology (MACT) standards for source categories established from a list of 189 toxic chemicals, and creates a Chemical Safety Board to investigate accidental releases of extremely hazardous chemicals

Among the criteria for listing a substance as a pollutant is whether it may be reasonably anticipated to endanger public health.

DEVELOPMENT OF THE LAW

The CAA, unlike several other environmental laws, was not drafted as a unified piece of legislation but expanded and grew as Congress decided more fine-tuning or regulatory authority was needed.

The original Clean Air Act was passed in 1955. Spurred by the smoky, dirty air that had plagued many industrial cities for decades, legislators decided to take action to control what were mainly unspecified particles of waste spewed into the air by factories. In subsequent years—1963, 1965, and 1967—the act was amended to add various provisions in response to new scientific knowledge about the effects and sources of pollution. The most notable amendments were those made in 1970, 1977, and 1990. These amendments made air pollution control a national rather than local goal and established the stringent federal clean air program that exists today.

1970 Amendments

In passing the amendments of 1970, Congress authorized the establishment of stringent uniform national ambient air quality standards to safeguard public health and environmental quality. Spurred by the environmental concerns of the late 1960s, Congress in the 1970 amendments set a general strategy for controlling air contaminants, including automobile exhausts.

The 1970 amendments called for a cooperative state–federal effort to control air pollution, but made it clear that state and local governments would have primary responsibility for limiting air pollution, with federal financial assistance.

1977 Amendments

The 1977 amendments drew on the state–federal experience under the 1970 law and were an effort to fine-tune the law while maintaining its general strategy. In 1977 Congress gave special attention to the criteria that must be met before a substance could be regulated under the act. Past experience with the law had shown some confusion among various groups that had read the act differently.

The 1977 amendments attempted to address these disparate requirements by adopting a standardized basis for rulemaking under the following sections of the act:

- Section 108 (criteria for national ambient air quality standards)
- Section 111 (new-source performance standards)
- Section 112 (hazardous air pollution standards where the risk would have to be more serious than for regulation under section 108)
- Section 202 (motor vehicle standards)
- Section 211 (fuel and fuel-additive provisions)
- Section 231 (aircraft emission standards)

In 1977 Congress also added provisions to guarantee that areas with clean air would not deteriorate. In addition, new provisions specified that any new source of pollution would have to meet a stringent set of technical standards, and additional pollution-causing development would only be permitted if offsetting reductions were made at existing pollution sources.

Degree of Proof

Chief among the concerns of Congress when it tackled the act in 1977 was the extent to which the judgment of EPA would apply to regulation under the act. Did the administrator need proof of harm in order to regulate or was there a preventive purpose contained in the act? The courts had answered this question in several key cases, among them a 1976 case brought by Ethyl Corporation which challenged the act's regulation of fuel additives. In a ruling that applied to the entire act, the District of Columbia Court of Appeals had ruled in the case that EPA should assess the risk of harm occurring and that if the risk was found to be significant, the act authorized the agency to act to prevent the harm from occurring (*Ethyl Corp. v. EPA*, 541 F2d 1, 8 ER Cases 1785 (D.C. Cir.), *cert. denied*, 426 U.S. 941, 8 ER Cases 2200 (1976)).

Before that ruling, it had been generally accepted at EPA and in Congress that the agency had this judgmental discretion in regulating air pollutants and that this judgment allowed consideration of all sources of human and environmental exposure to a substance. The court, however, clarified that EPA did not have to wait for actual harm to occur before regulating a pollutant; knowledge that a pollutant would contribute to the total amount of human and environmental exposure to a substance, and thus increase the risk of harm, was sufficient reason for deciding to regulate, the court said.

1990 amendments to the act expanded on that ruling in some sections. For instance, in a title dealing with the protection of the stratospheric ozone layer, Congress inserted a provision calling on the agency to accelerate the phaseout dates of harmful ozone-depleting substances if new scientific data reveal a need to do so.

Congressional Response

With an eye to such court decisions under the act, in 1977 Congress attempted to clarify its intention that EPA should have authority to use its judgment when deciding which pollutants to regulate and how to regulate them. The 1977 amendments clarified the role of EPA by stating the following:

- EPA may act to prevent harm before it occurs and does not have to prove that harm has occurred before it regulates.
- EPA must assess risks before regulating.
- In deciding that a public danger is being posed, the agency may consider cumulative risk from multiple sources of a pollutant.
- The degree-of-proof requirement that EPA must show risk, but not proof, of harm before regulating applies to all sources of pollutants under various sections of the act.
- The protection of public health required by the act should extend both to healthy and to particularly susceptible people.
- In reviewing any EPA actions under the act, the courts should base their decision on whether EPA has reached reasonable conclusions that are rationally justified.

Regulatory Alternatives?

Another factor bearing on Congressional changes to the act is the body of legal decisions (case law) concerning the act that indicates that setting ambient air quality standards is a primary purpose of the act. In 1977 Congress clarified that regulation of pollutants under other sections of the statute is a means, not a substitute, for attaining those ambient standards. Hazardous air pollutants, however, are somewhat of an exception to this, because section 112 expressly states that no ambient air quality standard is to apply to hazardous pollutants, which are regulated far more stringently, as discussed below. (Ambient standards may be set only for nonhazardous pollutants.) However, over the history of the air toxics program, only eight hazardous pollutants have been regulated.

Recognizing that the 1977 amendments failed substantially to reduce emissions of these very threatening substances, Congress included an entire title in the 1990 amendments that lists 189 pollutants for which source categories must be developed and then regulated.

1990 Amendments

By the end of the 1980s, it had been recognized for years that the CAA needed fixing. Repeated attempts to do so were thwarted by sharp political divisions. Roughly two years of intense negotiations preceded adoption of the 1990 amendments.

The 1990 amendments expanded the 1977 law to reduce certain criteria air pollutants. They set forth a strategy for states, with federal guidance, to clean up urban smog in the 100 most polluted cities by 2000. Moreover, they aim to cut toxic air pollution and emissions from motor vehicles each by at least 90 percent. The new law, EPA said, would remove 56 billion tons of pollutants from the air every year—or 224 tons per U.S. resident—at an estimated annual cost of $25 billion.

One of the most divisive issues of the bill that put the 1990 amendments in place was the section dealing with acid rain. The program that was finally agreed upon sets up a market-based system that allows polluters to reduce their acid-rain causing emissions by trading pollution credits. The goal is to halve these emissions by 2000.

The latest amendments also focus more attention on motor vehicles by requiring tailpipe emissions standards, providing a framework for reformulated fuels, and establishing a clean-fuel vehicle program in California, which has some of the worst urban air pollution problems in the country.

The new amendments also require phasing out certain chemicals that deplete the earth's protective ozone layer. The law is somewhat tighter than the international Montreal Protocol on Substances that Deplete the Ozone Layer, which was ratified to tackle the problem of a growing ozone hole.

A new permits provision was also placed in the law to make it more workable. In addition, under the new law many small businesses are subject for the first time to federal air pollution requirements.

Finally, new enforcement provisions embodying the "polluter pays" philosophy were added that include new criminal sanctions and change violations from misdemeanors to felonies.

PROVISIONS OF THE LAW

Although the CAA taken as a whole provides a broad scheme for controlling air pollution, implementation has not been smooth.

One reason is that the act has spawned probably more court challenges than any environmental law ever written. This occurred primarily because the act's provisions are so varied and overlap so much that the question of how EPA uses its authority under the act is always open to challenge. With respect to chemicals, a second reason for the act's implementation problems has been the need for scientific data to support such regulation. In many cases, such information is nonexistent or sketchy, and correlations of the data with actual health or environmental effects is difficult.

Then came the 1990 amendments. Their passage presented a new implementation challenge for EPA: it was required to issue 27 rules in the first year of enactment and 28 more the following year. Before this, the annual average number of rules issued for air pollution control was 6 to 8. EPA missed many deadlines, in large part because of delays from the White House Office of Management and Budget (OMB). OMB took issue with many of the agency's interpretations of the CAA and insisted that changes be made in proposed rules. As a result, EPA was on the receiving end of several lawsuits from environmental groups, and was criticized by members of Congress for being late. This happened in spite of the fact EPA hired 500 new staff members to work only on the Clean Air Act.

The main sections of the act that affect chemicals are:

- Section 109, which authorizes EPA to set ambient air quality standards
- Section 112, which authorizes regulation of hazardous air pollutants
- Section 111, which deals with new source pollution performance standards

Section 109: Ambient Air Quality Standards

National ambient air quality standards, authorized under section 109 of the CAA, are different from most other regulations issued under the act. The purpose of ambient standards is to provide a basic standard for air quality across the United States. Specific limits for states and local areas often are more strict because they are developed by those areas in line with local emissions and atmospheric conditions. State and local air quality standards, thus, need not be uniform across the country, as long as the overall ambient (basic) standard is met.

The focus of the standards is different as well from the focus of most other regulations issued under the CAA. The standards apply to specific chemicals with broad national impact emitted from both stationary and mobile sources of pollution and generally present in the ambient air in all areas of the United States. The cost and feasibility of achieving the limits set by the standard need not be considered. The timetable for local attainment of the standard varies from one locale to another, depending on the severity of the problem, and rules for attaining the standard are promulgated by states under State Implementation Plans.

The first six national ambient air quality standards were issued in 1971 to cover six of the more common air contaminants: carbon monoxide, hydrocarbons, nitrogen oxides, particulate matter, ozone, and sulfur oxides. A standard for lead was issued in 1978. No other standards have been issued, although several were revised or are in the process of revision. The standards are codified at 40 CFR 50.

The procedure for listing a pollutant under the ambient standards includes three steps:

- *Step One:* Announcing that a substance is to be listed
- *Step Two:* Issuing air quality criteria for the substance
- *Step Three:* Issuing proposed ambient air quality standards for the substance

Only after all these steps are taken is the pollutant actually regulated under an ambient standard.

Step One: Pollutant Listing

EPA must meet two statutory criteria before deciding to list a pollutant: it must determine the effect of the pollutant on public health and welfare, and it must show that the substance is emitted by numerous or diverse sources, both stationary and mobile.

Although both of these criteria may sound simple, only the second is fairly easy to ascertain. The legislative history of the act indicates that to meet the first criterion, EPA must evaluate separate issues: whether the substance in question *causes* or *contributes* to air pollution, and whether that pollution *may reasonably be antic-ipated* to endanger *public health*.

"Cause or Contribute"

This phrase allows EPA to list a pollutant based on its judg-ment after reviewing various data and epidemiological studies. It does not require that EPA prove that the pollutant *causes* an ad-verse health effect. Rather, EPA can determine that the pollutant may *contribute* to an unhealthy situation, a judgment reached after the agency considers all sources of exposure to the substance and all anticipated effects.

"Reasonably Anticipated"

This phrase as well gives EPA room for judgment in deciding whether a substance has proven harmful health effects or whether the best scientific thinking simply indicates that it most likely will cause adverse health effects.

"Endanger Public Health"

This phrase centers on the "endangerment" theory of public health protection. It was one issue addressed during enactment of the 1977 amendments to the act. At that time, Congress instructed EPA that it was the agency's duty to anticipate risks rather than to wait for ill effects to occur. It also emphasized the precautionary purpose of the act, saying that even the individuals most sensitive to the pollutant concerned could be taken into account when set-ting ambient standards.

Step Two: Air Quality Criteria

Within one year after listing an air pollutant, EPA must issue air quality criteria for the pollutant. These criteria do not specify allowable pollutant emission levels; those are specified in the stan-dards. Rather, the criteria must document the agency's scientific basis for deciding that regulation of a particular pollutant is needed.

In general, the criteria document for a listing must outline the following:

- The most recent scientific knowledge on identifiable effects of the pollutant on public health and welfare
- Variable factors that could alter the pollutant's effects
- Other pollutants that may interact with the designated pollutant to alter the pollutant's effects on public health and welfare

The provision for the issuance of criteria documents is contained not in section 109 but in section 108 of the CAA, which also provides that the documents and standards are to be reviewed at five-year intervals, beginning in 1981.

Step Three: Proposal of a Standard

At the same time that EPA issues the criteria document, it proposes standards. The act provides for establishment of both primary and secondary ambient air quality standards, though secondary standards have been issued for only a few listed pollutants. A single substance may be subject to both a primary and a secondary standard. The primary standard must be complied with first; the pollution limits set under the stricter secondary standard may be achieved later. The standards are promulgated as final rules after a public comment period and after any necessary revisions are made.

Primary Standards

Primary standards must reflect the concentration level necessary to protect public health and must allow for an adequate margin of safety to protect against the negative health effects cited in the criteria document.

In establishing primary standards, EPA has not precisely defined what is meant by "adequate margin of safety." In each case, the margin of safety is generally determined by the seriousness of the adverse health effects of the pollutant.

In addition, the margin of safety should protect against as-yet-unknown hazards, Congress decided. In a position backed up by various court rulings on the act, Congress has specified that EPA generally must use its best judgment in setting primary standards because in many cases there is no clear evidence as to when exposure to a given substance causes adverse health effects. Data from research using animals may indicate one level at which there is no adverse effect, yet this level may be different in other species and in humans. Furthermore, people who are particularly susceptible to the effect of a pollutant must also be protected, Congress decided. These people, who may suffer from asthma or emphysema, also are exposed to the ambient air as they go about their daily activities.

Given this situation, case law and congressional intent have merged to set a basis by which EPA develops primary standards. The agency must do the following:

- Specify the significance of the health effects
- Characterize the sensitive population
- Determine the probable-adverse-effect exposure level in the sensitive population
- Set a level below that probable-effect level to assure an adequate margin of safety

Secondary Standards

Secondary air quality standards are geared to protecting the public welfare as well as health from any known or anticipated adverse effect of a pollutant. Under the act, adverse effects on public welfare are defined as adverse effects on soils, water, crops, vegetation, synthetic materials, animals, wildlife, weather, visibility, and climate; damage to and deterioration of property; hazards to transportation; or adverse effects on economic values and on personal comfort and well-being.

Because secondary standards are designed to protect not only health but also all of the items just listed, they are set at more restrictive levels than primary standards. The three-hour secondary standard for sulfur dioxide, for instance, was set at a level low enough to prohibit any emission that would be concentrated enough to damage vegetation.

As of this writing, only lead, sulfur dioxide, and carbon monoxide are subject to both primary and secondary standards.

State Implementation Plans

Ambient air quality standards under the act are enforced by the states, each of which is divided for state regulatory purposes into various air quality control regions. Under rules in 40 CFR 52, each state must submit to EPA a state implementation plan that describes the methods it will use to meet the standards in the air quality control regions within its jurisdiction.

States may attain the national goals for ambient air quality in any number of ways, but each state's plan for doing so must be approved by EPA. For example, a state may allow emission of pollutants in an area with very clean air to be higher than in an area where the level of pollution is near the limit set by the ambient standard. Or it may not allow construction of new industrial plants in areas where pollution levels are near the limit set by the standard.

The control methods outlined in the state plan then must be enforced by the state air pollution control program. The state decides the requirements for each industry or region. States even may issue state ambient air standards on their own if they see a need for greater control of pollution than does EPA. For this reason, pollution control requirements vary from state to state and from one region to another within a state. All states, however, are supposed to meet the goals for attainment outlined in the EPA primary and secondary standards.

Ozone Presents a Challenge

Even with the setting of national standards that have significantly reduced the amount of air pollution, urban air problems persist, especially with ozone, carbon monoxide, and particulate matter.

Ozone presents by far the greatest challenge. The ozone that plagues urban areas, called *tropospheric* or *ground-level ozone*, is not to be confused with *stratospheric ozone*. The latter is a thin layer of ozone some 25 or 30 miles above the earth that protects the planet from harmful ultraviolet radiation. Tropospheric ozone is formed when certain compounds react with sunlight, and is commonly called smog. According to EPA, more than 100 million people live in cities that still fail to meet national standards set for the pollutant. CAA divides these mostly urban areas into five categories according to the severity of the problem and provides a time frame for when they are required to come into compliance: marginal areas have 3 years; moderate areas have 6 years; serious areas have

9 years; severe areas have 15 to 17 years; and extreme areas have 20 years. So far, only Los Angeles qualifies for mention on the extreme list.

Even though Congress gave states more time than prescribed under earlier amendments to meet the national air quality standards, states are also required to make constant formidable progress in reducing emissions. Emissions of volatile organic compounds (VOCs), many of which react with sunlight to form ground-level ozone, must be reduced by specific percentages depending on the area. EPA repeatedly missed deadlines set to meet the standards and received numerous extensions until passage of the 1990 amendments.

To address ozone pollution in the northeast where the problem crosses state lines, the act has set up an ozone transport region. A commission, including the governors and air pollution control representatives of each of the 11 states and the District of Columbia, would ensure that means to meet emission limits defined by EPA are incorporated into each state's control techniques guidelines. Urban centers within the transport region with populations over 100,000 must set up enhanced inspection and maintenance programs and vapor recovery devices at affected service stations.

Ozone, as well as carbon monoxide and particulate matter, comes from the diverse and numerous air pollution sources within an urban area. One component of urban smog—hydrocarbons—comes from motor vehicle emissions, petroleum refineries, chemical plants, gas stations, and dry cleaners. Nitrogen oxides (NOx), another key urban air pollutant, come from the combustion of fossil fuels, especially in electric power plants and other coal-fired industries. NOx is also a contributor to acid rain and is addressed later in the CAA.

State Implementation Plan Provisions for Ozone Nonattainment Areas

Areas that fail to meet air quality requirements for ozone are subject to a gradually increasing set of requirements depending on how polluted they are. States are required to submit to EPA plans to reduce emissions of pollutants based on the framework of requirements spelled out in the 1990 amendments.

Under EPA's mandatory permit program, new sources of air pollution must obtain sufficient offsetting reductions in emissions to ensure no overall increase in the amount of pollutants spewed into the air. The 1990 amendments make greater use of an emission offsets program prescribed in earlier versions of the act. Under the offsets program, a new facility that would add 100 tons per year of a pollutant to an area that already does not meet air quality standards must find offsetting reductions of that pollutant in another area. It can do so by reducing its emissions of that compound in another facility so long as it is owned by the same company, or it can buy offsets from another company. The key is that the offsetting reductions must be of the same pollutant.

Emission reduction plans for each category of nonattainment area include graduated offsets mechanisms. For example, a new source may have an offset requirement of 1.1-to-1 reductions of VOCs. If it emits 100 tons per year of VOCs, it must find a way to cut emissions of VOCs by 110 tons in another part of its facility. More polluted areas would have higher offsets ratios.

Marginal Areas   Marginal areas—those closest to meeting the standard—are required to inventory their emissions of pollutants that cause ozone. States must set up programs requiring construction and operating permits for each new and modified major stationary source.

States must incorporate *reasonably available control technology (RACT)* requirements into their plans to cut pollution. These are emissions limits defined by EPA and imposed on existing sources in nonattainment areas.

Crucial to plans to bring areas into attainment are the vehicle inspection and maintenance programs. The inspection programs must contain emission control diagnostic requirements within two years after EPA issues the rules for them.

Moderate Areas   Areas classified as moderate for ozone nonattainment contain additional requirements to those for marginal regions. Moderate areas must reduce their emissions of VOCs by 15 percent within six years of obtaining their designation. State implementation plans for these areas must contain RACT requirements for all major stationary sources—those emitting 10 tons per year or more—of VOCs and NOx. The NOx requirements can be waived if EPA determines they have no benefit.

Moderate areas must have basic inspection and maintenance programs for motor vehicles. However, they go a step further than programs in marginal areas. The state implementation plans must contain provisions for devices to be installed on the pumps at gas stations to collect escaping vapors during refueling of vehicles. Facilities that sell more than 10,000 gallons of gasoline per month—50,000 gallons for independent small business marketers—would be required to have these devices, called *Stage II systems*. This requirement will be superseded when EPA issues its rules under the mobile source provisions of the CAA. The act requires EPA to require onboard vapor recovery devices for automobiles as well as vapor recovery systems at gas stations in some areas. The gas station requirements for vapor recovery control can be waived once EPA determines that devices installed directly on vehicles are in widespread use.

Serious Areas   Major sources in serious areas are reclassified to include those that emit at least 50 tons per year of VOCs. States must enhance their monitoring of ozone, NOx, and VOCs in these areas. In addition to the 15-percent reduction in VOC emissions as required for those areas designated as moderate, serious areas must achieve additional cuts in VOCs of 3 percent from a baseline averaged over each consecutive 3-year period until the area comes into attainment.

States must include enhanced vehicle inspection and maintenance programs in their state implementation programs to reduce emissions of hydrocarbons and NOx from motor vehicles in areas with populations greater than 200,000. These stronger programs include computerized analyzers to measure emissions from vehicles in nonidle positions; no waivers for vehicles and parts covered by emission control warranties, with some exceptions; enforcement through denial of vehicle registration; annual emissions testing; and a centralized inspection and maintenance program to cut down on costs. Moreover, areas that are designated as serious, severe, or extreme and that have 1980 populations of 250,000 or more are required to implement a clean-fuel vehicle program. Such a program encourages the use of vehicles that burn fuels that pollute less. These include natural gas and alcohol-based fuels.

In serious areas a de minimis rule goes into effect for sources that incur physical changes or changes in their operations. If such changes result in an increase of 25 tons or less aggregated over a consecutive 5-year period, including the year the increase occurred, tough, time-consuming new source review requirements would not be triggered. Changes in major stationary sources emitting less than 100 tons per year would be considered a modification if they result in any increase in VOC emissions. However, if the company can offset that increase by a ratio of 1.3 to 1, new source review provisions could be avoided.

Severe and Extreme Areas   Even more stringent requirements apply to those areas listed as severe or extreme. A key requirement for states containing such areas is a program to reduce the number of vehicle miles travelled. These programs would enlist the help of the private sector. For example, companies employing 100 people or more must submit plans showing how they will reduce vehicle occupancy by at least 25 percent during rush hour. Some options include van pooling and use of flextime.

While all other nonattainment areas must reduce their emissions by 15 percent in the first six years and 3 percent thereafter, with some exemptions based on technological feasibility, extreme areas lose the exemption possibilities.

As of 1992, Los Angeles was the only area labeled extreme. Its air pollution problem is so extreme that even sources considered rather small in many areas—those with emissions of 10 tons per year—are given major source status.

In severe and extreme areas the CAA calls on utilities and other commercial sources with emissions per year of 25 tons or more to switch to cleaner burning fuels such as methanol, ethanol, or natural gas.

Provisions for Other Criteria Pollutants

The 1990 amendments also pay particular attention to NOx, which is produced from the combustion of fossil fuels. Major sources of NOx are subject to the same requirements as major emitters of VOCs. However, EPA may find that such drastic reductions in NOx emissions would have little benefit to air quality in that region, and the requirements would be waived. These "excess reductions" waivers may apply to areas that are not part of an ozone transport region or whose air quality would not be improved because of the reductions.

Programs similar to the ones implemented in ozone transport areas are also established for areas that do not meet national air quality standards for carbon monoxide and particulates. These programs, however, categorize areas only as moderate or serious.

Particulates are suspended pieces of matter, such as soot, dust, or even liquid droplets thrust into the air from various sources, including fossil fuel combustion, steel mills, diesel fuel combustion, and other industrial and commercial processes. EPA originally referred to them as *total suspended particulates (TSP)* and included in the definition all airborne matter. In 1987, it revised the definition and developed a standard for particles measuring less than 10 microns, which make up about half of the original TSP. These pose the greatest risk because they can penetrate the respiratory tract and cause damage or exacerbate existing health problems.

Controls in carbon monoxide and particulate nonattainment areas focus largely on reducing emissions associated with transportation. Aggressive oxygenated fuels programs may be imposed along with enhanced inspection and maintenance, depending on the severity of the problem.

Moderate areas that were not within the air quality limits for particulates when the law was enacted have until December 1994 to meet the standard; serious areas have until 2001. For carbon monoxide, moderate areas must meet the standard by the end of 1995, while serious areas must meet the standard by 2001. Both could acquire extensions to those deadlines if EPA determines the deadlines are too tight even with the most stringent controls.

Serious carbon monoxide and particulate areas must achieve a 5-percent yearly reduction in those pollutants once they fall out of attainment.

Mobile Sources

Motor vehicles today emit 60 to 80 percent less pollution than their 1960s counterparts, depending on the pollutant, according to EPA. However, they are still the primary source of carbon monoxide emissions in urban areas and account for about half of the emissions of VOCs and NOx, both of which contribute heavily to ozone formation.

Even with cleaner-burning cars and trucks, the problem continues simply because more vehicles are on the road and people are driving greater distances. This rapid—and for the most part, unforeseen—growth in traffic has offset the gains made in reduced emissions from individual vehicles. The 1990 amendments impose significant changes in this area over the old law.

These amendments attack the problem at its source: the tailpipe. New tailpipe standards for hydrocarbons, carbon monoxide, and NOx to take effect in model year 1994 will be imposed in two "tiers." These standards also vary according to the weight and type of vehicles. The agency will report to Congress in 1997 on whether the more stringent Tier II standards need to be applied beginning in model year 2003.

Fuels

The Clean Air Act of 1990 imposes new fuel requirements to ensure the increased use of alternative and cleaner-burning compounds. It also schedules reductions in gasoline volatility and sulfur content of diesel fuel.

Nine cities in the severe and extreme categories will be required to have reformulated gasoline measures beginning in 1995. These measures contain minimum-content requirements for various pollutants. Other areas with ozone problems may "opt in" to the program.

Beginning in 1996, the 26 dirtiest areas in the country will have to implement a program for centrally fueled fleets of 10 or more vehicles. The programs will incorporate emissions reduction mechanisms for those vehicles, such as converting to cleaner burning fuels.

Alcohol-based fuels with higher oxygen levels of 2.7 percent will be sold during the winter months in 41 areas that do not meet federal air quality standards for carbon monoxide.

California Pilot Program

Southern California has the worst air pollution problems in the country. Los Angeles's problem comes partially from the fact that while it is experiencing the most rapid population growth in the country, it lacks an adequate system of alternative transportation, such as a light rail. Thus, most people have to drive to reach their destinations.

The 1990 law requires phasing in even tighter emission standards in California for some 150,000 vehicles beginning in model year 1996, and upping that to 300,000 by model year 1999. The standards can be achieved through any combination of technology and cleaner fuels. In 2001, the standards become even tougher.

Section 112: Hazardous Air Pollutants

Section 112 of the CAA authorized EPA to set national emission standards for specific air pollutants that are particularly hazardous to health. These standards were based on the best available control technology for both new and existing emission sources of the pollutant and limited accordingly the amounts of the pollutants that could be discharged into the air.

In setting hazardous air pollutant standards, EPA was to consider both the beneficial and adverse economic, environmental, and energy impacts associated with the standard.

The guideline used to determine which pollutants fell into this category was whether the pollutant might reasonably be anticipated to result in an increase in mortality or an increase in serious and irreversible illness or incapacitating but reversible illness. The standards for the most part still include an ample margin of safety so as to protect the most sensitive individuals.

However, as of April 1986, only eight substances were listed in 40 CFR 61 as hazardous (asbestos, benzene, beryllium, mercury, vinyl chloride, inorganic arsenic, radon-222, and radionuclides). These remained until passage of the 1990 amendments. Emission standards for most listed substances were under review, and several other substances were slated to be listed. Each of the standards included specific limits on the amount of the pollutant that could be emitted in a given time period, specified controls for keeping emissions below this level, and required that any plant modification that would significantly increase emissions above the current level be reported to federal and state air pollution control agencies.

Congress viewed this section of the act as seriously lacking. The result was a complete revamping of the section with the amendments in 1990. These amendments changed the process for regulating what one EPA official called "the really nasty stuff."

Instead of the original two-step process whereby a substance was listed and a standard was written for it, the new amendments put forth a list of 189 substances. From these, EPA would establish source categories and write the regulations for them. EPA also was to issue guidelines on how to add or remove a substance from the list.

Carcinogen Controversy

For more than a decade, EPA has been trying to decide how to proceed with regulation of about 40 substances that are air pollutants and are known to cause cancer. As of this writing, only three of the substances have been listed under section 112.

One reason for the difficulty in meeting the mandates of the act is that the test for listing a substance under section 112 is difficult. The statute on the one hand gives the agency a mandate to control substances that cause or contribute to mortality or serious illness, but on the other hand requires that the substance be controlled with an ample margin of safety.

Data Problem

The act essentially gave EPA discretion to decide which air pollutants are to be considered hazardous under section 112. In doing so, the administrator weighs current scientific data on the suspect substances. Often, however, the data are faulty, controversial, or nonexistent because it is difficult to correlate the typically low levels of a pollutant in the ambient air with actual or even suspected health effects in a population exposed to a variety of substances that may cause illness.

In several cases, for example, the agency's Science Advisory Board flatly refused to approve health assessment documents for substances to be regulated under section 112 because of flawed or inadequate scientific data to back up the listing.

Safety Margin Problem

Another stumbling block to regulation under section 112 is its requirement that standards provide for an ample margin of safety. The agency and various environmental groups have taken the position that this phrase in the act means that cancer-causing chemicals have no safe level and thus must be controlled to a zero emission level. Industry, on the other hand, has criticized the agency's assumption that a small amount of a cancer-causing pollutant is hazardous.

For many suspect substances, reducing emissions to zero could force the shutdown of certain production processes and in effect would mean banning the manufacture of specific substances or products. An example of this occurred in 1983, when EPA under court order proposed a hazardous air pollution standard for arsenic from copper smelters. While the standard applied only to one plant in Tacoma, Washington, it forced the plant to lay off hundreds of workers and cease operation. In mid-1984, the plant announced its close in mid-1985 due to the cost of compliance.

Policy on Carcinogens in the Air

One way around the dilemma of regulating toxic substances in the air was the agency's attempt to adopt a policy on carcinogens in the air that would allow it to base its listing of substances as hazardous on the results of animal studies that show adverse health effects. First set out in 1979, the policy has gained more credence as the only way to operate within the constraints of section 112.

Under this policy, EPA requires emission sources to use the best available technology to control hazardous air emissions as much as possible. The agency then would go back to the emission source, measure any unreasonable residual risks, and regulate them in some other way or under another law if necessary.

Toxic Air Pollutants

Toxic air pollutants are those considered hazardous directly to human health or the environment. Toxic air pollution is widespread. Statistics from the Superfund Act's "Right-to-Know" reporting show that more than 2.7 billion tons of toxic pollutants are spewed into the air annually in the United States. EPA attributes 1,000 to 3,000 deaths per year to toxic air pollution.

From the list of 189 hazardous pollutants emitted by industrial processes, EPA will develop source categories that must meet maximum achievable control technology (MACT). Source categories include major sources emitting 10 tons per year a single substance or 25 tons per year of a combination, and area sources consisting of smaller emitters such as dry cleaners.

Industrial plants emitting these toxic substances will be regulated in four phases under the act. The first phase is the development of the numerous source categories that must meet the tough MACT standards. These standards, covering equipment leaks, vents, transfer stations, and waste-water operations, would be based on the best demonstrated control technology within the regulated industry. The controls would produce an emissions reduction of about 95 percent. While the act indicates the creation of at least 40 source categories for which controls were to be developed by Nov. 15, 1992, EPA has said the more probable number for which standards would be issued is about 350 because the preliminary list contains more categories than originally envisioned. Source categories beyond the first 40 will be regulated according to a schedule that ensures all controls will be achieved by 2000.

An early reductions provision is included under the act to offer industries incentive to cut their emissions earlier than required. Those sources that accomplish a 90-percent or better reduction by the time MACT standards are in place will receive a six-year extension on meeting those requirements.

Eight years after the MACT standards are issued, EPA must promulgate residual risk standards if necessary. The need would be triggered if any risks to health or the environment are evident after MACT is in place for most source categories. This is determined according to whether more than one source in the category exceeds a maximum individual cancer risk of one in one million.

The amendments also impose a general duty to prevent accidental releases of "extremely hazardous substances." EPA must issue rules for the prevention and detection of regulated substances within three years. EPA will develop a list of at least 100 extremely hazardous substances with their threshold quantities. Plant operators would have to develop risk management plans for the use of these substances.

An independent chemical safety board would be set up to investigate accidental releases of the listed substances if the incident causes death or injury, to conduct research, and to issue rules on reporting such releases.

Industries that will be regulated, many for the first time, under the amended act include coke ovens, municipal waste incinerators, and myriad small industrial sources.

EPA must also coordinate with other agencies to review how the deposition of hazardous air pollutants affects the Great Lakes, Lake Champlain, the Chesapeake Bay, and coastal waters.

Section 111: New Source Performance Standards

New industrial sources of pollutants must meet specific standards, called *new source performance standards,* to assure that individual industries will not unacceptably increase air pollution. Each standard is specific to a given industry and sets the limits that any new plant in the industry must meet. Each standard sets the maximum amounts of each kind of pollutant that can be emitted per individual unit of the plant's production. The standards are proposed after investigation of the various technologies available to that industry and of the cost to the industry.

These nationwide standards are intended to discourage plants from moving to states with less stringent air pollution regulations. Since the New Source Performance Standards are federal standards, they require compliance regardless of the plant's location.

The standards, which are published at 40 CFR 60, are applicable to facilities constructed, modified, or reconstructed after a standard is proposed. More than 50 such standards are in force, for a variety of industrial processes ranging from ammonium sulfate manufacturing to production of sulfuric acid. More than 50 other industrial processes or industries are listed on an EPA priority list for issuance of future proposals.

In some cases these new source standards are enforced by the states, while in others EPA is the responsible regulatory body. New Source Performance Standards take effect when proposed.

For those categories listed but not regulated before 1990, the newest version of the law sets a timetable for EPA to set performance standards.

Other Provisions

Studies of Specific Pollutants

In amending the act in 1977, Congress required EPA to study four pollutants and determine whether they will cause or contribute to air pollution that might reasonably be anticipated to endanger public health. The four were radioactive pollutants, cadmium, arsenic, and polycyclic organic matter. If the agency found that any or all of them met the criteria for endangerment, Congress specified that the pollutant or pollutants would have to be regulated under section 109, 110, or 112 or under any combination of the three sections.

Radionuclides and arsenic were subsequently regulated under section 112 as discussed above; regulation of the other substances is pending.

Acid Rain

Acid precipitation in the form of snow, rain, or fog occurs when pollutants—primarily sulfur dioxide and NOx—are emitted into the air and combine with water vapor. The result is highly acidic lakes and rivers that spell disaster for those ecosystems, damaged forests, and accelerated decay of buildings and monuments.

Approximately 20 million tons of sulfur dioxide are emitted annually, according to EPA. The Clean Air Act Amendments of 1990 aim to halve that by the turn of the century.

The acid rain section of the CAA reflects a pioneering approach to pollution control. It requires that emissions of sulfur dioxide be cut by 10 million tons from 1980 levels by 2000. It also mandates an emissions cap of 8.9 million tons.

One way of achieving this goal is through a unique, market-based strategy whereby emission credits, called *allowances*, can be traded. Credits are the equivalent of one ton of pollutant.

The program is set up in two phases. The first phase starts in 1995 and requires specific reductions from the 111 dirtiest emitters, mostly midwestern utilities. Those that install certain cleaner technologies may be eligible for a two-year extension. The second phase begins in 2000 and requires the 2,000 or so remaining utilities to cut their emissions. Key to the effectiveness of the program is the continuous emissions monitoring systems these plants must install.

Utilities have several options to meet the new acid rain requirements. They can install costly scrubbers that would virtually prevent the pollutants from being emitted; they can switch to cleaner fuels such as low-sulfur coal, natural gas, or an alcohol-based fuel; or they can buy credits from other utilities to cover their excess emissions. Without sufficient credits to cover their emissions, utilities can be fined $2,000 per ton.

Utilities must also reduce their emissions of NOx by two million tons from 1980 levels. However, no trading system is in place to accomplish these cuts. The lack of an emissions cap makes setting up a trading system difficult. Rather EPA will try to cut NOx emissions by imposing performance standards for some boilers in each of the two phases.

Permits

Perhaps the most crucial section of the 1990 Clean Air Act amendments is that pertaining to permits. It is essentially the administrative mechanism that makes the act work. The focus is to ensure compliance with all elements of the act.

Most sources of air pollution will be required to obtain an operating permit under an air program developed and maintained by each state. States must submit their plans to reduce air pollution to EPA, which oversees the states' efforts. When states fail to develop an adequate plan or to follow through with one already in place, EPA steps in with a federal permit program.

This permit program will ensure greater enforcement of the nation's air pollution laws. Furthermore, permits will contain all of a source's necessary obligations concerning its emissions, and each source will report periodically on its compliance.

Permit fees amounting to about $25 per ton of pollutant will eventually fund the state programs. Up to that point, states will receive only minimal assistance in activating these very complicated programs. EPA was required to issue rules within one year of enactment to guide states on the various aspects of implementing the permit program. However, because the program's effects are so broad—some 34,000 businesses would be regulated by federal air laws for the first time—ongoing disputes with the White House kept the rules from coming out on time. The delay did not mean an extension on the three-year deadline states had to incorporate the program into their SIPs.

Under the new system, facilities would receive a permit for a fixed term of up to five years. All sources subject to the program must submit the permit applications within a year from when the program becomes effective.

Permit amendments requiring public comment would be required if certain changes resulted in some levels of emissions increases. However, the law provides ways for states to include operational flexibility into their permit programs. This would enable sources to make certain changes in their processes or even physical structure of the plant without having to go through timely reviews required when permits are amended.

Protection of the Ozone Layer

Four sections were added to the CAA in 1977 to protect the ozone layer of the earth's stratosphere: sections 153, 154, 155, and 157. The first three directed EPA to study halocarbon emissions and any other emissions that might affect the ozone layer. Section 157 authorized EPA to regulate any substance, practice, process, or activity that might reasonably be anticipated to affect the stratosphere. These sections were added in light of scientific data showing a thinning of the ozone layer, mainly due to free chlorine tying up oxygen in the stratosphere. The thinning permits more ultraviolet light to reach the earth, causing a warming of the earth's surface, an increase in the incidence of cataracts and certain skin cancers, and damage to plants and oceanic plankton.

Aerosol uses of halocarbons were prohibited under section 6 of the Toxic Substances Control Act in 1978. In addition, the

United States, as a signatory to the Montreal Protocol (see page 37) must act to control production of ozone-depleting chemicals.

The 1990 CAA amendments address the problem of stratospheric ozone depletion more thoroughly. In light of new data showing a growing ozone hole, the act sets phaseout dates for many ozone-depleting substances. These dates in most instances correspond with those established in the Montreal Protocol. Targeted substances include chlorofluorocarbons, halons, carbon tetrachloride, and methyl chloroform. The act also lays out provisions on safe substitutes for these important substances.

Clean Water Act
(CWA)

AT A GLANCE

Public Law Number: Pub. L. No. 92-500

U.S. Code citation: 33 USC 1251 *et seq.*

Enacted: October 18, 1972; effective when enacted
  Amended: 1973, 1974, 1975, 1976, 1977 (major amendments, Pub. L. No. 95-217), 1978, 1979, 1980, 1981, 1982, 1983, 1984, 1985, 1987 (major amendments, Pub. L. No. 100-4)

Regulations at: 40 CFR 100–140, 40 CFR 400–470

Federal agencies with jurisdiction: Environmental Protection Agency (EPA), Army Corps of Engineers

Congressional committees/subcommittees with jurisdiction:
  House of Representatives: Water Resources Subcommittee of the Public Works and Transportation Committee
  Senate: Environmental Pollution Subcommittee of the Environment and Public Works Committee

BNA reporting services: *Daily Environment Report, Environment Reporter, Toxics Law Reporter*
  Text of law appears in *Environment Reporter* Federal Laws at 71:5101 *et seq.*
  Text of regulations in *Environment Reporter* Federal Regulations
  Legal decisions appear in Environment Reporter Cases (ER Cases)

What the CWA regulates and why: The act provides the legislative vehicle for regulating the discharge of nontoxic and toxic pollutants into surface waters by municipal sources, industrial sources, and other specific and nonspecific sources.

Clean Water Act—Contd.

The act's ultimate goal is to eliminate all discharges of pollutants into surface waters. Its interim goal is to make all waters in the United States usable for fishing and swimming.

Under the act, EPA sets effluent guidelines for various types of industries and municipal sewage treatment plants. These guidelines are minimum, technology-based levels of required pollution reduction. Using these guidelines, states issue every individual facility, whether municipal or industrial, a permit to discharge wastes into surface waters. The individual permit, called a National Pollutant Discharge Elimination System (NPDES) permit, specifies the types of control equipment and discharge limits for the specific facility and is written with the quality of the receiving waterway in mind.

Extensive amendments made in 1987 phase out the subsidy program for local sewage treatment plants, replacing it with state revolving loan funds. The amendments also set up programs to reduce polluted runoff from "nonpoint" sources, such as city streets, farm land, and mining sites; and establish a new program to control the discharge of toxic pollutants.

Latest developments: The CWA will be one of the environmental issues Congress will have to contemplate in 1993. Central in the water debate is the definition of wetlands and whether to include this definition in the act. President Bush pledged in his 1988 campaign that there would be "no net loss" of wetlands. However, the battle between conservationists and developers continues over what that means.

Legislation to reauthorize was introduced by Sen. Max Baucus (D-Mont.) in May 1991. It seeks to guarantee that all of the $18 billion authorized in 1987 for the revolving fund program used to build sewage treatment facilities will be made available to address water pollution problems. It also would provide $3 billion to help states combat the problem of nonpoint source pollution.

COVERAGE OF THE LAW

The goal of the Clean Water Act (CWA; also called the Federal Water Pollution Control Act after the original law in this field, which the CWA revised) is to restore and maintain the chemical, physical, and biological integrity of the surface waters of the United States. To achieve this, the act provided that discharge of pollutants into navigable waters was to be eliminated by 1985. An interim goal of the act is to provide for protection and propagation of fish, shellfish, and wildlife in the waters of the country, and to ensure that waters can be used for recreation.

To achieve this goal, the act regulates the discharge of both toxic and nontoxic pollutants into waterways by municipal sources, industrial sources, and other sources of pollution. These sources generally are divided into *point sources* (well-defined places such as discharge pipes at which pollutants enter waterways) and *nonpoint sources* (ill-defined runoff from farmlands, roads, and city streets that enters waterways).

Protection of underground water sources is accomplished under the Safe Drinking Water Act (see chapter on SDWA).

Types of Pollution

The CWA attacks several major types of pollution—municipal, industrial, nonpoint source, and dredge and fill.

Municipal pollution is controlled through federally aided construction of municipal sewage treatment plants, and discharge requirements for those plants. Industrial pollution is controlled by imposing discharge requirements on industrial plants, by placing special controls on discharges of toxic substances, and by requiring a variety of safety and construction measures (in some cases mandated under a variety of other laws as well) to reduce spills of substances that could pollute waterways.

Both industrial and municipal pollution are considered point source pollution. Discharges from point sources are regulated under the source's individual National Pollutant Discharge Elimination System (NPDES) permit. Each NPDES permit specifies the standards that the point source must meet. These standards are composed of effluent *guidelines* (minimum, technology-based levels of pollution reduction that all point sources must attain) and effluent *limitations* (specific control requirements directed at a specific discharge site). The effluent limitation is usually a quantitative restriction imposed on individual pollutants from a single industrial or municipal site.

NPDES permits are issued by state officials or—in the absence of an adequate state permit program—by EPA officials, who base the restraints contained in the permit not only on the type of pollutants being discharged but also on the amount of pollution the receiving body of water can tolerate. This permit system forms the basis for much of the federal pollution control program.

Since most domestic or household waste is relatively nontoxic, the construction, operation, and maintenance of most municipal sewage treatment plants under this system would be relatively simple were it not for one feature of the CWA: the act allows industry to discharge its wastes into publicly owned treatment plants if the industries pretreat the wastes to remove some of the worst or more toxic pollutants. The act therefore also calls for use of pretreatment standards for such wastes discharged into municipal treatment plants as part of the overall effluent limitations and guidelines for a specific industrial operation or pollutant.

The two other major sources of pollution—nonpoint source pollution and pollution from dredge and fill activities—are regulated differently.

Nonpoint source pollution is controlled by state and local agencies through a system of individual programs aimed at improving and maintaining local water quality. Stormwater runoff restrictions written into local zoning and building regulations are examples of these controls. Authorized under section 208 of the act, the nonpoint source programs have generally been ineffective in controlling most toxic substance and chemical runoff, especially from farmland. At the federal level, nonpoint source pollution was the subject of a major EPA study for regulatory schemes.

Nonpoint source pollution is thought to be responsible for more than half of the water pollution problems nationwide. With that in mind, Congress is expected to make it a key issue in reauthorizing the Clean Water Act, anticipated in 1993. According to EPA, despite the successes of traditional technological controls on more than 70,000 facilities, nonpoint source pollution still causes many bodies of water to be in violation of water quality standards.

Pollution from dredge and fill activities is controlled through a system of permits issued by the Army Corps of Engineers. Authorized under section 404 of the CWA, the program is intended to protect water quality and to prevent pollution of streams, waterways, and marshlands that might be subject to dredging or to filling with soil removed from another location. Preservation of wildlife habitats is another goal of this program.

Nonpoint source and dredge and fill pollution will be discussed only in passing because these are not the major provisions of the act oriented toward dealing with toxic substances.

DEVELOPMENT OF THE LAW

The CWA as it exists today is a complete revision of federal legislation dating back to the Refuse Act of 1899. This act, and major modifications made in 1948, 1956, 1965, 1966, and 1970, failed to control major and increasing pollution of waterways across the United States. Massive fish kills were common, rivers and streams near industrial plants were often orange or green because of discharges from the plants, and many streams and bodies of water were closed to swimming and fishing because of bacterial or chemical contamination. The pollution was so bad that one river, in Ohio, caught fire in 1969.

1972 Amendments

In the face of past failure to control water pollution, Congress in 1971 decided that a radical new approach to controlling such pollution was needed. The Senate Committee Report on the 1972 amendments to the Federal Water Pollution Control Act (amendments that subsequently became the Clean Water Act) outlined several of the key deficiencies that Congress felt were in need of remedying:

- Past efforts at allowing states to set water quality standards had failed, mainly because it was difficult to determine which source of pollution along a given stream or river was responsible if the quality of the water failed to meet state water quality standards. Because there was no firm enforcement mechanism, court battles and negotiations went on for years while pollution continued.
- State water quality programs were so diverse that many industries faced with imposition of stronger requirements simply moved to other areas with weaker standards. Faced with this type of threat, many states issued no standards or deliberately issued weak standards to lure industry from neighboring states.
- Under the laws in effect at the time, the federal government had authority only over interstate navigable waters. This left the federal government with no backup authority should states fail to protect streams, lakes, or rivers within their borders. In addition, money to build the needed treatment facilities was in short supply. Although some federal money was available to help states and localities build such plants, it was never enough. Many jurisdictions undertook no construction, waiting instead until more federal money was available.

During extensive hearings in 1971 and 1972, Congress gathered testimony on these and other issues and drafted major changes that would totally revise the old Federal Water Pollution Control Act and make it into the Clean Water Act. The bill, which set out an entirely new scheme for water pollution control, was to be the first comprehensive federal water pollution control statute. Not only would conventional pollutants such as bacteria be regulated, but so would toxic pollutants and pollution caused by storm water runoff.

The bill as sent to the White House was vetoed by President Richard M. Nixon. Congress overrode the presidential veto and the Clean Water Act became law on October 18, 1972.

1977 Amendments

As expected, and in fact promised, the 1972 law was reviewed and revised in 1977 to correct some of the deficiencies and unworkable sections drafted in 1972. The 1977 amendments to the law strengthened and extended its regulation of toxic substances in water, and extended some deadlines written into the 1972 law.

Kepone Incident

Key to much of the congressional action in 1977 was the discovery that discharges from a small chemical factory in Hopewell, Virginia, had polluted the James River and made workers ill. The discharges into the river had been contaminated with Kepone, an insecticide. In addition, some of the wastes from the plant were discharged into municipal sewers and treated at the Hopewell municipal plant, where the Kepone had destroyed the bacterial process by which most conventional wastes were treated and caused the sewage treatment plant to inadequately treat its wastes. Therefore, not only the effluent discharged into the sewage system and into the river but also the sludge produced by the sewage treatment plant had been contaminated.

With this incident in mind, Congress in 1977 strengthened the authority granted EPA under the CWA to control industrial waste discharges into bodies of water and into municipal treatment plants.

Toxic Pollutants

Congress also in 1977 required EPA to regulate discharges from 34 industries and to set controls for 65 toxic compounds and classes of compounds containing about 125 chemicals. This congressional action was not entirely original, however. By the mid-1970s, EPA had failed to set many of the best-available-technology (BAT) rules mandated by the 1972 amendments to the CWA. The National Resources Defense Council sued EPA, and in a 1976 settlement agreement, the agency agreed to promulgate effluent limitations and pretreatment standards for 65 toxic pollutants discharged by 34 industries (*Natural Resources Defense Coun-*

cil v. Train, 8 ER Cases 2120 (D.D.C. 1976)). The terms of the settlement and the list of pollutants were incorporated into the law as part of the 1977 amendments as an indication of the congressional intent that toxic substances in water were to be controlled.

Since then, EPA has gotten court approval for several extensions of the original court-ordered deadlines in the course of preparing and issuing rules; under the schedule, the last of the 34 rules was scheduled to become final in late 1985, but the agency has consistently missed the deadlines. The rules are published at 40 CFR 129.

1987 Amendments

The Clean Water Act was reauthorized and extensively amended by the Water Quality Act of 1987 (Pub. L. No. 100-4), which Congress passed twice (once at the end of the 99th Congress). President Reagan vetoed the legislation in each session of Congress, but the second veto was easily overridden. The 1987 amendments phase out the subsidy program for local sewage treatment plants, replacing it with state revolving loan funds. The amendments also set up programs to reduce polluted runoff from "nonpoint" sources, such as city streets, farmland, and mining sites; and established a new program to control the discharge of toxic pollutants.

Another key provision of the act is a requirement that states list all navigable waters that are not expected to meet water quality standards because of toxic pollutants even after dischargers meet all existing effluent limitations requirements, including installation of "best available technology economically achievable" by industrial dischargers. These list requirements have come to be known as "toxic hot spots." States also must identify the sources of these toxic pollutants for each affected segment of navigable waters, their quantity, and individual control strategies that will enable the segments to meet applicable water quality standards.

States had two years from enactment to complete these listings, and the EPA administrator had nine months from enactment to issue guidance to states on performing the identifications. The control strategies were required to be designed to attain compliance with water quality standards no later than three years after implementation, under the legislation. The administrator would approve or reject states' control strategies.

The amendments also require states, when reviewing or revising their water quality standards, to develop specific numerical criteria for certain priority toxic pollutants identified by EPA, if those pollutants interfere with the designated uses of affected water bodies.

Another provision prohibits "backsliding" by dischargers; this means no permits can be issued with less stringent effluent limitations than previously were in effect.

That the amendments represent to some extent another oscillation is a control strategy that moves between the use of direct water-quality standards and the imposition of technological control requirements.

PROVISIONS OF THE LAW

The CWA regulates the discharge of nontoxic and toxic pollutants into waterways by municipal, industrial and other point sources and by nonpoint sources of pollution. Under the CWA, pollution is defined as the "man-made or man-induced alteration of the chemical, physical, biological, and radiological integrity of water." Types of pollution include toxic substances, organic wastes, sediment washed from agricultural or construction operations, acid, bacteria and viruses, nutrients, heat, and oil and grease.

Because of difficulties that arose with other efforts to control water pollution, the act gives authority to the federal government and covers all surface waters in the United States. The federal government may delegate some provisions under the act to state or local jurisdictions, but the jurisdictions must implement the act according to federal regulations and specifications.

Through a variety of programs, the act attacks municipal and industrial pollution, pollution from nonpoint sources and spills, and pollution from dredging or placing fill material in bodies of water, including wetlands.

Major provisions of the act that deal with chemicals are:

- Section 303: water quality criteria and standards

- Sections 301, 304, and 307: effluent guidelines and limitations
- Section 311: control of discharges of oil and hazardous substances

Section 303: Water Quality Criteria, Standards

Central to the operation of the act are state standards for water quality and federal criteria outlining the water conditions that must be present to support a particular use of a body of water.

Although EPA sets effluent limitation guidelines for industrial categories, these guidelines often are not stringent enough to protect the water quality in a particular body of water. In such cases, the state water quality standards, which may incorporate the EPA criteria for water quality, can be used to impose more stringent pollution control requirements on a specific water pollution source. These more stringent control requirements are written into the pollution source's NPDES permit issued by state or federal officials.

Water Quality Criteria

Criteria for water quality (40 CFR 125) are set by EPA to describe what level of certain pollutants ambient water can contain and still be suitable for certain uses. Regulations under the act establish four specific use categories:

- Class A—primary water-contact recreation (suitable for swimming)
- Class B—able to support fish and wildlife
- Class C—public water supply
- Class D—agricultural and industrial use

While the goal of the act is to bring all surface waters up to the specific fishable/swimmable levels, in practice this has been difficult to accomplish.

The criteria used to describe water quality are analogous to the ambient air standards of the Clean Air Act in that they set national guidelines (see chapter on the CAA). After scientific analysis, EPA determines how much dissolved oxygen is needed to support various types of fish and aquatic life in various types of bodies of water. This figure then is proposed as the dissolved oxygen criterion. Similar criteria are set for scores of chemicals, fecal coliform count, acidity (pH), and other substances or conditions that can be used to describe the water quality of a body of water.

Once these criteria are set, states use them to establish water quality standards and to determine the discharge limits for individual NPDES permits granted to pollution sources in the state. States may set criteria based on site-specific conditions.

Water Quality Standards

Under the act, states are required to set, submit to EPA for approval, and enforce water quality standards that classify all waters in the state with respect to intended use and the conditions necessary to maintain that use. Each standard must include limitations on any pollutant that might affect the use of the body of water it applies to, *e.g.*, oxygen-depleting wastes, suspended solids, toxic chemicals, acidity (pH), and heat.

Water quality standards must be reviewed by the issuing state every three years. Regulations concerning state standards are published at 40 CFR 131.

Components of a Standard

Each standard is composed of the following four parts:

- The use classification of the body of water (Class A, Class B, etc.)
- The water quality criteria that must be met to maintain that use
- An antidegradation clause stating that discharges that would downgrade the existing use classification will not be permitted
- An implementation and enforcement plan

Under the CWA, existing uses of a body of water must be maintained. For example, construction of a treatment plant or industrial facility that would degrade water quality from Class C to Class D would not be permitted except under certain very stringent conditions. In general, if a stream now is used for swimming, the state is required under the act to protect that use in setting the related water quality standard.

Standard Setting

The CWA requires each state to encourage full public participation in the process of setting a water quality standard. This can entail gathering public testimony when a new facility applies for a discharge permit, or can involve public pressure to upgrade the current use category of a stream or body of water.

As noted earlier, the ultimate goal of the act is to make all surface waters in the United States fishable/swimmable. EPA encourages states to upgrade their water quality standards for individual bodies of water to come closer to this goal. This approach, however, and the act's emphasis on public participation, often bring citizens' groups and conservationists into conflict with industrial development and pro-industry government groups. The primary reason for this is that industry often must install costly pollution control equipment to meet even the existing water quality standard for a stream. The cost to that industry could be far larger should a state decide to upgrade the water quality standard for a particular stream into which the industry discharges pollutants. For this reason, state water quality standards and the process for setting and reviewing them constitute one of the most central provisions of the act, but also one of the most controversial.

Sections 301, 304, and 307: Effluent Guidelines, Limitations

Under the CWA, all municipal and industrial point sources of water pollution are subject to effluent limitations. These limitations, based on effluent limitation guidelines and water quality standards, are embodied in an NPDES permit issued for that specific pollution source, the terms of which must be adhered to.

An effluent limitation is a limit on the amount of specific pollutants that a specific source may discharge. The limitation is custom-tailored for each discharger based on the EPA effluent limitation guideline for the type of facility and on the water quality of the particular body of water into which the discharge will be made. The quality of water that must be maintained is set out in the state water quality standard, discussed earlier.

Effluent Guidelines

Under section 301 of the CWA, EPA sets uniform national guidelines (40 CFR 401 *et seq.*) for discharges of each type of pollutant from each type of industrial point source. The guidelines, set on an industry-by-industry basis, are the minimum standards that every discharger in the specific industrial category must meet. Despite the use of the term *guidelines,* these requirements are not advisory. Rather, they form the skeleton of a mandatory program which is fleshed out by the insertion of specific discharge limits for individual pollution sources within the category.

To illustrate, the effluent *guideline* established by EPA and applicable to the pesticides chemical manufacturing industry (40 CFR 455) limits the release of organic pesticide chemicals and pollutants that create chemical or biological oxygen demand. The guideline also specifies the acidity (pH) of the discharge and the amount of total suspended solids it may contain. The amount of the discharge that is permitted is based on units of production, with a maximum allowable daily and monthly level specified. The effluent *limitation,* however, established by a state for a specific plant discharging an effluent into a specific body of water and written into the NPDES permit, may be more stringent than the release level set by the guideline, depending on the quality of the body of water into which the effluent is discharged.

More than 50 industries are covered by effluent guidelines, including the fruit and vegetable canning industry and manufacturing industries for cement, iron and steel, fertilizers, paint, plastics, and pharmaceuticals.

A separate set of effluent guidelines applies to municipal discharges, mainly those from sewage treatment plants. Pollutant discharges also are regulated according to whether the source is old or new. In addition, pretreatment of industrial discharges into treatment plants is required.

The U.S. Appeals Court for the Ninth Circuit ruled in 1990 that EPA must amend its CWA regulations to require states to identify all sources of toxic pollutants in their waterways by expanding their facilities lists (*NRDC v. EPA,* 915 F.2d, 31 ER Cases 2089, 9th Cir., 1990). Moreover, the court directed the agency to reconsider whether individual control strategies should be required for states' expanded lists of point source pollution.

The "toxic hot spots" rule under section 304 of the act has been successfully implemented by the majority of states. More than 500 waters are now listed for individual control strategies. The section requires states to list waters adversely affected by toxic, conventional, and nonconventional pollutants described below, to identify the point sources discharging to certain listed waters, and to develop individual control strategies.

Types of Pollutants

For purposes of regulating under the CWA, pollutants are divided into three categories: conventional, toxic, and nonconventional. In recent years, control of substances in the second category, toxic pollutants, has been EPA's top priority.

Conventional pollutants are those that deplete oxygen in the receiving waters; alter its pH level; or add suspended solids, fecal matter, or oil and grease.

Toxic pollutants include the 65 chemicals and classes of chemicals added to the act in 1977 (see discussion of 1977 amendments). When the various compounds and classes involving the 65 are broken out, the total number of substances to be regulated is about 125 priority pollutants, ranging from acenaphthene through zinc compounds. EPA has termed these *priority pollutants*. Although the act allows EPA to draft specific effluent standards under section 307 for these substances, the agency has issued only a few. Instead, EPA has been developing water quality criteria for all the priority pollutants and is incorporating limits on the pollutants into its industrial and municipal effluent guidelines and pretreatment standards. Ambient water quality criteria for 64 of the 65 chemicals were issued in 1980. The final one, for 2,3,7,8-tetrachlorodibenzo-*p*-dioxin, was issued in February 1984.

Nonconventional pollutants are those that are neither toxic nor conventional. Added to the act in 1977, the nonconventional pollutant category can encompass hundreds of pollutants. Pollutants in this category may be reclassified as toxic if scientific data indicate a toxic hazard, or may be reclassified as conventional if conditions warrant. Examples of nonconventional pollutants include ammonia and phosphorus.

Types of Controls Required

Under the act, pollutants must be controlled to various degrees, by various types of treatment technology, and by various deadlines. The type of control required is written into the effluent guidelines and into individual NPDES permits. The types of controls include the following, in ascending order of stringency:

- *Best Practicable Technology (BPT).* This is the minimum acceptable level of effluent treatment for existing plants discharging directly into surface waters. Most facilities already meet this level of pollutant removal.
- *Best Conventional Technology (BCT).* More stringent than BPT controls, the BCT controls apply to conventional pollutants and were mandated by Congress in the 1977 amendments to the act. The act required dischargers of conventional pollutants to use BCT to meet effluent limits by July 1, 1984. EPA has been slow in completing the regulations on BCT controls and this deadline was not met. It is likely a new deadline will be established under an amendment to the law.
- *Best Available Technology (BAT).* This is the most stringent type of control requirement for existing dischargers and applies to the priority pollutants discussed earlier and to nonconventional pollutants. About 57,000 dischargers that treat their own wastes became subject to BAT regulations as of July 1, 1984, but EPA has issued only a few of the regulations outlining what pollution control devices and engineering controls are needed for specific industrial categories and which priority pollutants must be controlled to meet this standard.
- *Best Engineering Judgment (BEJ).* In writing discharge permits for pollution sources for which EPA has not issued regulations, the permit writers use BEJ, *i.e.,* their best professional judgment, to determine what types of pollution controls to require.
- *Best Available Demonstrated Control Technology (BADCT).* The most stringent category, this applies only to new industrial sources of pollution. These standards aim for zero pollutants in a plant's effluent and operate on the rationale that it is easier and less costly to build stringent pollution control equipment into a new facility than it is to add it to an existing one.

Because Congress recognized the difficulty and cost of requiring industry to install pollution control equipment that satisfies the requirements of the various types of controls, it allowed for a phase-in provision that takes into account both environmental and economic considerations.

Needless to say, determining what pollution control equipment a pollution source must install to meet the goals of the CWA is an elaborate and technical process involving both EPA and the states. The effluent guidelines that specify the type of control (BAT, BCT, etc.) required of an industry often are the subject of court challenges and extensive arguments between the affected industries on the one side and environmental groups on the other. These arguments often continue even at the point when states write control requirements into an individual plant's NPDES permit.

Effluent Limitations

Effluent limitations are specific control requirements imposed on specific point sources of water pollution. The limitations incorporate both the effluent guidelines and the state's limits on specific pollutants to allow standards to be achieved or maintained. Each limitation, therefore, is custom-tailored to the specific pollution source by state or federal officials who take into account the type of industry or facility, the body of water receiving the waste and its designated use category, and the criteria for the pollutants being discharged.

Limitations for Municipal Plants

All municipal wastewater treatment plants are subject to effluent limitations under section 304 of the CWA. The limitations, which are written into the plant's NPDES permit, generally include effluent limits based on both the content of the discharge and the water quality standard for the body of water receiving the discharge.

Treatment by publicly owned treatment works (POTWs) is classified as being one of several types:

- Primary treatment, in use at some older plants and small facilities, removes only 35 percent of the oxygen-demanding pollutants, primarily by filtration of solid matter.
- Secondary treatment removes at least 85 percent of the pollutants in municipal waste water and is roughly equivalent to the BPT controls imposed on industrial sources.
- Advanced treatment, employing the most sophisticated treatment equipment, removes 95 percent of the pollutants in the waste water.

All POTWs originally were to meet secondary treatment standards by July 1977, but Congress repeatedly has extended the deadline when it has become apparent that most plants would not be able to meet it. The federal government provides up to 85 percent of the funding to build POTWs that will meet the secondary treatment standards and encourages use of innovative technology to move toward advanced treatment levels of pollution removal. It takes between four and seven years, however, for planning, funding, and construction of a new POTW.

NPDES Permits

The cornerstone of the effluent guideline and limitations system of regulating water quality is the NPDES permit. All point sources discharging wastes into surface waters must have an NPDES permit issued by the state, or by EPA if the state has not taken over this responsibility. Permits must be reviewed and considered for renewal every five years. Regulations on the issuance of NPDES permits are published at 40 CFR 122, 123.

Content of a Permit

The NPDES permit is the tool for listing the specific effluent limitations for a point source. In issuing the permit, the issuing agency incorporates the federal effluent limitation guidelines and specific state limits.

The permit describes allowable discharges in terms of amount and concentration. It may also outline pollution control requirements and specify the date by which the controls must be in place, and it describes monitoring (testing) and reporting that the permit holder must perform. Any variances, such as peak load variances or exemptions from some types of control, also are listed in the permit.

The permit's monitoring and reporting provisions set up a system of self-monitoring by the permit holder. Reports on tests of effluent must be made periodically to the agency issuing the permit, and are available for public scrutiny. The state or EPA may revoke the permits of holders who violate the conditions of their NPDES permits.

In drafting the NPDES requirements, Congress decided that public access to and scrutiny of the permits and reports filed by holders would ultimately have a beneficial effect on regulatory attempts to improve water quality. For this reason, permits issued by states or by EPA often are the subject of court challenges, not only by industrial firms that feel the rules are too stringent and costly, but also by environmental groups that feel the rules do not go far enough.

Many industrial plants, generally small ones, have no NPDES permit because they do not discharge wastes directly into surface waters. Instead, the wastes are discharged into local sewer systems. These firms generally must pretreat their wastes, as discussed below.

Pretreatment Standards

Treatment of ordinary household waste poses few problems for municipal treatment plants, but only 75 percent of the wastes treated by such plants are from such sources. The remainder come from various industrial facilities that discharge their wastes into the local sewer system. Best estimates are that about 15,000 firms in about two dozen industries discharge wastes into public treatment works.

Most POTWs are not equipped to handle industrial wastes, which either travel through the plant untreated or disrupt operation of the plant and make it malfunction. In addition, the toxic substances in industrial wastes may contaminate sewage sludge with chemicals and heavy metals, making it unusable, or may cause sewer fires, corrosion, or explosions.

To address this concern, Congress under section 307 of the act authorized EPA to issue pretreatment standards, codified at 40 CFR 403. These standards, usually written into industrial effluent guidelines, require firms discharging directly into municipal treatment works to pretreat their wastes to remove certain toxic substances from the waste water before it enters the public sewer system. These pretreatment standards are based on achieving end treatment results equivalent to those obtained using best available control technology (BAT). In general, the standards are enforced through the effluent limitations imposed on the POTWs, *i.e.*, the effluent of the POTW must be in compliance with limitations established in its NPDES permit.

Pretreatment of these wastes is needed for two reasons. The first is to protect water quality and sewage plant operation. The second is to prevent firms that discharge into local sewer systems from having an unfair economic advantage over firms that must pay to install equipment to treat their own wastes.

Local Controls

The CWA also allows states and local governments to impose pretreatment requirements more stringent than EPA's on industrial firms that discharge wastes into the local sewer system for treatment by POTWs. Some local POTWs, as a result of the stronger conditions imposed on them in their NPDES permits, require greater pretreatment than the EPA mandates for industrial firms, usually because of the type of wastes received or the quality of the receiving surface waters. Pretreatment standards prevent the discharge of pollutants directly to the treatment plant.

In addition, the CWA provides that municipal plants that treat large amounts of industrial waste must be constructed with additional capacity and equipment to handle such wastes. Industrial waste generators that discharge into the plant must pay a portion of the additional construction and operation costs of such POTWs. Because of the controversy it has caused, this provision of the act is rarely used.

Section 311: Discharges of Oil, Hazardous Substances

The third major section of the CWA that protects surface waters is section 311, which established mechanisms for cleaning up spills and other releases of oil and hazardous substances into navigable waters. Related EPA regulations appear at 40 CFR 109–117.

Under section 311, EPA has designated about 300 substances as hazardous when spilled or discharged. For many of the substances, the agency also has established a "reportable quantity" designation—the minimum amount of the substance that when spilled must be reported to the federal government's National Response Center. The center provides information on proper cleanup and disposal procedures and can dispatch federal, state, or local authorities with expertise on dealing with a spill.

Also authorized under section 311 were establishment of an emergency fund that may be used to pay the costs of cleaning up discharges of hazardous substances; initiation of planning to prevent spills; and the drawing up of a National Contingency Plan, which outlines response powers and responsibilities for cleanup of discharges into the environment.

Section 311 also provides for civil penalties of up to $250,000 for those responsible for the discharge of a substance into the environment and makes the discharger responsible for removal and cleanup costs.

This section of the CWA works closely with the cleanup provisions of the Comprehensive Environmental Response, Compensation and Liability Act, the superfund law enacted in 1980 (see chapter on CERCLA). In many cases, cleanup provisions of the two laws are virtually identical, and the cleanup fund authorized under the CWA has been incorporated into the cleanup fund established under the 1980 superfund law. The provision for the drawing up of a National Contingency Plan, originally written into the CWA, also was incorporated into the superfund law but in a revised form so as to encompass all cleanup actions that may be authorized by the federal government under either the CWA or the superfund law. For this reason, federal activities regarding cleanup of spills and chemical contaminations are covered in the chapter on CERCLA and the superfund.

Oil Pollution Control Act of 1990

In August 1990, President Bush signed the Oil Pollution Control Act of 1990 (Pub. L. No. 101-380) which established new liability limits for owners and operators of tankers that cause damaging oil spills. The action came largely in response to the *Exxon Valdez* disaster in March 1989. In that incident, the tanker *Valdez* rammed into Bligh Reef in Alaska's Prince William Sound. Some 11 million gallons of Alaskan crude oil gushed into the sound's pristine waters in what would turn out to be the worst oil spill in U.S. history. The spilled oil washed up on more than 700 miles of Alaska shoreline, killing fish and wildlife, and spawning litigation that sought billions of dollars in damages.

The new law also amended the Clean Water Act, principally section 311, relating to liability for spills of oil and hazardous substances in U.S. waters. Jail penalties under section 311(b)(5) for failure to provide prompt notification of spills were increased to a maximum of five years. Administrative penalties under section 311(b)(6) were similarly increased.

Prospects for Reauthorization

Reauthorization of the Clean Water Act will be a high priority for Congress in 1993. Legislation (S. 1081) to renew the act was introduced in May 1991 by Sen. Max Baucus (D-Mont.).

Federal funding for the state revolving fund program, which provides loans to build sewage treatment facilities, expires in 1994. The Baucus bill would guarantee that all of the $18 billion authorized under the 1987 amendments for the program will be made available to address water pollution problems.

A key provision in the reauthorization bill focused on nonpoint source pollution, an area of interest to the White House. The bill would provide a new $3 billion grant program to help states deal with nonpoint source pollution, such as runoff from urban and agricultural areas. It also would provide $2.5 billion in grants to solve the contamination problem from combined sewer overflows. Another $2.5 billion would be earmarked to help small communities comply with the act.

A similar bill introduced in the House by Rep. Gerry Studds (D-Mass.) would extend funding for the state revolving loan fund through 1999. It would also establish a permit fee system on all industrial dischargers to address coastal water pollution.

The reauthorized act would probably employ new market-based strategies similar to those adopted under the 1990 Clean Air Act amendments. EPA is urging Congress to consider new pollution control efforts including pollution prevention for industrial sources and economic incentives. Such a plan might include a pollution credits trading program that could be used to control nonpoint source contamination.

Safe Drinking Water Act
(SDWA)

AT A GLANCE

Public Law Number: Pub. L. No. 93-523

U.S. Code citation: 42 USC 300(f) *et seq.*

Enacted: December 16, 1974; effective when enacted
  Amended: 1976, 1977, 1979, 1980, 1984, 1986 (major amendments, Pub. L. No. 99-339)

Regulations at: 40 CFR 140–149

Federal agency with jurisdiction: Environmental Protection Agency (EPA)

Congressional committees/subcommittees with jurisdiction:
  House of Representatives: Health and the Environment Subcommittee of the Energy and Commerce Committee
  Senate: Toxic Substances and Environmental Oversight Subcommittee of the Environment and Public Works Committee

BNA reporting services: *Daily Environment Report, Environment Reporter*
  Text of law appears in *Environment Reporter* Federal Laws at 71:6041 *et seq.*
  Text of regulations appears in *Environment Reporter* Federal Regulations
  Legal decisions appear in Environment Reporter Cases (ER Cases)

What the SDWA regulates and why: The act mandates establishment of uniform federal standards for drinking water quality, and sets up a system to regulate underground injection of wastes and other substances that could contaminate underground water sources. (Surface water is protected under the CWA.)

Safe Drinking Water Act—Contd.

Under the law, EPA sets two types of drinking water standards. Primary standards apply to substances that may have an adverse effect on health. These are enforced by the states. Compliance is mandatory. Secondary standards provide guidelines on substances or conditions that affect color, taste, smell, and other physical characteristics of drinking water. These standards are advisory, not mandatory. Drinking water obtained from underground sources must be tested to see that it meets the primary standards. Some states also require that water meet the secondary standards.

The law also bans underground injection of certain materials in or near an underground water source, and requires issuing of permits, monitoring, and recordkeeping for underground injection that is allowable.

The act was amended in June 1986 to take away the EPA's discretion in deciding whether to set standards for contaminants in drinking water. EPA was required to issue binding standards for 83 drinking water contaminants within three years. However, as of the middle of 1990, only 55 of the standards had been issued or proposed. The agency said the rest would not be ready until sometime in 1992. EPA said it wants to bring further improvements by issuing standards for another 25 contaminants by 1995.

EPA was given power under the 1986 amendments to order operators of public drinking water systems to comply with federal standards by issuing administrative orders instead of having to obtain a court order.

The amendments create a federal groundwater protection program, under which EPA will give grants to states to prevent contamination of wellfields that provide public drinking water. Although regulation of groundwater is retained by the states, EPA can require that minimum criteria be met before the grants are awarded.

COVERAGE OF THE LAW

The goals of the Safe Drinking Water Act are to establish federal standards for drinking water quality, to protect underground sources of water, and to set up a system of state/federal cooperation to assure compliance with the law and its standards. While the law technically applies only to public water systems serving 25 or more persons, its provisions on groundwater contamination also provide a form of protection to individual and agricultural users of groundwater.

The protection afforded under the act is based on a system of drinking water standards set by EPA. Each standard limits the amount of a specific contaminant that may be present in drinking water. Primary standards, which apply to substances that may have an adverse effect on health, are enforced by the states and must be complied with. Secondary standards, which provide guidelines on substances that affect the color, taste, smell, and other physical characteristics of water, are advisory. Both types of standards are set by EPA but enforced by the states, with state enforcement of secondary standards optional. States may also establish more stringent standards than those of the federal government.

A second major component of the act is regulation of underground injection of chemicals and other substances that could enter the aquifer and harm it. Injection of liquid wastes into underground wells as a way of disposal may only be carried out if it will not damage the quality of the aquifer.

The intent of the SDWA was to fill the gap left by the enactment of the Clean Water Act (CWA) passed two years earlier. While the CWA was passed to clean up and protect streams and other surface waters, the SDWA was intended to protect underground water sources.

DEVELOPMENT OF THE LAW

The SDWA was passed by Congress on December 3, 1974, to address a growing concern that earlier efforts to assure safe drinking water had failed.

The earliest federal efforts to control the quality of drinking water began in 1912 when the Public Health Service issued standards aimed at preventing diseases caused by contaminated water. Amended many times in the ensuing years, the standards applied only to water provided on interstate vehicles such as buses and trains; however, the standards also were used by states and localities as guidelines on tolerable levels of contaminants in water.

The growing recognition that groundwater used for drinking must be protected was born out of the same concern that prompted Congress to set uniform national standards for clean surface water and clean air under the CWA and CAA.

In the early 1970s, Congress was looking at natural resources with long-term protection in mind, and drinking water presented a particular problem. Water tends to move underground, carrying with it contamination from nearby or far away, depending on the aquifer. In many cases, this movement is slow, thereby allowing contaminants to be filtered out as the water travels through various types of soil and rock formations. But if the contamination level in the aquifer exceeds that with which the earth is able to cope through this cleansing process, the contamination can show up miles away and persist for many years.

Decades of experience with state programs to preserve natural resources had shown that these programs varied as to their effectiveness. Only some of the states had adopted drinking water programs using the federal Public Health Service standards as guidelines, and even in these states enforcement, monitoring, and funding were spotty. For example, a 1970 federal study had found that more than one-third of drinking water samples tested were contaminated with harmful chemicals and bacteria. This was especially upsetting since the U.S. Geological Survey had found that half the U.S. population, including almost all of the rural inhabitants, depended on groundwater rather than lakes, rivers, or other surface water for drinking water and for other domestic uses. Moreover, about 40 percent of the water used for agricultural irrigation was groundwater rather than surface water, the survey had found. These results raised the possibility that unknown contaminants in groundwater could enter the food chain or harm those drinking it.

In addition, many cities and towns were serving growing populations with outdated and deteriorating water supply systems that had been built decades before. Seepage into the underground systems from industrial areas and sewers was widespread.

Authority to regulate the quality of drinking water used for interstate purposes had already been transferred to EPA from the Public Health Service before the SDWA was passed. With the relatively new agency deep in efforts to protect the environment, it made sense to Congress that groundwater protection should be made a national rather than state activity. Primary responsibility for enforcement is given to the states, however, if possible. States submit their plans for enforcing the SDWA to EPA. If the agency approves the plan, the state receives "primacy" and the authority to enforce the law within its borders.

EPA's Broad Congressional Mandate

In passing the SDWA in 1974, Congress gave EPA several stringent timetables for setting maximum levels of contaminants in water. The first set of standards was to be set nine months after the date of enactment of the law. These so-called "interim" regulations would specify contaminants that may have an adverse effect on human health. Congress anticipated that the interim standards would be based on the Public Health Service standards, and was careful to use the word "may" in giving EPA jurisdiction, thus allowing the agency latitude in deciding which contaminants should be controlled.

Congress also gave the agency the option in establishing interim regulations of specifying either maximum contaminant levels for pollutants that could be measured or water treatment techniques to control contaminants. In either case, Congress specified that the levels to which persons would be exposed should provide an "ample margin of safety." In setting the standards, EPA was to consider epidemiological, toxicological, physiological, biochemical, and/or statistical research, and extrapolations from such data. EPA subsequently issued the interim regulations (40 CFR 141, 142).

NAS Study

The legislation also provided for revising the interim standards after a study by the National Academy of Sciences (NAS). According to the law, NAS was both to recommend maximum contaminant levels that would protect health and to list contaminants that may harm health but for which maximum tolerable amounts in water could not be determined. As was the case under several other environmental laws, this study was not to take costs of compliance into account. It was only to assess the health impact of contaminants in water, the impact on particularly susceptible individuals, the synergistic effect of contaminants, and the level at which a given contaminant in the human body would be expected to increase the risk of adverse health effects.

EPA was given a series of timetables for proposing the levels recommended by NAS. The agency was to set the allowable contamination at the level where no known health effects would occur and was to provide for an ample margin of safety. The agency also was to list treatment techniques that would reduce the contaminants in drinking water to below the level recommended by NAS.

When NAS reported the results of its study in June 1977, it provided extensive research on drinking water contaminants and/or their health effects. It refused, however, to set maximum contaminant levels, saying this was the duty of a regulatory body, not a research body.

EPA then decided that the interim regulations (40 CFR 141, 142) would suffice and left the interim primary standards in effect. The standards, however, have been modified several times since enactment of the law.

Underground Injection

In drafting the SDWA, Congress also provided for control of underground injection into wells of fluid that might enter drinking water sources. In enacting this section of the law, Congress gave EPA a long lead time to allow states time to devise an underground injection control program that conformed with the federal regulations. Such wells, used for disposal of liquid wastes, must be covered by permits obtained before operations begin. The permits, which are issued by the states, are issued only after a study of the operation indicates that wastes from the injection site will not enter the underground water supply and contaminate public drinking water supplies. Congress drafted the program to be technology-based and did not list chemicals that may or may not be disposed of in underground wells. Rather, it mandated that any such activity be designed, monitored, and inspected so that no contamination would occur.

The 1986 Amendments

The Safe Drinking Water Act Amendments of 1986 required EPA to issue binding standards for 83 drinking water contaminants within three years. The binding standards would require many drinking water utility companies to install treatment systems, including systems that use granular activated carbon, or in some cases to find new sources of drinking water. However, as of the middle of 1990, only 55 of these standards had been issued or proposed. The remaining standards were expected to be issued by the end of 1992.

The measure also created for the first time a substantial federal role in protecting groundwater by authorizing EPA to give grants to states to develop and carry out plans to protect from contamination wellfields used as sources of public drinking water. While states must include certain elements in their plans to qualify for the grants, states rather than EPA have primacy in setting future regulations governing groundwater.

The law also does the following:

- Streamlines the procedures EPA must follow to set drinking water standards, thereby speeding the process
- Makes tampering with a public drinking water supply a federal crime
- Provides state and local governments federal aid for protecting aquifers that serve as the only source of drinking water for a community

- Requires companies that inject wastes into the ground to monitor for contamination of groundwater
- Gives EPA the power to order someone who contaminates drinking water to provide an alternate supply that is clean

PROVISIONS OF THE LAW

As mentioned earlier, in enacting the SDWA Congress in effect was closing the gap left when it enacted the CWA; while the CWA was intended to protect surface waters, the SDWA was intended to protect underground water sources and assure that public water supplies met certain minimum national standards.

The major chemical control provisions under the SDWA are found in sections 1412 (drinking water standards) and 1421 (underground injection).

Section 1412: Drinking Water Standards

Drinking water standards under the SDWA apply to public water systems, defined as those piping water for consumption by 25 or more people or having at least 15 service connections. Under the definition, the regulations subsequently issued under the act cover small water supply systems serving a small housing development or commercial building, as well as cities and towns providing water to hundreds or thousands of people. Under the act, EPA sets both primary and secondary standards.

Primary Standards

Primary standards (40 CFR 141, 142) set limits on contaminants that may affect health and are enforced by the state under the "primacy" system discussed earlier, unless the state is unwilling or unable to do so. Among the primary standards are Maximum Contaminant Levels (MCLs) for fluoride, arsenic, a variety of pesticides, mercury, lead, nitrates, and several additional inorganic and organic chemicals. In July 1990, EPA issued MCLs for radon, uranium, radium, and other compounds.

States must measure and monitor the amounts of the primary contaminants in public water supplies and report the results to EPA periodically. Municipal governments and private water companies that supply water to the public must test water quality to make certain that any contaminants do not exceed federal limits.

The water supplier must also keep records of water quality, notify customers if a standard is being exceeded, and take prompt corrective action if a violation occurs. Federal funding is available to help pay for construction of water supply systems and for upgrading of existing systems.

Secondary Standards

Secondary standards (40 CFR 143), also mandated under section 1412 of the act, specify the maximum contaminant levels consistent with protection of the public welfare. These standards are advisory only, and may not be enforced by the federal government if states fail to require compliance with them.

Secondary standards include limits on various physical characteristics which may not harm health but may make water less pleasing to drink or use. Among the secondary standards are limits on chloride, copper, iron, and manganese, all of which impart an unpleasant odor or taste to water. Other characteristics regulated under the secondary standards are color, foaming, acidity, and total dissolved solids (cloudiness).

Section 1421: Underground Injection Control

Under section 1421 of the SDWA, the federal government is directed to establish an underground injection control (UIC) program to be enforced by the states. The UIC program (40 CFR 144–147) focuses on subsurface emplacement of fluids that may result in contamination of groundwater that is used for, or may be used for, a public water supply. Types of contamination that may result in noncompliance with the primary drinking water standards and types of contamination that may affect human health are both regulated.

Under the law, EPA sets the UIC program in place, while states enforce it through a system of permits and required monitoring by well operators.

Classes of Wells

Under the UIC program, states must conform to federal regulations that became effective in 1980. Those regulations (40 CFR 144–147) establish the following five types of underground injection wells:

- Class I—wells into which highly toxic industrial and/or municipal wastes are injected beneath the deepest layer of the earth containing an underground source of drinking water
- Class II—wells used to inject fluids in the course of producing oil and gas, and for liquid hydrocarbon storage
- Class III—wells used to extract minerals or energy from the earth
- Class IV—wells where hazardous wastes or radioactive materials are injected into or above a formation within one-quarter mile of an underground source of drinking water
- Class V—wells not included in the other categories, encompassing those used for cesspools, draining, storage of gaseous hydrocarbons, cooling-water return, or a variety of other uses

According to the program set up by EPA, a state must phase out operation of Class IV wells within six months after the state UIC program is approved. No new Class IV wells will be permitted. Class I, II, and III wells must be evaluated every five years and must be issued a new state permit after each evaluation in order to continue to operate. Class V wells are not affected by the program.

Under the UIC program, well operators must file quarterly reports on the physical and chemical characteristics of the injected fluids. Records on the injected fluids must be kept for five years after the well is closed or abandoned. In addition, the state must be notified 180 days before the well is converted or abandoned, and the state must be informed within 24 hours if the well is out of compliance with its permit or if the injection system malfunctions.

Because of the long lead time written into the law—states had over two years to establish a program to conform to the 1980 regulations—many state UIC programs are only now beginning to operate.

Other Provisions

The SDWA also provides special protection for so-called "sole-source aquifers," those underground water supplies that serve as the only source of drinking water in an area. Specific areas in the United States may be designated under this provision, thereby triggering more stringent protective measures. An example is San Antonio, Texas, where extensive research is required and a permit must be obtained before any activity that could damage the aquifer can be undertaken.

The SDWA also allows the EPA administrator to issue orders or begin civil action if a contaminant entering a public water system poses an imminent or substantial hazard and if the state fails to take action.

In addition, the law allows citizens to file suit against any person alleged to be in violation of the act or to sue EPA if it fails to perform a duty under the law.

Regulations Under 1986 Amendments

New regulations issued in 1987 codified the prohibition in the 1986 amendments against the use of lead pipes, solder, and flux in the installation or repair of any public water system or any drinking water plumbing connected to a public water system. The regulations included the law's definition of "lead free" and noted that the deadline for state enforcement of the prohibition was June 19, 1988.

The new regulations also reflected the changes in the conditions under which public water systems may receive variances from national primary drinking water regulations. Changes of cleanup requirements were also codified.

Lead levels in drinking water received widespread public attention early in the summer of 1988 when a government study showed that 8 out of 12 water coolers tested contained lead liners. Lead from coolers was leaching into the drinking water at levels greater than the standard of 50 parts per billion (ppb).

EPA revised the standard in May 1991 to one that corresponds to a 5 ppb average. In addition, lead will be monitored at the tap where the highest concentrations are found. The purpose of this plan is to control lead leaching from pipes, solder, and plumbing fixtures. Water supply systems will be required to monitor for lead in hundreds of thousands of homes and to curb lead levels by treating water to reduce its acidity and control corrosion.

By 1993, large water systems will be required to begin developing corrosion-control systems. Such programs are scheduled to go into effect for smaller systems in 1994.

This rule is expected to cut the amount of lead in the blood of more than one-half million school children with elevated lead levels.

The Natural Resources Defense Council released a survey in July 1991 showing that fewer than 1 percent of U.S. schools and day-care centers had sampled and analyzed their drinking water for lead. Thirty-two states had no information on testing at day care facilities. Legislation (S 1445, AR 2840) introduced soon after sought to reduce lead exposure by doubling to $40 million per year funding for lead testing for children. It would require residences to be tested before they are sold or rented, and would require testing in schools. It also calls for public water systems to remove lead from the entire system if any home shows contamination above 10 ppb.

In 1988 EPA released a list of 53 drinking water contaminants that may require future regulation, as well as changes of contaminants to be regulated by June 30, 1989.

The agency was to develop final numerical standards and regulations for 25 of the 53 contaminants by January 1991, under the 1986 amendments. Under a court-approved agreement, the deadline was extended to 1993.

Prospects for Reauthorization

Although discussions concerning reauthorizing the Safe Drinking Water Act have been going on since 1990, it is unlikely that the bill will be reauthorized in 1992. EPA's programs on protecting drinking water can continue without reauthorizing the act as long as Congress appropriates the funds.

The EPA Administrator has been pushing for Congress to remove the statutory provisions requiring the agency to regulate 25 new contaminants every year, saying such a requirement is not scientifically justified.

Part III

Chemical Waste and Disposal Laws

Resource Conservation and Recovery Act
(RCRA)

Public Law Number: Pub. L. No. 94-580

U.S. Code citation: 42 USC 6901 *et seq.*

Enacted: October 21, 1976
> *Amended:* 1978, 1980, 1984 (major amendments, Pub. L. No. 98-616), 1988

Regulations at: 40 CFR 240–271

Federal agency with jurisdiction: Environmental Protection Agency (EPA)

Congressional committees/subcommittees with jurisdiction:
> *House of Representatives:* Commerce, Transportation, and Tourism Subcommittee of the Energy and Commerce Committee
> *Senate:* Environmental Pollution Subcommittee of the Environment and Public Works Committee

BNA reporting services: *Daily Environment Report, Environment Reporter, Toxics Law Reporter*
> Text of law appears in *Environment Reporter* Federal Laws at 71:3101 *et seq.*
> Text of regulations appears in *Environment Reporter* Federal Regulations
> Legal decisions appear in Environment Reporter Cases (ER Cases)

What RCRA regulates and why: Although the act was passed to control all varieties of solid waste disposal and to encourage recycling and alternative energy sources, its major emphasis is control of hazardous waste disposal.

167

Resource Conservation and Recovery Act—Contd.

The law establishes a system to identify wastes and track their generation, transport, and ultimate disposal. Standards for disposal sites and state hazardous waste programs also are included.

Under the law, EPA lists substances that are considered hazardous when disposed of on land. Anyone who generates listed wastes above a certain amount must register with EPA and comply with requirements applying to generators of waste. Transporters of hazardous wastes and disposal sites also must be registered with the agency and a permit must be obtained for disposal sites to receive hazardous wastes. A multi-copy manifest must accompany each batch of such wastes from generator to ultimate disposal site so that waste may be tracked and so that each site has a record of its contents. Records on wastes generated, shipped, and disposed of must be available to regulatory authorities and submitted to them periodically.

Major amendments made in 1984 expand waste management requirements, ban land disposal of bulk liquid hazardous wastes, require regulation of underground storage tanks, and bring generators of smaller amounts of hazardous waters under the law's regulatory requirements.

Latest developments: In early 1992, Congress was considering legislation to reauthorize RCRA (S. 976, 102d Congress). The bill started out with broad provisions, but by the time the Senate passed it in June 1992, it was scaled down. As passed by the Senate, the measure would allow states and localities to control the flow of out-of-state municipal solid waste headed for disposal in their borders.

As of mid-1992, it was unclear whether an out-of-state municipal solid waste bill or a broader RCRA bill would reach the House floor.

COVERAGE OF THE LAW

The Resource Conservation and Recovery Act was passed by Congress in 1976 to close the circle of environmental laws enacted in the previous six years. While other laws regulated air and water pollution, chemical hazards, and drinking water, RCRA was enacted to deal with recycling and disposal of the by-products of an industrialized society.

While RCRA was primarily drafted as a disposal/recycling law, its actual implementation has focused heavily on one section: the provisions on hazardous waste. As an indication of the reason for this, an EPA survey released in 1984 indicated that about 265 million tons of hazardous wastes are generated in the United States each year. Since that time, EPA said the number has decreased for various reasons to about 240 million tons. One reason given for the decline is that companies are trying to generate less hazardous waste because of tougher regulations. But one agency official said that actually hazardous waste generation is between 240 million tons and 275 million tons per year.

RCRA is designed to regulate the activities of all parties dealing with wastes that EPA lists as hazardous. Wastes are considered hazardous if they exhibit any of four characteristics: ignitability, corrosivity, reactivity, or toxicity (see "Section 3001: Identification and Listing"). Once a waste is listed as hazardous, those who generate, transport, or dispose of such materials must comply with a variety of notification and recordkeeping requirements so that such a substance generated, transported, stored, or disposed of in the United States may be tracked for 30 years.

The law also provides for monitoring of disposal sites to make certain that no environmental contamination occurs, and provides stringent penalties and enforcement mechanisms.

DEVELOPMENT OF THE LAW

RCRA had its beginnings in 1965 with passage of the Solid Waste Disposal Act. As open dumps smoldered in cities across the United States, Congress enacted the waste disposal act to help cities turn their dumps into soil-covered sanitary landfills, thereby reducing health hazards and air pollution. In 1970, Congress further amended the act to require a comprehensive investigation of hazardous waste management practices in the United States.

Shortly after its enactment, responsibility for administering the waste disposal law was passed to the newly created EPA from the Department of Health, Education, and Welfare (now the Department of Health and Human Services). EPA, however, was deeply involved in the new air and water pollution control laws, and simply ignored the hazardous waste management studies and surveys called for by the 1970 amendments. According to an EPA official, the hazardous waste programs called for in those amendments suffered from "benign and malignant neglect" because EPA seemed to regard "only air and water pollution as legitimate offspring."

In 1975 the issue arose again when Congress began holding hearings to update the 1970 waste disposal law. At that time, pro-environment feelings were strong in the United States. Congress had in recent years enacted several anti-pollution laws that were popular with the public, if not with the industries being regulated, and the sludge and other debris generated by air and water pollution control equipment had to be disposed of.

The law that came out of those 1975 hearings gave little indication of the effect it would eventually have on the American public and industry. After almost a year of hearings, Congress enacted RCRA, a law that was concerned primarily with recycling wastes and obtaining energy from the three billion to four billion tons of materials that are discarded in the United States annually. Even used motor oil and tires came under the purview of the act.

The Resource Conservation and Recovery Act became law October 21, 1976, giving the United States a new statute that replaced the earlier Solid Waste Disposal Act. In subtitle B the new law contained provisions on solid waste and resource recovery, including disposal of used oil and waste, and called for closing most open dumps. Under subtitle E, various new technologies and new markets for recycled materials were to be promoted by EPA in concert with the Department of Commerce.

The new law also contained a subtitle C, titled "Hazardous Waste Management," which embodied what many considered to be Congress' effort finally to get EPA moving on evaluating hazardous waste as an emerging potential national problem.

Original Congressional Goals

The original text of RCRA itself gives an indication of congressional thinking in passing the law, and of the lack of emphasis on hazardous waste. Of the eight objectives originally listed in section 1003 of the law, only one mentioned hazardous waste.

The other objectives of the law chiefly dealt with solid waste (i.e., garbage), prohibited open dumps, and promoted recycling. Furthermore, in section 1002 of RCRA, where Congress listed an 800-word summary of its reasons for enacting the law, hazardous waste was mentioned only twice. The first time occured when the law said that disposal of "solid waste and hazardous waste" in or on the land could present a danger to human health and the environment.

The second mention was more significant. The summary went on to say that "hazardous waste presents, in addition to the problems associated with non-hazardous solid waste, special dangers to health and requires a greater degree of regulation than does solid waste."

It is interesting to note, however, that in 1984 when Congress performed a major overhaul of the law, section 1002 was changed so that 4 of the 8 findings listed focused exclusively on hazardous waste. Furthermore, the original 8 objectives listed in section 1003 were expanded to 10, with 4 of them focusing solely on the hazardous waste issue.

Congress also added section 1003(b), which states the following:

> (b) NATIONAL POLICY.—The Congress hereby declares it to be the national policy of the United States that, wherever feasible, the generation of hazardous waste is to be reduced or eliminated as expeditiously as possible. Waste that is nevertheless generated should be treated,

stored, or disposed of so as to minimize the present and future threat to the environment.

Despite the seeming lack of emphasis on hazardous waste in the original law, it stipulated that EPA was to issue regulations on hazardous waste management within 18 months of passage, i.e., by April 1978. This date apparently was specified in an effort to end the procrastination that EPA had exhibited in failing to act on the hazardous waste study requirements contained in the Solid Waste Disposal Act; the real need for RCRA, and especially for its hazardous waste provisions, was not truly recognized until 1978.

Despite the April 1978 deadline established in RCRA for issuing rules under the new RCRA legislation, EPA again was slow to act. In fact, the only rules issued at all by the deadline were still at the "proposed" stage and applied only to transporters. The remainder of the year, however, was a busy one in this area for EPA and a landmark period for hazardous waste regulation.

Love Canal

In August 1978 President Carter declared a state of emergency in an area near Niagara Falls, New York, where more than 82 different long-buried chemicals had begun bubbling out of the ground and seeping into basements. Almost 40 families were evacuated immediately, a nearby school was closed, and barbed wire fencing was strung around the heart of the working-class neighborhood now known around the world as Love Canal.

The canal was basically an uncompleted half-mile-long waterway dug around the turn of the century by William T. Love. Beginning in the 1930s, the trench, with its clay-lined bottom, had been used as an industrial dump. In 1947, the land where the trench was located was purchased by Hooker Chemical and Plastics Corporation and until 1953 was used as a depository for tons of industrial wastes. In 1953, under threat of having the property condemned to allow government acquisition, Hooker sold the site to the Niagara Falls Board of Education. The education department constructed a neighborhood school on part of the site and sold the unneeded portion to a developer who constructed several hundred tract homes on it. In 1976, heavier-than-normal rains over a period of years raised the water table sufficiently to send the chemicals buried on the site into basements and playgrounds.

EPA was called in to investigate in 1976, and two years later issued a report that would become the rallying cry for congressional and environmental critics of EPA's failure to regulate hazardous waste disposal. In that report, EPA identified 82 different chemicals on the Love Canal site, many of them known carcinogens and highly toxic. The need for hazardous waste regulation exploded into the public consciousness.

Response to the Situation

Within months after Love Canal gained national prominence, Congress began 13 days of hearings on hazardous waste. After compiling 1,800 pages of testimony, the House Interstate and Foreign Commerce Subcommittee on Oversight and Investigation issued a scathing report critical of both government and industry efforts at hazardous waste control.

In reporting on the results of the hearings, Subcommittee Chairman Bob Eckhardt (D-Texas) said, "EPA has failed to meet statutory deadlines for regulations on disposal of hazardous wastes; has failed to determine the location of all hazardous waste sites; and has not taken vigorous enforcement actions." The report also chastised industry for "laxity, not infrequently to the point of criminal negligence, in soiling the land and adulterating the waters with its toxins." Also criticized was Congress itself, for "lethargy in legislating controls and appropriating funds for their enforcement."

During the year after Love Canal burst into national prominence, a number of studies performed by EPA and others determined that Love Canal was only one of an estimated 50,000 sites where more than 750,000 hazardous waste generators had deposited almost 60 million tons of wastes. And according to EPA, only 10 percent of the waste had been disposed of in a way that would assure that incidents similar to Love Canal would not occur.

The state of Illinois and several environmental groups sued EPA and obtained a court-ordered schedule under which the agency would issue final hazardous waste regulations by December 31, 1979 (*Illinois v. Costle*, 12 ER Cases 1597 (D.D.C. 1978), *aff'd sub nom. Citizens for a Better Environment v. Costle*, 14 ER Cases 1198

(D.C. Cir 1980)). The litigation continued, however, and EPA was later ordered to issue final hazardous waste land disposal regulations by February 1, 1982 (*Illinois v. Gorsuch,* 530 F. Supp. 340, 16 ER Cases 2024 (D.D.C. 1981)).

The magnitude of the potential hazardous waste crisis prompted Congress to increase funding for regulatory programs and to give EPA specific recommendations on how the program should operate to prevent future Love Canals. The General Accounting Office, after studying the hazardous waste situation, issued two reports recommending that a self-sustaining national trust fund be established to close hazardous waste sites permitted under RCRA as they became full. Envisioned was a system under which RCRA would regulate existing waste sites to make sure wastes were disposed of safely, and the post-closure fund would pay to close sites and monitor them for environmental contamination.

At the same time, there was a growing sentiment that some type of law was needed to provide for cleanup of sites that were old, abandoned, and/or constructed prior to issuance of stringent regulatory controls under RCRA. Two years later, in 1980, the Comprehensive Environmental Response, Compensation, and Liability Act (the Superfund Law) was enacted (see chapter on CERCLA).

Regulatory Program Delayed

Despite the furor caused by Love Canal and the myriad of congressional hearings, actual regulation of hazardous wastes was slow to occur.

After proposing the first regulations in 1978, EPA found itself buried under stacks of public comments on the rules. Some complained that the rules would place an impossible burden on industry, while others charged that the rules were not stringent enough to prevent future Love Canals. In trying to respond to legitimate criticisms on the hastily written rules, the agency found itself hampered on two fronts: it was facing the court-ordered deadline of December 31, 1979, for issuing final rules, and it was forced to repropose several portions of the rules because of the breadth of the needed changes.

In October 1979, EPA went back to court to plead for more time to prepare the rules. EPA Administrator Douglas M. Costle said: "I have made every effort to assure myself that the agency has a management system and plan of action which, with a high degree of confidence, can achieve the promulgation of a high-quality, legally defensible, operational hazardous waste regulatory program by next April."

In explaining the delay, Costle noted that the agency had a seven-foot-high stack of comments to consider. "These comments are designed to stake out territory on which industry lawyers can subsequently sue, seeking court-ordered stays and remands of pro-mulgated regulations. In other words, these comments are a mine field with the potential of blowing our hazardous waste regulatory program right out of the water. . . . If we do not take such care, industry lawyers can, in the courts, undo everything we have been trying to achieve," Costle said. "So to achieve effective regulation of hazardous waste we must take time to do our homework," he said, promising to issue immediately any rules that were ready before the new target date of April 30, 1980. The court approved the delay.

Final Rules Unveiled

On February 26, 1980, EPA issued some of the hazardous waste rules under RCRA in final form. These rules—which cov-ered for generators and transporters, and created a comprehensive registry of those handling hazardous waste—were considered the least onerous of those needing to be issued under RCRA.

The more controversial rules—defining which wastes were considered hazardous and dealing with treatment, storage, and disposal facilities—were issued May 5, 1980. Review of the rules by the Office of Management and Budget, which objected to the cost of compliance, caused part of the delay. In addition, the site chosen for unveiling the rules, a chemical waste dump in New Jersey, had to be changed when it blew up shortly before the announcement of the new rules was to be made.

Two days later, on May 7, 1980, the Department of Trans-portation completed a package of final rules that would aid in the enforcement of RCRA. The package provided for identification of hazardous wastes in transit and brought the wastes under the labeling, packaging, and spill reporting provisions of the Hazardous Materials Transportation Act (see chapter on HMTA).

EPA subsequently mailed 400,000 sets of forms requiring registration by August 18, 1980, of those who generated, transported, treated, stored, or disposed of hazardous wastes. Even this, EPA conceded, was just the beginning of what would become one of the largest and most controversial regulatory programs in environmental history. According to one EPA official at the time, "The program is merely the catalyst which will bring legal pressure to bear on a number of deeply ingrained social and industrial bad habits. . . . It sets in motion a process which at best may significantly alter the texture and social fabric of a future some five to ten years over the horizon."

1984 Amendments

On November 8, 1984, President Reagan signed into law Pub. L. No. 98-616, which made major amendments to the hazardous waste law enacted in 1980. In light of EPA's past performance in meeting congressional goals set out in the 1980 law, the new law expanded the scope of hazardous waste regulation and imposed stringent deadlines on EPA.

In fact, the law enacted in 1984 contained a regulatory scheme that would take effect whether EPA issued implementing regulations or not. The law told EPA when it had to publish regulations, what the rules could contain, when the agency had to issue final permits to certain facilities, and what the permits could contain.

The measures that were designed to keep EPA on schedule prohibited land disposal after July 1988 of substances on the first third of a list of 450 hazardous materials identified, unless EPA could show that human health and the environment would not be harmed thereby. After June 1989 the same provisions applied to the first two-thirds of the list. And after May 1990 all substances on the list had to be covered by regulations, standards, or actions showing that land disposal was safe. If by that time EPA had not acted, the law would have prohibited land disposal of the hazardous wastes. The schedule for the final third was released May 8,

1990, but EPA granted a three-month extension to allow industry time to read the rule and develop a compliance strategy. Industry and EPA estimated that compliance could cost $440 million per year. Those industries affected include electric, gas, and sanitary services; chemical and allied products; and petroleum refiners.

Congress also gave citizens greater ability to sue past and present waste generators, handlers, transporters, and owners and operators of waste sites for activities that pose an imminent hazard.

Reasons for the Rewrite

In 1976, the primary objectives of RCRA were to control the handling of wastes and to encourage recycling and conservation of energy and natural resources. As noted earlier, EPA was slow to act in any of these areas, and it took four years before hazardous waste management regulations were issued and a permitting system for hazardous waste facilities was set up.

Subsequent experience and a variety of studies conducted over the years, however, found that in 1983 an estimated 40 million metric tons of hazardous wastes were escaping control each year because of loopholes in the regulatory and legislative scheme. By 1984, Congress was taking a serious look at the gaps in the "cradle to grave" regulatory program and decided that major changes were needed.

Among the 1980 law's major shortcomings were its failure to regulate the many generators of small amounts of waste, to regulate waste oil, and to assure that land disposal facilities were constructed and operated on an environmentally sound basis.

Furthermore, the preceding years had shown a real need to control chemical contamination of groundwater. Leaking underground storage tanks were found to be a major cause of this contamination. In fact, at one point in 1984, it was estimated that as many as 75,000 such tanks were leaking a variety of chemicals, oil, gasoline, and other substances.

The major amendments enacted in 1984 do the following:

- Set stringent timetables for EPA to issue operating permits to hazardous waste treatment, storage, and disposal facilities.
- Impose technical criteria on various types of waste facilities and set deadlines by which the facilities had to meet the requirements or close.

- Require treatment, storage, and disposal facilities to take corrective action for all releases of hazardous waste or constituents from any waste unit regardless of when the waste was placed in the unit. The corrective action must be taken before a final permit is issued or, if this is impossible, the permit must contain a schedule for the corrective action to be completed and proof that the money is available to carry out the cleanup or other corrective action.
- Restrict disposal on land of a variety of wastes. The law set dates, ranging from November 1986 through May 1990, when land disposal of hazardous wastes would be prohibited unless EPA proved before that date that land disposal was "protective of human health and the environment."
- Add a new subtitle I to regulate underground storage tanks and require such tanks to meet certain technical standards.
- Bring generators of between 100 and 1,000 kilograms of hazardous waste per month under the hazardous waste program.
- Require EPA to regulate those who burn wastes and used oils in boilers and industrial furnaces because such facilities are not technically incinerators but still may pollute the environment.
- Give citizens expanded rights to sue past or present generators, transporters, or disposal facility owners and operators for current or past practices or omissions that are alleged to create an imminent hazard.
- Require EPA to inspect every permitted hazardous waste facility at least every two years and to inspect government-owned facilities annually.

EPA missed many of its regulatory deadlines, and in March 1989, the Environmental Defense Fund sued. In June 1991, the agency and the EDF agreed to resolve the so-called "megadeadline suit" (*EDF v. EPA.*, 31 ER Cases 1046 (D.D.C. 1991)). Under a court agreement, EPA was to issue 20 or more rules including those listing determinations and studies, with deadlines ranging from 1992 to 1998. EPA began proposing the rules at the end of 1991.

PROVISIONS OF THE LAW

RCRA was passed in 1976 to control disposal of solid wastes and to mandate procedures for the management and handling of hazardous waste materials. As mentioned earlier, recovery of usable materials from wastes and recycling of wastes into energy also are goals of the act, although these goals have been overshadowed in recent years by the act's emphasis on control of hazardous wastes.

In the area of hazardous waste, the act's goal is to provide what EPA officials have called a "cradle to grave" tracking system that will ensure safe disposal of wastes considered hazardous to health or the environment.

In general, the act authorizes EPA to list wastes that it considers hazardous. Once a waste is listed, firms that generate, store, or transport such wastes become subject to the related standards and facility permit requirements issued under the act. Penalties for violations of RCRA are severe in order to prevent so-called "midnight dumping" (illegal dumping of wastes) and to assure that hazardous wastes will be disposed of in an environmentally safe manner.

RCRA has the following major chemical control provisions:

- Section 3001: Identification and listing of hazardous wastes and provisions requiring regulation of generators of small quantities of hazardous wastes
- Sections 3002, 3003: Standards applying to hazardous waste generators and transporters, including a manifest (shipping document) system for tracking wastes from generation through final disposal
- Section 3004: Standards applying to facilities for treatment, storage, and/or disposal of hazardous wastes, including burning and blending of wastes used as fuels
- Section 3005: Permit standards applying to hazardous waste facilities, including incinerators, landfills, surface impoundments, and land treatment units
- Sections 3007, 3008: Enforcement of standards through compliance orders, administrative orders, and consent decrees
- Subtitle I: Regulation of underground storage tanks

Section 3001: Identification and Listing

Section 3001 of RCRA provides for the identification and listing of hazardous wastes. Once a waste is listed by EPA as hazardous, those generating, transporting, storing, or disposing of it become subject to the other applicable requirements of the act.

Those who generate solid wastes are responsible for determining if a waste is hazardous, either because it is listed by EPA or because it exhibits the characteristics of a hazardous waste as defined in the RCRA regulations. Conversely, if a waste is not listed and does not exhibit any of the characteristics of a hazardous waste, those who handle it are not subject to the requirements of RCRA.

Certain wastes, however, are automatically excluded from coverage under RCRA. These include domestic sewage; household waste; agricultural and animal wastes used as fertilizers; industrial wastewater discharges regulated under the Clean Water Act; irrigation return flows; and certain nuclear, mining, coal, and oil-drilling wastes.

Definition of a Hazardous Waste

According to regulations set by EPA (40 CFR 260, 261), a hazardous waste is any solid waste that may cause substantial hazard to health or the environment when improperly managed. In deciding which wastes meet this definition, EPA developed a set of criteria for measuring the characteristics of wastes. Hundreds of specific wastes, waste sources, and processes that exhibit at least one of the characteristics discussed below are included in the RCRA hazardous waste list.

Criteria for Listing a Hazardous Waste

EPA considers a waste to be hazardous if it exhibits any of the following chemical characteristics:

- *Ignitability*. It poses a fire hazard during routine management.
- *Corrosivity*. It has the ability to corrode standard containers or to dissolve toxic components of other wastes.
- *Reactivity*. It has a tendency to explode under normal management conditions, to react violently when mixed with water, or to generate toxic gases.
- *EP Toxicity*. It exhibits the presence of one or more specified toxic materials at levels greater than those specified in the agency's regulations when it is analyzed by a specific "extrac-

tion procedure." Under the 1984 amendments, EPA revised the procedure then in effect so that it accurately predicted leaching potential.

In addition, EPA may list a waste as hazardous based on several other factors, including the following:

- General toxicity of the waste
- Degree of toxicity of the constituents of the waste
- Concentration of the hazardous constituents and/or the potential for these constituents to migrate from the waste into the environment
- Persistence and potential for bioaccumulation of the waste once it is in the environment
- Susceptibility of the waste to improper management
- Quantity of the waste generated
- Whether the waste has a past history of damage to the environment or to human health

As required by the 1984 amendments, EPA also added additional characteristics of hazardous waste, including those that indicate toxicity.

EPA has published a list of about 450 specific chemicals that are defined as toxic wastes. Wastes containing specified concentrations of certain heavy metals or certain pesticides are also defined to be toxic (40 CFR 261.24–261.30).

Exemptions and Delisting

A generator may get an exemption from the RCRA regulations even if the waste it is generating is listed. To do so, the generator must show that its waste is fundamentally different from the waste listed. In demonstrating this, the generator must provide, or make reference to, test data showing that the specific waste does not meet the criteria that caused EPA to list the waste as hazardous.

According to EPA, the "delisting" process was established because individual waste streams vary depending upon raw materials, industrial processes, and other factors. If EPA delists a waste, notice that it is being removed from the lists of wastes subject to RCRA is published in the *Federal Register*.

A 1984 amendment to section 3001 of RCRA brings generators of small volume of hazardous wastes under the law. These
requirements are discussed below.

Sections 3002, 3003: Generator, Transporter Standards

Regulations covering hazardous waste generators and transporters are authorized under sections 3002 and 3003 of RCRA;
they have been issued by EPA and are published at 40 CFR 262
and 263 respectively. In general, these regulations establish the
duties of generators and transporters of hazardous wastes, including steps to be taken to register with EPA, to analyze wastes, and
to keep records so that wastes can be tracked from the point of
generation to the point of final disposal.

Generator Requirements

As mentioned earlier, those who create solid wastes must determine whether the substances are hazardous wastes as defined
by EPA under section 3001 of the law and in the regulations at 40
CFR 261. If the waste is not listed by EPA, the generator is responsible for determining if the waste exhibits any of the characteristics of a hazardous waste, i.e., ignitability, corrosivity, reactivity, or toxicity. In addition, a generator may know that a waste is
hazardous simply because of the materials or processes used in
producing the waste.

Once a person or firm determines that it is generating a hazardous waste, the person or firm must do the following:

- Obtain an EPA identification number for the firm.
- Get a permit for the facility where the waste is generated if the
  waste is held on the site for more than 90 days before disposal.
- Use appropriate shipping containers for the waste and label it
  properly as specified by the Department of Transportation.
- Prepare a manifest (shipping form) for tracking the waste once
  it leaves the generation site.
- Assure through use of the manifest that the waste reaches the
  designated disposal facility. (A copy of the manifest is returned
  by the facility to the generator after the facility receives the
  waste.)

- Periodically submit a summary of hazardous waste activities to EPA.

These requirements are discussed in greater detail below.

Small-Quantity Generators

The 1984 amendments to RCRA expanded the scope of the hazardous waste program to include generators of hazardous wastes in quantities of between 100 and 1,000 kilograms per month. Before the amendments, only generators of 1,000 kilograms or more per month were covered.

As required by the 1984 amendments, EPA published regulations for these smaller quantity generators, estimated to be about 175,000 businesses, in March 1986. The regulatory scheme proposed in July 1985 to carry out this new congressional mandate in general paralleled existing generator standards, but exempted smaller generators from the full manifest provisions; allowed this class of generators to store wastes on site for a longer period of time; and imposed reduced requirements for planning for emergencies, training employees, and contingency planning.

EPA estimated that the regulations would bring many small firms, such as laundries, printers, and garages, under the RCRA requirements at an average startup cost of $2,180 and an annual cost of $200.

Identification Number

Generators of hazardous wastes must get an identification number from EPA within 90 days of beginning operation. The number is obtained from the EPA regional office with jurisdiction over the facility site.

Preparing Wastes for Shipment

Generators must prepare a manifest to accompany all shipments of hazardous wastes sent to off-site treatment, storage, or disposal facilities. The manifest will travel with the waste to the disposal site.

Generators also must use transporters that have an EPA identification number, must keep records of all waste shipments, and must report to EPA any shipments that do not reach the designated disposal facility.

The Manifest

EPA and the Department of Transportation (DOT) require that a uniform manifest form accompany all hazardous waste shipments. The manifest, a copy of which is published at 40 CFR 262, must contain the following:

- Generator's name, address, and EPA identification number
- Names and EPA identification numbers of all transporters
- Name, address, and EPA identification number of the facility designated to receive the waste
- Description of the waste (proper shipping name, hazard class, and identification number) from the DOT hazardous materials table (49 CFR 172.101) issued under authority of the Hazardous Materials Transportation Act (see chapter on HMTA)
- Quantity of waste and number and type of containers
- Generator's signature certifying that the waste has been labeled, marked, and packaged in accordance with EPA and DOT regulations
- A certification that the volume of waste has been minimized and that the planned method of treatment, storage, and/or disposal minimizes the present and future threat to health and the environment (added in 1984)

When the generator turns over the waste to the transporter, both transporter and generator sign the manifest. The generator then keeps one copy and provides the transporter with additional copies. Each person/organization handling the waste in transit to the disposal site keeps a copy of the manifest, including the transporter. When the waste is received at the disposal facility, the facility must return a copy of the manifest to the generator, thereby letting the generator know that the waste was received. If no copy is received, the generator must notify EPA.

Generators who store wastes on their property for more than 90 days are considered to be waste storage facilities and must obtain a storage-facility permit under section 3005 of RCRA. The date accumulation of the wastes began must be marked on the waste container.

Small-quantity generators, however, may store wastes on site for 180 days (or 270 days if over 200 miles from the disposal site) without a storage facility permit.

Transporter Requirements

Regulations governing transport of hazardous wastes were devised jointly by EPA and DOT. DOT also regulates the labeling, packaging, placarding, and transport of hazardous materials. In promulgating transporter rules under RCRA (40 CFR 263), EPA incorporated by reference the DOT hazardous materials transport rules. DOT, in turn, amended its hazardous materials table (49 CFR 172.101) to include the hazardous wastes listed by EPA (see chapter on the HMTA).

The rules on transport of hazardous wastes, authorized by section 3003 of RCRA and published at 40 CFR 263, require waste transporters to do the following:

- Get an EPA identification number
- Use the uniform manifest system in transporting the wastes
- Deliver all of the wastes as specified on the manifest
- Keep a copy of the manifest for three years
- Comply with DOT requirements on reporting discharges and spills of wastes (see chapter on the HMTA)
- Clean up any hazardous wastes discharged during transit

The manifest must accompany the waste at all times during transit and until it reaches its ultimate disposal site.

Rail and Water Shipments

A uniform manifest need not accompany shipments of wastes that travel by rail or in bulk by water. Instead, DOT has developed shipping papers that must accompany such shipments (see chapter on the HMTA). If transportation other than by rail or water takes place at any stage of the shipping process, however, the manifest must accompany the shipment at all times, even on the water and/or rail segments.

The three-year retention time for keeping a copy of the manifest also applies to shipping papers covering rail and/or water shipments.

Discharges in Transit

Accidental or intentional spills, leaks, or other discharges of hazardous wastes on land or into water while the substances are in transit must be cleaned up by the transporter. In some cases, however, this requirement will be waived if an emergency is such that parties other than the transporter are needed to clean up the discharge.

In most cases, the discharge must be reported immediately to the National Response Center, the government agency charged with coordinating response to hazardous substances spills in the environment. A written report of the discharge also must be submitted to DOT, which will forward a copy to EPA. (For more information on requirements concerning the reporting of discharges, see chapters on the Comprehensive Environmental Response, Compensation, and Liability Act (CERCLA) and the HMTA.)

Section 3004: Treatment, Storage, Disposal Facilities

Central to the hazardous waste control plan authorized by RCRA are the requirements imposed on owners and operators of facilities that treat, store, or dispose of hazardous wastes. Authorized by section 3004 of RCRA and published by EPA at 40 CFR 264, 265, and 267, these rules are intended to ensure the safe handling of hazardous wastes. Included are provisions on emergencies, manifest handling, recordkeeping, waste treatment and storage, monitoring, closure of a facility, and financial liability during operation and after a facility is closed.

Under RCRA, a hazardous waste facility must comply with regulations under one of the three CFR parts just mentioned, in line with the following:

- A facility in operation in 1980 must operate under interim status standards (40 CFR 265) until EPA issues it a final facility permit. (This procedure is still in progress.)

- A facility opened after the regulations took effect in 1980 must operate under interim status standards (40 CFR 267) until EPA issues it a final facility permit.
- A facility with a final facility permit must operate under permanent standards (40 CFR 264).

Although the requirements under the sections are similar, EPA issued separate requirements so that facilities in existence when the rules were promulgated in 1980 would not have to close down because they lacked a permit. Under the two-pronged system, facilities that apply for a permit may continue to operate under the part 265 or part 267 rules until the permit is issued, after which they must operate under part 264 rules. Because of the large number of facilities that need permits, EPA estimated that it would take many years for all final permits to be issued. In fact, in 1984, only 2 percent had been issued final permits.

Sites that accept hazardous wastes for treatment, storage, and/ or disposal are considered waste facilities under RCRA. In addition, plants that generate wastes but store them on site for more than 90 days or that treat or dispose of the wastes themselves are considered hazardous waste facilities and must apply for a facility permit and comply with the treatment, storage, and disposal regulations.

Changes Made in 1984

The 1984 amendments to RCRA made major changes to the provisions of section 3004. While most are geared to forcing EPA to meet specific permitting deadlines, they also do the following:

- Require EPA to ban land disposal of a variety of liquid wastes and all wastes listed as hazardous under RCRA according to a series of dates that stretched into 1990 unless EPA proved that the prohibition was not needed to protect human health and the environment
- Ban use of waste or used oil contaminated with dioxin or other listed wastes as dust-control agents on roads
- Set out waste treatment methods that would allow land disposal of wastes that otherwise would be banned from land disposal

- Require monitoring of air emissions at hazardous waste facilities
- Impose minimum technological standards on landfills and surface impoundments, and require surface impoundments, waste piles, land treatment units, and landfills to conduct groundwater monitoring
- Regulate hazardous wastes used as fuel
- Require corrective action at all permitted facilities and require that the action extend beyond the facility's boundaries when necessary to protect human health or the environment
- Require permits for underground storage tanks that cannot be entered for inspection

As of May 1990, EPA had issued all the land ban rules.

General Facility Requirements

According to EPA regulations (40 CFR 260), facilities involved in treatment, storage, and/or disposal must file a permit application under section 3005 of RCRA (see discussion of section 3005 below) and must obtain an EPA identification number. The owner or operator of a facility must have on hand written plans for inspecting the facility and for dealing with emergencies. In addition, the owner or operator must do the following:

- Analyze wastes entering the facility to make certain that substance identities are as specified on the manifest.
- Provide security to exclude unauthorized entry into the storage or disposal site.
- Inspect the site for malfunctions, operator errors, and discharges. (Included must be inspections of monitoring, safety, security, operating, and structural equipment.)
- Train employees in the handling of emergencies and in inspection and monitoring of emergency equipment.
- Take special precautions to prevent accidental reaction between, or ignition of, incompatible wastes, and to make sure that waste mixing does not pose a risk to health or the environment. (The regulations contain listings of incompatible wastes.)
- Maintain accessible and operating emergency equipment, including fire extinguishers, spill control equipment, and telecommunications equipment.

- Inform local police, fire, and emergency response teams about the layout of the facility and the hazards they may encounter.
- Have a written plan for responding to emergencies and an emergency coordinator to handle such situations.

The Manifest, Recordkeeping, and Reporting

The Manifest

Upon receiving a hazardous waste at the facility, the owner or operator of the facility must sign, date, and return a copy of the manifest to the transporter who delivered the waste. Within 30 days, another copy of the manifest must be returned to the generator of the waste. The facility must keep a copy of the manifest for three years.

It is also the responsibility of the operator to check to make sure the waste listed on the manifest is what actually was delivered to the site. Discrepancies that cannot be resolved must be reported to EPA. Any waste that arrives at the facility without a manifest must be reported to EPA within 15 days.

Recordkeeping and Reporting

The site operator must keep records of the type, quantity, and origin of the wastes received at the site. Records of method of treatment, storage, and/or disposal must also be kept, along with records of waste analyses, inspections, personnel training, and monitoring results. Information on how often the emergency facility contingency plan was used, and on cost estimates for closing the site and for monitoring it after it is closed, also must be kept on file. All such records may be inspected by EPA.

In addition to reporting unmanifested wastes, owners and operators must report to EPA any releases of wastes, fires, or explosions; groundwater contamination and monitoring information; and information on any facility closure.

Operating Criteria

As mentioned earlier, owners and operators of hazardous wastes facilities must comply with operating requirements listed in

40 CFR 264, 265, or 267. Among these are requirements concerning groundwater monitoring, waste storage and treatment criteria, and financial liability, all of which are discussed in greater detail below.

Groundwater Monitoring

Facilities where hazardous waste is purposely placed onto or into the land must conduct groundwater monitoring to assess the facility's impact on the uppermost aquifer underlying the facility. The monitoring must be performed according to a written plan and must be done at the owners' and operators' expense both during operation of the facility and after it is closed.

Under the RCRA rules, facilities that engage in land disposal must drill enough wells to monitor migration of wastes from the site. One well must be on the up-gradient from the site to assess normal water quality in the area (this well will measure the quality of underground water before it gets to the site). At least three wells must be drilled on the down-gradient to monitor underground water flow for waste migration. The wells should be placed at the edge of the facility to allow early detection of leakage. Among the items to be checked are the aquifer's suitability for drinking as measured by the water quality parameters of the Safe Drinking Water Act (see chapter on SDWA), the overall quality of the water, and the amount of contaminants in the water. The level of the water also must be measured and recorded.

Any suspicious findings, as outlined in the regulations, must be reported to EPA. During the first year of monitoring, a quarterly report on the monitoring results must be submitted to EPA. Records of the monitoring must be kept for the life of the site and for the period of its post-closure monitoring.

Medical Waste Monitoring

Congress amended RCRA to include the Medical Waste Tracking Act of 1988 soon after several highly publicized incidents of medical waste washing up on East Coast beaches. This law required EPA to develop a two-year demonstration program of tracking medical waste. Medical wastes include blood and blood products, bandages, any contaminated equipment that has been discarded, and animal or human body parts. EPA would submit three reports to Congress on the program. EPA said the final report would be sent by the end of 1992.

Since the act was amended, 45 states have issued regulations defining medical waste and how it should be disposed of.

Other Management Requirements

Among other requirements that hazardous waste facilities must comply with are criteria for the following:

- Containers to prevent leakage, explosion, or other discharges
- Tanks used to store wastes (with criteria including analysis and testing, segregation of incompatible wastes, and daily inspection)
- Design and maintenance of surface impoundments (waste pits, ponds, and lagoons)
- Waste piles (with criteria including protection from wind and leaching)
- Land treatment of wastes (with criteria including runoff rules and recordkeeping, monitoring, and analysis requirements)
- Landfills, incinerators and other heat-treatment disposal methods, biological and chemical destruction, and underground injection

Closure, Post-Closure, and Financial Responsibility

Under RCRA, hazardous waste treatment, storage, and disposal facilities must have a written plan to provide for closing the site when wastes no longer are accepted. The closure plan must explain how the facility will be closed down and estimate how much and what type of waste has been in the site at any given time during the site's lifespan. The closure plan must be submitted to EPA 180 days before closure begins. Closure must begin within 30 days after the last load of waste is delivered.

Disposal facilities must in addition have a post-closure plan, which must include provisions for groundwater monitoring and other maintenance activities to guard against environmental harm. This plan also must be submitted to EPA 180 days before the date of expected closure, and must provide for care of the site for 30 years after closing.

Owners and operators of hazardous waste sites must guarantee the costs of closure and post-closure care of the site. The owner/operator must make cost estimates and then assure that the money needed is available in one of the following five ways:

- By establishing a guarantee
- By posting a surety bond
- By arranging for a letter of credit
- By obtaining an insurance policy
- By meeting a financial test that sets up the owner/operator as a self-insurer

Section 3005: Facility Permits

Section 3005 of RCRA requires that any facility that treats, stores, or disposes of hazardous wastes must obtain a permit from EPA, or from the relevant state if it has taken over operation of the hazardous waste program by adopting rules equivalent to the federal rules. Rules on issuance of permits, published at 40 CFR 270, require a facility to seek interim status if the facility was in existence or under construction in 1980. Facilities that have been granted interim status under RCRA get a final permit by submitting a second application within six months after EPA requests it.

Permit applications are reviewed by EPA, which informs the public that a request for a hazardous waste facility permit is pending. If EPA decides to grant the permit, it announces this fact and schedules time for public notice, public comment, and, in some cases, public hearings.

Once issued, permits are effective for 10 years, but may be reviewed, modified, or revoked by EPA if deemed necessary.

The 1984 amendments to RCRA require review of permits after five years and inspection of facilities every two years.

Permit Application

In general, the permit application consists of two parts. Part A, used to apply for interim status, includes a description of processes used to treat the wastes, the design of the facility, and the wastes to be treated. Part B is more detailed, and requires submission of information on how the facility will meet technical standards promulgated under RCRA. For example, in part B detailed information on the following must be included:

- Contingency plans for emergencies
- Waste analysis procedures
- Inspection schedules
- Operating procedures to prevent environmental contamination at the site
- Facility design and layout
- Engineering
- Groundwater protection
- Closure and post-closure plans
- Containers, tanks, and incinerators used at the site

Virtually all the permit deadlines set out in the 1984 amendments to RCRA deal with part B. Under the amendments, EPA has four years to issue final permits for land disposal, five years for incinerators, and eight years for all other types of waste facilities. Interim status will expire and the facility must be closed if the deadlines are missed.

Sections 3007, 3008: Enforcement

Enforcement of RCRA is carried out by states, EPA, and DOT, with DOT monitoring transporters and shippers of hazardous wastes.

Under section 3008 of the law, EPA is authorized to use compliance orders, administrative orders, and consent decrees to force compliance with the law. In addition, section 3007 authorizes EPA inspectors to enter sites to inspect for compliance, collect samples of wastes, and examine and copy records relating to the wastes.

The 1984 amendments require EPA to inspect a facility every two years (every year for facilities operated by federal government or by states or local governments).

Compliance Orders

EPA is authorized to issue a compliance order to anyone it finds to be in violation of RCRA. The order explains the violation, sets a deadline for compliance, and may include a penalty assessment. Civil penalties of up to $25,000 per day are authorized for missing the compliance deadline, as is suspension or revocation of the violator's hazardous waste permit.

Interim Status Corrective Orders

Under the 1984 amendments, EPA may issue a corrective order to any interim status facility from which there is or has been a release of hazardous waste into the environment. The order, which must state the specifics of the situation, must specify a time for compliance with the corrective measures. Failure to comply carries a civil penalty of up to $25,000 for each day of noncompliance with the order.

Criminal Penalties

RCRA makes it a criminal offense to knowingly violate certain provisions of the law. For example, a $50,000 penalty and/or up to two years in jail is authorized for transporting wastes to a facility not having a permit or for treating, storing, or disposing of a hazardous waste without a permit or while violating any material condition of a permit.

A penalty of up to $50,000 per day or imprisonment is authorized for giving false information in any required hazardous waste document or for destroying, altering, or concealing any records required under the law. Penalties are doubled for repeat convictions.

"Knowing Endangerment"

A keystone in the RCRA enforcement scheme is its provision on "knowing endangerment." Authorized by section 3008 of the law, this provision calls for penalties of up to $250,000 or 15 years' imprisonment or both for knowingly violating RCRA in a way that places another person in imminent danger of death or serious bodily injury or that manifests an extreme indifference for human life. A defendant that is an organization is liable for a $1 million fine in such cases.

Under this section, "serious bodily injury" includes any injury that involves substantial risk of death, unconsciousness, extreme physical pain, protracted and obvious disfigurement, or protracted loss or impairment of the function of a bodily member, organ, or mental faculty.

Virtually all transportation, treatment, storage, and disposal requirements under the act are subject to the "knowing endangerment" penalty provisions if the requirements are knowingly violated and danger to human life is present.

Subtitle I: Underground Storage Tanks

A new subtitle I added to RCRA by Congress in the 1984 amendments provides for regulation of underground storage tanks that contain petroleum or other regulated substances. The program, which exempts only certain residential tanks, septic tanks, and tanks regulated under other provisions of the law, is expected to affect the estimated 100,000 to 400,000 tanks containing such substances and possibly allowing them to leak into groundwater.

Under the amendments, the tanks are not subject to a permit, but rather must meet certain technical performance standards issued by EPA in 1987.

The first step in the process was imposition of a requirement that tank owners notify EPA or a designated state agency about the age, size, type, location, and use of their tanks by May 8, 1986.

The tank program also sets up a variety of notification provisions that affect manufacturers and distributors, who must inform tank owners about their obligations under RCRA.

The program also covers tanks taken out of service since 1974, and sets penalties of up to $10,000 for failure to notify EPA or the appropriate state agency about the tank.

In addition, the amendments set up a series of deadlines by which EPA must issue standards for leak detection, inventory control, tank testing, recordkeeping, reporting, corrective action, financial responsibility, and closure. Most of the deadlines fell in 1987 and 1988. Rules were issued in September 1988 in two parts: One setting technical standards and one laying groundwork for state enforcement programs.

A new underground storage tank program was included in the Superfund Amendments and Reauthorization Act of 1986 at section 205. First, under the law, states must make two inventories of underground storage tanks—one for petroleum tanks and one for other regulated substances. Second, EPA must establish financial responsibility regulations for owners of underground storage tanks—both for petroleum and for other regulated substances. EPA is authorized by the act to require owners and operators of tanks to undertake whatever corrective action is necessary to protect human health and the environment from tank leaks.

Prospects for Reauthorization

By the end of 1991, reauthorization of RCRA was in limbo. Congressional staff members predicted a bill probably would not be passed until late 1992. One obstacle to reauthorization was the insistence of both the House and the Senate that it be tied to legislation to implement the Basel Convention, a treaty regulating the international transport and disposal of waste. Contentious issues in the RCRA debate include the expected higher costs of waste disposal, the addition of federal recycling provisions, and disagreement over interstate transport regulations. Because of opposition from industry and environmentalists and disagreement within the Senate over recycling provisions as well as other issues, reauthorization legislation cleared committee but never made it to the Senate floor. However, a bill on the interstate transportation of municipal solid wastes, based on language similar to a provision of the reauthorization legislation, was passed by the Senate in July 1992. This measure (S. 2877) would allow states and localities to restrict the import of out-of-state municipal solid waste for disposal. As of mid-1992, it was unclear whether an out-of-state municipal solid waste bill or a broader RCRA bill would reach the House floor.

Comprehensive Environmental Response, Compensation, and Liability Act
(CERCLA)

Public Law Number: Pub. L. No. 96-510

U.S. Code citation: 42 USC 9601 *et seq.*

Enacted: December 11, 1980
 Amended: 1982, 1986 (major amendments in the Superfund Amendments and Reauthorization Act, Pub. L. No. 99-499 (SARA))

Regulations at: 40 CFR 300

Federal agency with jurisdiction: Environmental Protection Agency (EPA)

Congressional committees/subcommittees with jurisdiction:
 House of Representatives: Subcommittee on Commerce, Transportation, and Tourism of the Energy and Commerce Committee
 Senate: Environmental Pollution Subcommittee of the Environment and Public Works Committee

BNA reporting services: *Daily Environment Report, Environment Reporter, Toxics Law Reporter, Due Diligence Reference Guide*
 Text of law appears in *Environment Reporter* Federal Laws at 71:0701 *et seq.*
 Text of regulations appears in *Environment Reporter* Federal Regulations
 Legal decisions appear in Environment Reporter Cases (ER Cases)

What CERCLA requires and why: The act, commonly called the superfund law, requires cleanup of releases of hazardous substances in air, water, and groundwater and on land. Both new spills and leaking or abandoned dumpsites are covered. Releases of reportable quantities of a substance listed as hazardous must be immediately reported to the National Response Center at (800) 424-8802.

CERCLA also establishes a trust fund to pay for cleaning up hazardous substances in the environment and gives EPA authority to collect the cost of cleanup from the parties responsible for the contamination.

Money for the various types of cleanups authorized under the law comes from fines and other penalties collected by the government, from a tax imposed on chemicals and petrochemical feedstocks, and from the U.S. Treasury. A separate fund established under the law is authorized to collect taxes imposed on active hazardous waste disposal sites, to finance monitoring of sites after they close.

The Superfund Amendments and Reauthorization Act (SARA) passed in 1986 added strict cleanup standards strongly favoring permanent remedies, stronger EPA control over the process of reaching settlement with responsible parties, a mandatory schedule for initiation of cleanup work and studies, individual assessments of the potential threat to human health posed by each waste site, and increased state and public involvement in the cleanup decision-making process.

A separate title III of SARA provides a framework for emergency planning and preparedness and requires chemical manufacturers to provide community groups with information on their inventories of hazardous chemicals and of releases of chemicals to the environment.

Latest developments: In 1991, Congress extended superfund for three years with an allocation of $5.1 billion to continue from October 1991 to September 1994. The federal taxing authority was extended to petroleum and some feedstock chemicals, which are used to make other chemicals, to ensure that hazardous waste sites would continue to be cleaned up while Congress debated other issues. Talks on CERCLA reauthorization began in the fall of 1991.

COVERAGE OF THE LAW

The Comprehensive Environmental Response, Compensation, and Liability Act (CERCLA, or the superfund law), unlike other environmental laws affecting chemicals, does not regulate hazardous substances. Instead, CERCLA provides a system for identifying and cleaning up chemical and hazardous substance releases into any part of the environment. The law also provides authority for EPA to collect the cost of cleaning up a release from the responsible parties and establishes a $1.6 billion fund to pay for cleaning up environmental contamination where no responsible party can be found or where those responsible for the release will not or cannot pay for cleanup. EPA can subsequently go to court to secure reimbursement to the fund by responsible parties who will not pay voluntarily.

CERCLA incorporates the spill-cleanup provisions of the Clean Water Act, which addressed only spills that threatened navigable waters. The National Contingency Plan (the federal scheme for responding to hazardous substances in the environment originally established under the CWA) also was revised to include all releases of hazardous substances and was incorporated into the CERCLA regulatory sphere. The law thus collects in one place the provisions for responding to releases of hazardous substances into the environment, whether intentional or accidental and whether one-time (e.g., from a spill) or continuing (e.g., from an old waste disposal site).

DEVELOPMENT OF THE LAW

Congress enacted CERCLA in 1980 after it became apparent that a law was needed to close the final loophole in environmental regulation. The law was a direct result of the August 1978 emergency that arose when long-buried chemicals were discovered seeping into homes and out of the ground in the Love Canal area of Niagara Falls, New York. Remedial measures at the site and relocation of more than 200 families cost the state of New York in excess of $35 million and there was no federal program to help pay the costs.

This situation and the realization that Love Canal was only one of hundreds of such abandoned dumpsites prompted the Carter administration to propose legislation creating a superfund to pay for cleanup and authorizing the government to recover the costs where possible from those responsible for the disposal or release.

In its proposed form the legislation also was intended to give the government authority to monitor and respond to releases of hazardous substances into the environment, to compensate victims injured by exposure to hazardous substances, and to pay for medical costs incurred as a result of the exposure. Many of the provisions authorizing the government to accomplish the latter two objectives, however, were dropped in the course of congressional consideration of the proposed legislation.

During its trip through the House and Senate, the superfund legislation underwent many changes, with often as many as three or four bills under active consideration at a given time. During congressional deliberations, the amount of the fund was reduced from more than $4 billion to $2.7 billion to $1.6 billion. The duration of the fund was limited to five years, with 1985 the last year unless the law was reauthorized. Provisions on compensating those injured by exposure to hazardous substances, including out-of-pocket medical expenses, were deleted. Only provisions to collect for damages to natural resources owned by a state or the federal government were left intact in the final legislation.

Sen. Robert T. Stafford (R-Vt.), one of the prime proponents of the legislation, felt the final superfund law eliminated 75 percent of what was sought in the original administration bill. "But knowing of the urgent need for legislation, we were willing to [accept] that," Stafford said of the compromise superfund bill approved by the Senate on November 24, 1980.

PROVISIONS OF THE LAW

The superfund law gave the federal government authority for the first time to respond directly to releases or threatened releases of hazardous substances that may endanger public health or the environment.

As signed by President Carter on December 11, 1980, CERCLA established a five-year, $1.6 billion fund to finance cleanup of abandoned hazardous waste sites and other cleanup actions needed to protect the environment. The government was authorized to recover the cleanup costs from those responsible for the release. If no responsible party could be found or if, as in the case of many abandoned hazardous waste sites, that party was the owner of a defunct company and had no money, the cleanup could be paid from the fund. The law provided that 87.5 percent of the $1.6 billion for the fund was from a tax on crude oil, petroleum products, and about 40 feedstock chemicals. The remaining 12.5 percent was funded by the U.S. Treasury from general tax revenues.

The law also set priorities for cleaning up abandoned hazardous waste sites and required development of a plan for government response to hazardous substance releases. Also written into the law was a provision to reimburse states and localities retroactively for waste-site cleanup costs incurred after January 1, 1978. One of the first superfund expenditures thus was for cleanup of Love Canal.

The main provisions of the superfund law included the following:

- Expansion of the National Contingency Plan for responding to releases of hazardous substances
- Establishment of requirements for reporting discharges of hazardous substances above certain quantities to the federal government and for federal government responses to emergencies.
- Imposition of cleanup requirements and cost recovery from those responsible for hazardous substance releases
- Imposition of taxes on crude oil, petroleum products, and hazardous wastes.

National Contingency Plan

First required to be prepared in 1968 under the Federal Water Pollution Control Act, which was replaced by the Clean Water Act, the National Contingency Plan now outlines how the federal government will respond to discharges of hazardous substances into all parts of the environment.

The plan originally served as the vehicle through which the Clean Water Act authorized coordination of federal hazardous cleanup and response efforts in regard to discharges affecting navigable waters. When CERCLA was passed in 1980, Congress directed that the National Contingency Plan be broadened to encompass a wide variety of emergency responses and substances. Included in the revised plan, published in 1982 at 40 CFR 300, is federal policy on responding to oil spills and other discharges not only into navigable waters but also at abandoned and/or uncontrolled hazardous waste sites. The plan, authorized under section 105 of CERCLA, is the only set of federal regulations that has been issued under the superfund law.

The plan establishes the National Response Team to oversee the federal response to emergencies involving hazardous substances. The team, headed by an EPA representative, is composed of representatives of the 12 federal agencies having authority to deal with health or environmental hazards. When the team is activated in a hazardous substance emergency, the representative of the federal agency with lead responsibility for the emergency becomes the leader. The plan also establishes Regional Response Teams to provide local assistance in an emergency, and provides for a system of on-scene coordinators. An on-scene coordinator is assigned to respond to each discharge into the environment and to assess what type of response is needed.

The plan also sets out how responsibilities will be divided among the federal agencies and outlines the functions of state and local governments and emergency response personnel in responding to hazardous substance discharges.

National Priorities List

One of the requirements of CERCLA is that EPA establish a list of abandoned or uncontrolled hazardous waste sites and update it annually. Using a rating system set out in the plan to determine the degree of hazard, EPA is to rank each site with respect to its priority for cleanup.

About 1,200 sites are on or have been proposed for the National Priorities List, set out as Appendix B of the National Contingency Plan (Appendix B, 40 CFR 300). Sites on the list are eligible for cleanup using superfund money. The agency has identified about 17,000 hazardous waste sites that are in need of cleanup, and expects that number to increase to about 22,000. Of the 22,000, about 2,000 will have to be cleaned up with superfund money, EPA estimates, with the remainder to be cleaned up by those responsible for disposal of the wastes.

Reporting and Responding to Discharges

Under CERCLA, spills or discharges into the environment of certain amounts of substances designated as hazardous must be reported immediately to the National Response Center, which was originally established under the Clean Water Act. The center will notify all appropriate government agencies, which will coordinate response to the discharge.

Listed Substances

Under the superfund law, the following substances are considered hazardous:

- Hazardous wastes listed in regulations issued under the Resource Conservation and Recovery Act (40 CFR 261)
- Hazardous substances listed in regulations issued under section 311 of the Clean Water Act (40 CFR 110, 112-114))
- Toxic pollutants listed in regulations issued under section 307 of the Clean Water Act (40 CFR 116, 117)
- Hazardous air pollutants listed in regulations issued under section 112 of the Clean Air Act (40 CFR 61)
- Imminently hazardous substances and mixtures regulated under section 7 of the Toxic Substances Control Act (none to date)
- Any additional substance that EPA designates as hazardous under CERCLA

Reportable Quantities

Section 102 of CERCLA establishes one pound as the reportable quantity for all listed substances, except that the 300 substances listed as hazardous under the Clean Water Act must be reported if discharged in the amounts stipulated under the CWA.

Because of the problem caused by use of the blanket "one pound" designation written into CERCLA, EPA in May 1983 proposed as an alternative a list of 696 substances that would be considered hazardous under the superfund law when spilled or discharged, and designated reportable quantities for each. The new proposed reportable quantity was based on the substance's degree of hazard when discharged and ranged from one pound to 5,000 pounds.

The list and accompanying new quantities, which became final in 1984, were required because the general "one pound" designation was impractical in many situations. For example, since copper is listed as a hazardous substance under CERCLA because it is on several of the lists incorporated by reference in CERCLA, a copper pipe falling from a truck and weighing more than one pound would be a reportable quantity and thus the "discharge" would have to be reported. The new proposed reportable quantity for copper would be 1,000 pounds, and the definition of "discharge" would take into consideration whether the substance was a solid mass.

Emergency Response Arrangements

As mentioned earlier, under CERCLA the party responsible for a release of a reportable quantity of a substance listed as hazardous must immediately notify the National Response Center. Originally established under the Clean Water Act, it is operated by the U.S. Coast Guard and maintains a 24-hour telephone line for reporting spills—(800)-424-8802. When the center is notified, lead responsibility for dealing with the release is immediately assumed by either the Coast Guard or EPA, depending on the location and type of emergency. In general, the Coast Guard handles responses to discharges that threaten navigable waters, while EPA deals with those into nonnavigable inland waterways and on land.

On-Scene Coordinator

When a discharge occurs, the lead agency, either EPA or the Coast Guard, appoints an on-scene coordinator (OSC) to coordinate and monitor all protective and precautionary activities in order to make certain that everything possible is done to protect public health and the environment. Upon reaching the scene of the discharge, the OSC assesses the nature and magnitude of the situation. A decision is then made on whether to (1) assist or monitor cleanup efforts by local officials and responsible parties, or (2) seek specialized assistance from federal agencies represented on the National Response Team.

Federal Response Groups

The superfund law establishes, under the National Contingency Plan, an Environmental Response Team and a National Strike Force (not to be confused with the National Response Team or National Response Center). The Environmental Response Team is composed of 11 experts with expertise in every discipline considered necessary in dealing with hazardous substances, and is part of EPA. The National Strike Force is a Coast Guard group with similar expertise in responding to emergencies in navigable waters. Both the team and the strike force are able to plan and conduct emergency operations, including scientific analysis, treatment of hazardous substances, and safety measures. The OSC may request the assistance of either the team or the strike force in dealing with an emergency if local emergency response groups lack the expertise needed to deal with the situation.

Cleanup and Cost Recovery

CERCLA provides a flexible national policy for responding to a wide variety of hazardous substance releases. In most cases, the cost of cleanup is paid for by the party or parties responsible for the release. The law, however, allows EPA to use superfund money to pay for cleanup when the discharger is unknown, when the discharge is caused by an act of God or war, or when the responsible party cannot or will not respond adequately.

Types of Responses

The superfund law authorizes three types of emergency responses for incidents involving release of hazardous substances: immediate removal, planned removal, and remedial actions. The first two were also authorized under the Clean Water Act but were modified with passage of CERCLA; the third was added when Congress enacted the superfund law in 1980.

Immediate Removal

Immediate removal may include cleanup of spills or installation of fencing or other barriers to contain a discharge. Generally, immediate removals are limited by CERCLA to a maximum time period and expenditure level of six months and $1 million respectively. The term refers to any action needed to be taken immediately to deal with a hazardous substance emergency, and can include evacuation of nearby inhabitants.

Immediate removal is called for when a hazardous substance release incident threatens significant harm to health, life, or the environment. For example, an immediate removal may be ordered to prevent fire or explosion, to prevent exposure of humans to acutely toxic substances, or to protect drinking water or a stream from contamination.

Planned Removal

A planned removal is an expedited response to a hazardous substance release situation when an immediate response is not needed. The same time and dollar limits apply as in the case of immediate removals.

Remedial Actions

Remedial actions are longer term (and usually more costly) actions to provide a permanent remedy for a hazardous substance situation.

Remedial actions may only be taken at sites listed on the National Priorities List of hazardous waste sites. Such actions may include sealing or capping a waste site, construction of drainage systems or leakage collection systems, or drilling of wells for monitoring, etc. In general, any action required to clean up a site may be authorized, including temporary or permanent relocation of residents.

Before authorizing a superfund expenditure for remedial actions, EPA generally attempts to get the responsible party to clean up the site voluntarily or to get the state or local government to take over most or all of the responsibility for site cleanup. The agency also tries to use legal action to force cleanup of the site. If none of these approaches works, the CERCLA fund may be used to pay for cleanup of a site. In such cases, EPA later will attempt to recover the cleanup cost through legal action.

Several conditions must be satisfied before a superfund remedial action can begin. The state must be willing to pay part of the cost, usually 10 percent, and must agree to maintain the site after cleanup is completed. Because of the nature of remedial actions, significant scientific study and analysis must be performed, much of it to determine the most cost-effective method for cleaning up the site and to decide how clean the site must be when the remedial action is completed.

The superfund may not be used to pay for removals if those responsible for the situation are already cleaning up the site. In practice, about 90 percent of all cleanup actions are performed by the responsible parties. Few of these cleanups, however, are at sites on the National Priorities List, a situation EPA is attempting to overcome. To do so, EPA is encouraging private parties to clean up listed sites and in 1983 adopted a policy stating that beginning to clean up a site (whether on the list or not) would not mean those undertaking action would be considered legally responsible for all cleanup costs.

Cost Recovery

In enacting CERCLA, Congress authorized EPA to take legal action to force those responsible for hazardous substance release situations to pay for cleanup.

Section 106 of the law allows EPA to issue administrative orders to require responsible parties to clean up the releases. The orders are enforceable by federal courts and those who fail to comply are subject to a $5,000 fine per day.

Section 107 of the law states that any party who transports or disposes of a hazardous substance in such a way that it is released or threatens to be released into the environment is liable for all costs of removal or remedial action to clean up the release and for legal damages for injury to or destruction of natural resources.

Limits of Liability

Under the law, liability of a responsible party is as follows:

- The total cost of an emergency response to deal with releases from waste facilities and other facilities that do not fall in one of the other categories below, plus $50 million for damages covered under the law
- Up to $5 million for releases from any vessel that carries a hazardous substance as cargo or residue
- Up to $500,000 for releases from other vessels
- Up to $50 million for releases from any motor vehicle, aircraft, pipeline, or rolling stock

Liability is waived, however, if the release is caused by an act of God, an act of war, or an act or omission of a third party other than an employee or agent of the responsible party.

Liability is tripled if the responsible party fails to perform a removal or remedial action ordered under the law.

Legislation (S. 1557) was introduced in 1991 to protect cities from third-party lawsuits. The bill would give municipalities legislative relief from lawsuits by large corporations seeking financial contributions for cleaning up municipal garbage at superfund sites. EPA plans to develop national guidelines to allocate cleanup costs and a model settlement agreement for municipalities.

Fund in Action

Key to the operation of the superfund law is the concept of "responsible party." In the case of a chemical spill or accident, the party who caused the spill is fairly easy to identify; the government then can force the responsible party to clean up the spill or can proceed against the party for cost recovery if the government carries out the cleanup. The situation is different with uncontrolled or abandoned waste disposal sites. Frequently dozens or even hundreds of persons or companies contributed wastes to the site. Some of them contributed hazardous substances, while others disposed of trash or other nonhazardous substances in the site.

Since the Resource Conservation and Recovery Act now requires that records be kept of hazardous waste disposal activities (see chapter on RCRA), identifying who is responsible for a more recently established uncontrolled site will be relatively simple in the future. In the meantime, EPA under CERCLA has inventoried some 36,000 older uncontrolled waste sites and has identified up to 2,000 sites (of which about 1,200 of the worst have been put on the National Priorities List) where cleanup under the superfund law may be needed. Cost estimates for cleaning up those sites range from $8 billion to $16 billion, but it is expected that the responsible parties, rather than the superfund, will bear much of the expense.

For each of those older sites, EPA will have to identify the parties responsible for having placed the hazardous substances in the site. Once EPA identifies these persons, it frequently can negotiate a cleanup plan with them, thus avoiding depletion of superfund monies. For example, 246 firms that disposed of wastes at a site in Indiana have agreed to pay $2.9 million to clean up the site, with the agreement formalized as an EPA administrative order.

If responsible firms are not willing to negotiate a cleanup settlement, EPA can force them to pay through court action. Cleanup of sites where responsible parties cannot be determined or where the responsible parties are out of business or no longer exist will be paid for from the CERCLA fund.

In June 1992, EPA issued guidelines to allow small-volume waste contributors at superfund sites to reach early settlements with the federal government. The agency said it is encouraging these early "de minimus" settlements to reduce the number of parties that EPA must negotiate with for site cleanups.

Lender Liability

EPA issued a rule in April 1992 designed to shield private and governmental lending institutions from liability for hazardous wastes at facilities in which they hold a security interest (57 FR 18344).

The issue of lender liability came to a precipitous head with the May 1990 federal appeals court ruling in *U.S. v. Fleet Factors Corp.*, 901 F.2d 1550, 31 ER Cases 1465 (2d Cir. 1990); *cert. denied*, 111 S.Ct. 752 (1991). In that case, the U.S. Court of Appeals for the Second Circuit held that a secured creditor may be liable, without being a facility operator, if it participates in the management of a facility "to a degree indicating a capacity to influence the corporation's treatment of hazardous wastes."

Congress considered legislation in 1990 to change CERCLA's language on liability, and EPA promised to issue a rule on the subject. In its February 1991 draft proposal, EPA said the court's language on creditors' management activities was not a legally binding precedent.

The final rule specifies a range of activities that lenders can take to manage and protect their collateral without being held liable under CERCLA. It also establishes when a financial institution is considered to be participating in management of contaminated property and therefore liable. Lenders are able to foreclose and sell the collateral without being considered the "owner" or "operator" of the collateral.

The potential liability of government agencies that involuntarily acquire property as part of the assets of failed or insolvent lending and depository institutions was also addressed. The Federal Deposit Insurance Corporation and the Resolution Trust Corporation have the same security interest exemptions as the failed institution.

In July 1992, Michigan and the Chemical Manufacturers Association challenged the EPA rule (*Michigan v. EPA*, No. 92-1312 (11th Cir.); *Chemical Manufacturers Association v. EPA*, No. 92-1314 (11th Cir.)). Michigan is arguing that EPA went beyond its authority to interpret CERCLA in the rule when the agency created liability exemptions for secured creditors. The chemical industry trade group is raising substantive and procedural objections to the rule, saying CERCLA gives the agency rule-making authority only in the area of the National Priorities List, not in liability. The American Bankers Association has said it would intervene in support of the rule.

Many senators in the 102d Congress believed that further legislation was needed to give lenders even more protection than the EPA rule provides. In July 1992, the Senate passed a bill containing an amendment to shield municipalities and lenders from cleanup liability at superfund sites. The bill (S. 2733) was designed to improve the regulatory structures of the Federal National Mortgage Association and the Federal Home Loan Mortgage Association.

AMENDMENTS AND REAUTHORIZATION

Major amendments and the reauthorization of CERCLA occurred in 1986 with passage of the Superfund Amendments and Reauthorization Act (Pub. L. No. 99-499, October 17, 1986) (SARA). The amendments made major changes in the original law by adding strict cleanup standards that strongly favor permanent remedies at waste sites, stronger EPA control over the process of reaching settlement with parties responsible for waste sites, a mandatory schedule for initiation of cleanup work and studies, individual assessments of the potential threat to human health posed by each waste site, and increased state and public involvement in the cleanup decision-making process.

The amendments kept the concept of strict, joint, and several liability, which EPA has found to be its most powerful enforcement tool in inducing responsible parties (landowners, owners, and operators) to clean up waste sites. The law also codified many existing agency enforcement practices that evolved under the first five years of CERCLA.

The reauthorization provided $8.5 billion over five years to EPA and other federal agencies for the cleanup of abandoned and inoperative waste sites. These funds were raised through a $2.5 billion broad-based tax on business income and a sharply increased tax on petroleum. Taxes on chemical feedstocks were raised to $1.4 billion, from $1.2 billion in the original law.

A major change in the law was the passage of required cleanup schedules. Under the amended law, EPA was required to begin cleanup activities at 175 superfund sites by October 17, 1989, with work underway at 375 sites by 1991. It was required to begin 275 remedial investigation and feasibility studies by October 1989. This goal represented an effort by Congress to speed the pace of the program.

The agency said it had begun actual cleanup at 178 sites and had performed 318 remedial investigations and feasibility studies by the deadline. Controversy arose when the agency's inspector general said the numbers were overstated because of the criteria it used to determine what constituted when work was begun. EPA Administrator William Reilly defended the agency's work, saying it had begun remedial action at more than 600 of 1,200 sites identified for remedial action.

The 1986 law established formal procedures for settlements between EPA and responsible parties to ensure that agreements are embodied in consent decrees lodged before a federal court and are subject to public review and comment before being made final.

Health Studies

Due to concern over the dearth of information on the health effects of toxic waste for people who live near superfund sites, Congress greatly expanded the role of the Agency for Toxic Substances and Disease Registry (ATSDR), which was created under the original law. ATSDR not only performs health assessments at each superfund site, but also prepares lists of toxic substances, does toxicological profiles, and performs research on health effects.

Emergency Planning

The Resource Conservation and Recovery Act provides a framework for the safe storage, transport, and disposal of hazardous chemicals, and CERCLA provides a means of cleaning up hazardous waste sites. A third facet of industrial safety was emphasized when a release of methyl isocyanate in Bhopal, India, in December 1984 killed an estimated 2,000 people and injured many more.

The Bhopal disaster gave great impetus to a need for catastrophe planning and preparedness. SARA contains, in addition to the amendments to CERCLA, a self-contained law—Title III—the Emergency Planning and Community Right-to-Know Act.

The act requires companies that make, process, or use chemicals to:

- Work with community groups that must be set up under the law to define how government, the public, and the firms themselves should respond to chemical emergencies.
- Provide information, including the disclosure of information on hazardous chemicals that are used or stored at a plant site, and help the local groups develop emergency response plans.
- Notify the local groups if an extremely hazardous chemical is released into the environment.
- Provide for each plant site general information on all chemicals that are considered hazardous under the Occupational Safety and Health Administration's Hazard Communication Standard, and be prepared to provide more detailed chemical data upon request.
- Submit lists or copies of Material Safety Data Sheets on all chemicals falling under the OSHA standard to the community groups.
- Produce an annual inventory of toxic chemicals that each facility routinely releases into the environment, including data on the average volume of the chemical on hand and the quantities and method of emission. Annual reports must be sent to EPA and the states.

In November 1986, EPA issued a list of 369 chemicals that it considers to be extremely hazardous (called the Chemical Emergency Preparedness Program (CEPP) list) and required companies to report if they have any of the chemicals on hand above a set threshold. The reporting thresholds range from 2 to 10,000 pounds depending on the toxicity of the chemical.

The law also provides for emergency notification of the community if a hazardous chemical is released into the environment. Notice must be given immediately for releases of any CEPP list or superfund list chemicals above EPA release threshold.

Part IV

Chemical Transport Laws

Hazardous Materials Transportation Act
(HMTA)

AT A GLANCE

Public Law Number: Pub. L. No. 93-633

U.S. Code citation: 49 USC 1801 *et seq.*

Enacted: January 3, 1975; effective when enacted
  Amended: 1976, 1979, 1981, 1983, 1990 (major amendments Pub. L.
  No. 101-613)

Regulations at: 49 CFR 106, 107, 171–179

Federal agency with jurisdiction: Department of Transportation (DOT)

Congressional committees/subcommittees with jurisdiction:
  House of Representatives: Surface Transportation Subcommittee of the
    Public Works and Transportation Committee, Transportation
    and Hazardous Materials Subcommittee of the Energy and
    Commerce Committee
  Senate: Surface Transportation Subcommittee of the Commerce, Sci-
    ence, and Transportation Committee

BNA reporting service: *Chemical Regulation Reporter, Daily Environment
  Report*
  Text of law appears in *Chemical Regulation Reporter* Hazardous Ma-
    terials Transportation binders at 215:1001 *et seq.*
  Text of regulations appears in *Chemical Regulation Reporter* Hazard-
    ous Materials Transportation binders

What HMTA regulates and why: The act gives authority to the Secretary
  of Transportation to regulate hazardous materials transportation in
  intrastate, interstate, and foreign commerce. Hazardous materials

that are shipped by road, rail, air, or water must be correctly packaged, labeled, marked, and placarded. In addition, hazardous materials loads must be handled according to instructions laid out by DOT's Research and Special Programs Administration (RSPA).

The law originally was enacted in 1975 to prevent the release of dangerous chemicals that threaten public safety and health. The current law also is designed to protect the life, property, and the environment from unintentional releases. Today DOT estimates that 4 billion tons of regulated hazardous materials are transported annually in the United States, and about 500,000 U.S. shipments of hazardous materials occur each day.

Under HMTA, RSPA shares regulatory authority with the Federal Highway Administration, the Federal Railroad Administration, the Federal Aviation Administration, and the U.S. Coast Guard, all DOT agencies. Transport of single-mode shipments are enforced by the corresponding DOT modal agency (for example, air shipments are enforced by the Federal Aviation Administration). RSPA enforces hazardous materials shipments transported by more than one mode (for example, by air and highway). RSPA also promulgates and enforces nonbulk packaging requirements, and shares jurisdiction with other modal agencies.

Various types of accidents and releases of reportable quantities of a substance listed as hazardous must be immediately reported to the National Response Center at (800) 424-8802. Information necessary for immediate handling of spills (such as, how to identify contents, how to contact shipment owner) is available to registered members toll-free from CHEMTREC, a service of the Chemical Manufacturers Association (CMA), at (800) 424-9300.

Latest developments: In 1990, HMTA was reauthorized by Congress, which made significant changes to the statute for the first time since it was enacted in 1975. These changes seek to achieve greater uniformity of hazardous materials transportation rules at the federal, state, and local levels. Training of hazardous materials employees is required to prevent releases of such materials during loading, unloading, and transport. Training of emergency response officials is being enhanced to improve incident coordination, and a national registration system is being established for shippers, carriers, and possibly package manufacturers.

Hazardous Materials Transportation Act—Contd.

In 1991, RSPA issued a final rule called HM-181, which represents the biggest changes to the hazardous materials transportation rules since they were consolidated under DOT in 1967. The new rule adopted a performance-oriented approach to packaging, eliminating most of the construction specifications for nonbulk packaging. The rule also changed the classification system of hazardous materials, basing the new system on United Nations provisions.

COVERAGE OF THE LAW

The Hazardous Materials Transportation Act (HMTA), which became law in 1975, gives the Department of Transportation (DOT) authority to regulate the movement within the United States of substances that may pose a threat to health, safety, property, or the environment when transported by air, highway, rail, or water. Only substances shipped in bulk by water are excluded, being regulated instead by the U.S. Coast Guard under the Ports and Waterways Safety Act of 1972 (see part V for summary of PWSA).

More than 30,000 hazardous materials are regulated under HMTA. These include explosives, flammables, oxidizing materials, organic peroxides, corrosives, gases, poisons, radioactive substances, and etiologic agents (materials causing disease in humans). Hazardous substances and wastes, although regulated by EPA under the Clean Water Act; the Comprehensive Environmental Response, Compensation, and Liability Act; and the Resource Conservation and Recovery Act (see chapters on CWA, CERCLA, and RCRA), are considered subgroups of hazardous materials regulated under HMTA when transported, and are then subject to the corresponding DOT regulations.

Rules issued under HMTA require special packaging, labeling, handling, placarding, and routing when materials shipped in commerce are listed as hazardous. These requirements apply within the United States, and are based on the system recommended by the United Nations.

On December 20, 1990, RSPA issued a final rule that completely revamped the domestic hazardous materials transportation packaging regulations. The rules were revised to correspond more closely with international regulations that took effect worldwide January 1, 1991.

The U.S. final rule—commonly called HM-181, after the docket number assigned by DOT—adopted performance packaging requirements for containers carrying hazardous materials. RSPA disposed of 400 pages of rules, mostly small-package construction specifications, that gave hazardous materials shippers and package-makers detailed instructions on how to construct drums, boxes, and other packages designed to carry hazardous materials.

The new performance packaging rules are designed to allow shippers flexibility in choosing a package. Performance packages must meet certain tests corresponding to the degree of hazard of the material to be shipped, but the rules do not specify exact manufacturing instructions.

In addition, the new U.S. rules adopted the U.N. classification scheme, dividing hazardous materials into nine classes. Though the classification system is similar to that of the old U.S. rules, some criteria have changed. To be sure that a hazardous material is classified correctly, a shipper should test its materials for flash point, boiling point, toxicity, pressure, corrosivity, and other chemical characteristics.

The new rules took effect October 1, 1991, but very few provisions were immediately required. The only provisions that took effect in 1991 are classification and communication requirements for new explosives and classification requirements for materials poisonous by inhalation. Under the new regulations, the words "Poison-Inhalation Hazard" or "Inhalation Hazard" are required to appear on all shipping papers identifying those materials.

October 1, 1992, is the effective date for all hazard communication requirements for materials poisonous by inhalation, and classification and communication requirements for infectious substances (etiologic agents).

Classification and communication requirements for all other regulated materials take effect October 1, 1993. Also on this date, packaging requirements for materials poisonous by inhalation are effective, as are modal segregation requirements.

After October 1, 1994, the manufacture of most DOT-specification packages is prohibited. That is, a package that does not meet the performance tests cannot be marked or certified for hazardous materials service. Also on this date, placarding requirements take effect.

Packaging manufacturers and shippers have until October 1, 1996, to deplete the supply of DOT-specification packages.

Other transitional period provisions allow packages that were filled prior to October 1, 1991, to be transported under the old requirements until October 1, 2001.

During this transition period, shippers and carriers may mix and match most of the old provisions with most of the new requirements. For example, a specification package can be shipped marked and labeled under the new requirements. Most any combination of old and new requirements are allowed until each effective date passes.

DEVELOPMENT OF THE LAW

When the HMTA was passed in 1975, it consolidated almost a century of hazardous materials transportation regulations. These rules had been enacted piecemeal, with each mode of transport (highway, rail, air, water) subject to a different set of requirements. In practice, this meant that a shipment that traveled by several modes was subject to several different sets of labeling, packaging, and handling regulations.

After passage of the act a new division within DOT, the Research and Special Programs Administration (RSPA), was created and given authority over all intermodal transport. Within this division was the Materials Transportation Bureau (MTB). All hazardous materials regulations for all modes of transport—plus exemptions, registrations, and packaging requirements—were drafted by MTB. This assured requirements were uniform, although enforcement of regulations covering hazardous materials traveling by a single mode of transport is the task of the DOT branch with jurisdiction over that mode. In addition, MTB enforced regulations other than those applicable to a single mode of transportation.

As of November 1985, MTB was abolished and all of these authorities and functions were assumed by RSPA, and under it, the Office of Hazardous Materials Transportation.

History of Transport Rules

The original hazardous materials rules were developed by the railroads following the Civil War because of a proliferation of poorly identified and packaged explosives and ammunition transported by train. The regulations were drafted by the Bureau of Explosives, a division of the Association of American Railroads.

In 1908 Congress passed the Explosives and Other Dangerous Articles Act, vesting regulatory authority in the Interstate Commerce Commission (ICC) and authorizing the Bureau of Explosives to help the ICC develop regulations. Initially, the ICC simply adopted the regulations used by the railroads but it subsequently expanded them in the early 1900s to include flammable liquids, compressed gases, and other hazardous materials.

The goal of these early regulations was to assure use of proper containers for the substance being shipped and to make sure those handling it were aware of the hazard posed. These goals, according to DOT, were based on the common law precept, still accepted, that the common carrier is the insurer of goods in transit but the shipper (*i.e.*, the party submitting the goods to the carrier for shipment) may be liable for damage or injury in transit if the carrier was not adequately warned of the hazard involved. This "duty to warn" precept is involved in injury and/or damage litigation under many environment and safety laws. In the hazardous materials area, the method of providing a warning usually takes the form of entries on shipping papers and identifying marks on packages.

According to DOT, the early regulations thus were a codification of the relationship between carriers and their customers. Over the years, other modes of transport were added to the ICC regulatory scheme.

Creation of the CAB, DOT

In 1938, Congress passed the Civil Aeronautics Act to govern air carriers. The Civil Aeronautics Board (CAB) developed the first air hazardous materials regulations in the early 1940s by simply cross-referencing the rail requirements adopted by the ICC but originally developed by the Bureau of Explosives. The bureau retained this rule-writing function until 1967, when the Department of Transportation Act created the DOT.

The new agency took over the hazardous materials functions of the ICC and CAB and placed them under one of the newly created modal authorities—the Federal Aviation Administration, the Federal Railroad Administration, or the Federal Highway Administration. The U.S. Coast Guard also was transferred into DOT, but retained the regulatory authority over transport by water that it still holds today.

Each of the administrations had authority over transport in its mode and was prohibited from delegating that authority outside its area. The result was that shipments traveling by several different modes (*i.e.*, air and highway, railroad and highway) had to comply with several sets of requirements and might be inspected by several different authorities.

In 1974, the Secretary of Transportation sought to have the fragmented approach to regulation of hazardous materials transportation centralized. The HMTA was enacted on January 3, 1975, to facilitate this goal.

The law authorized the secretary to issue regulations that apply to "any person who transports, or causes to be transported or shipped, a hazardous material, or who manufactures, fabricates, marks, maintains, reconditions, repairs, or tests a package or container which is represented, marked, certified, or sold by such person for use in the transportation in commerce of certain hazardous materials." The regulations promulgated by DOT through formal proposal and final rulemaking may govern "any safety aspect" including "packing, repacking, handling, labeling, marking, placarding, and routing (other than with respect to pipelines) of hazardous materials, and the manufacture, fabrication, marking, maintenance, reconditioning, repairing, or testing of a package or container which is represented, marked, certified, or sold by such person for use in the transportation of certain hazardous materials."

The new law consolidated hazardous materials rulemaking and container approval and gave the secretary the power to delegate authority over specific hazardous materials situations to DOT branches.

Reauthorization of HMTA

Though some attempts had been made in the early 1980s to reauthorize the act, Congress was not successful until HMTA was

15 years old. In the 101st Congress, about 30 bills were introduced to amend the law. But only a few proposals—those that called for sweeping changes—were taken seriously.

Key provisions that lawmakers addressed included required emergency response training, tougher preemption standards for state and local laws, highway routing, and national registration. Up until Congress passed the Hazardous Materials Transportation Uniform Safety Act (HMTUSA) in the waning hours of the 101st Congress, consensus on those issues still was being hammered out.

As the reauthorization was enacted, important new provisions require DOT to establish a national registration system for people involved in hazardous materials transportation. DOT proposed in an October 1991 *Federal Register* notice (56 FR 51294) that those subject to register with the department annually include chemical manufacturers and carriers of certain quantities of radioactive materials, the most sensitive explosives, materials toxic by inhalation, and bulk hazardous materials.

Congress suggested registrants pay a fee of between $250 and $5,000. It required the final rule to be issued by March 31, 1992, but built in a six-month extension. A final rule issued by RSPA July 9, 1992, requires shippers and carriers of hazardous materials to register with DOT and pay an annual registration fee of $300 (57 FR 30620). This fee provision took effect August 31, 1992. Under the rule, foreign shippers and carriers also are subject to the registration requirements and must comply by assigning a U.S. representative.

The money RSPA collects from the registration fees will be used to give grants to state and local governments to plan for emergency response and to train firefighters to respond to hazardous materials incidents.

Congress gave RSPA more power in HMTUSA to decide preemption issues. The law made binding the agency decisions on preemption of state and local laws, and also established five hazardous materials transportation activities that fall under exclusive federal jurisdiction. If state or local governments want to regulate hazardous materials transportation in any of the five designated areas, the rules have to be "substantively the same" as the federal language. All other state or local rules must pass the obstacle and dual compliance tests the agency has used for 15 years in deciding preemption.

Congress also authorized DOT to establish highway routing guidelines for restricting or designating the roads on which hazardous materials shipments can be transported. State and local governments must follow these federal standards in establishing restricted or preferred routes. Congress created a dispute resolution process to protect against "exporting" hazardous materials shipments from one jurisdiction to another. The Federal Highway Administration was delegated the authority to establish those guidelines, and the agency was working on the proposed rules as of mid-1992.

Modal Administrations

The delegations of authority subsequently made by the secretary left RSPA plus the four other DOT administrations with specific functions as shown below:

- *RSPA.* This organization, with its Hazardous Materials Safety Office, drafts and issues hazardous materials regulations, exemptions, registration certificates, and packaging and container certifications for all transport modes. RSPA also oversees intermodal enforcement and pipeline safety. Other functions of RSPA include transportation research, transportation crisis management, and safety training.
- *U.S. Coast Guard.* This organization carries out inspections and enforcement of regulations governing shipping of hazardous materials by vessel. It also has regulatory and exemption authority for bulk transportation of hazardous materials by water, and authority under the Clean Water Act and the Comprehensive Environmental Response, Compensation, and Liability Act to respond to releases of oil and hazardous substances into water (see chapters on CWA, CERCLA).
- *Federal Aviation Administration.* This body carries out inspection and enforcement for air shipments of hazardous materials.
- *Federal Highway Administration.* Primarily through its Motor Carrier Safety Office, this organization carries out inspection and enforcement functions relating both to transport of hazardous materials by road and to the manufacture and use of containers used in bulk transportation by highway. It also cooperates with the ICC on highway routing of hazardous materials shipments and enforces motor carrier safety rules (49

CFR 390–397) and financial responsibility (insurance) requirements for carriers of hazardous materials and for other highway carriers (49 CFR 387).
- *Federal Railroad Administration.* This agency carries out inspection and enforcement activities for rail shipments of hazardous
materials, regulates manufacture and use of containers for
bulk rail shipments, and cooperates with the ICC on rail routing of hazardous materials shipments.

PROVISIONS OF THE LAW

Regulations under the HMTA require that all shipments of
hazardous materials be packaged, labeled, and transported in accordance with requirements based on the nature of the material.
Specific responsibilities fall on the shipper of the material, the
carrier of the shipment, and the manufacturer of the shipping
container or packaging material.

Under the act, RSPA designates materials as hazardous under
49 CFR 172 and imposes requirements on all shippers under 49
CFR 173. Other sections of the DOT rules deal specifically with
shipments by rail (49 CFR 174), air (49 CFR 175), water transport
vessel (49 CFR 176), or highway (49 CFR 177); set forth container
specifications (49 CFR 178); and list requirements for tank cars (49
CFR 179).

Under the act, DOT has authority to apply regulations to
anyone who transports, ships, causes to be shipped, or makes a
packaging that is sold for shipping hazardous materials in
commerce.

Provisions of the HMTA include:

- Requirements that shippers classify, package, mark, label, placard, and provide shipping papers for hazardous materials
shipments
- Requirements that carriers of hazardous materials transport
the shipment in line with DOT rules, and respond appropri-
ately to spills and other emergencies
- Standards for manufacture of approved containers
- Enforcement through inspections by local, state, and federal
officials

Shipper Requirements

Shippers, including brokers and freight forwarders, are the main group responsible for assuring compliance with the HMTA. It is the shipper who makes the decisions that affect the actions of carriers, emergency response personnel, and others handling hazardous materials. A shipper is anyone who offers a hazardous material for transportation or anyone who performs a shipper's packaging, labeling, or marking function. Rules promulgated by RSPA set out the requirements for shippers.

The shipper must carry out the following activities, discussed in grater detail below:

- Classify the shipment according to DOT requirements
- Select a proper shipping name
- Select authorized and effective packaging
- Mark the package with a variety of information
- Label the package in accordance with 49 CFR 172
- Describe the shipment on the shipping paper
- Certify compliance with DOT regulations
- Give the materials to the carrier in proper condition for shipment

Classification

The first decision a shipper must make is what classification to assign the material being offered for transport. All later regulatory requirements are based on the classification.

The classification notifies all who handle the shipment or respond to an emergency how the substance must be dealt with. If the classification chosen is incorrect, then all other regulatory system requirements chosen by the shipper as having to be followed will be incorrect.

Each hazardous material must be classified according to the hazard it presents. Each class has certain packaging and handling requirements based on the classification to ensure the safety of the package during transport. In the rule changes under HM-181, the hazard classes were pared from 22 to 9 major classes. Because some classes are divided into more than one part, the classes are similar to the ones under the rules before HM-181 was made final, but are numbered after the U.N. classification system. They are:

Class 1

1.1 Explosives (with a mass explosion hazard)
1.2 Explosives (with a projection hazard)
1.3 Explosives (with predominantely a fire hazard)
1.4 Explosives (with no significant blast hazard)
1.5 Very insensitive explosives, blasting agents
1.6 Extremely insensitive detonating substances

Class 2

2.1 Flammable gas
2.2 Non-flammable compressed gas
2.3 Poisonous gas

Class 3

Flammable and combustible liquid

Class 4

4.1 Flammable solid
4.2 Spontaneously combustible material
4.3 Dangerous when wet material

Class 5

5.1 Oxidizer
5.2 Organic peroxide

Class 6

6.1 Poisonous material
6.2 Infectious substance (Etiologic agent)

Class 7

Radioactive material

Class 8

Corrosive material

Class 9

Miscellaneous material

Other hazardous materials that are regulated but do not fall into any of these classes include forbidden materials that are not allowed to be transported because they present too high a danger. On the other end of the scale are materials that are less dangerous that do not have to meet all the packaging and classification requirements. These are called *ORM-D materials*, a nomenclature left over from the old U.S. hazard classes. *ORM* stands for *other regulated material*.

Forbidden materials are listed in the Hazardous Materials Table in 49 CFR 172.101, and also are described in 49 CFR 173.21. ORM-D, which also are listed in the table, usually are consumer commodities, which may be materials that are regulated in another hazard class but that present little danger during transport because of their quantity, form, or packaging.

The definitions of each of the hazard classes are listed in 49 CFR 173.50–173.140.

It is important to identify correctly the substance being shipped, and then to refer to the hazardous materials table. The table provides the proper shipping name which must be written on shipping papers, the primary hazard class number, and any subsidiary risk labels that may be required.

Sometimes materials may present more than one hazard. When this occurs, shippers should refer to the Precedence of Hazards Table in 49 CFR 173.2.

Hazardous Materials Table

The hazardous materials table constitutes the meat of the regulations, listing the substances RSPA regulates by name. The table consists of 14 columns, giving information on the proper shipping name of materials, the hazard class or division, the U.N. or domestic number assigned to the material, labeling requirements, special packaging or handling requirements, packaging authorizations, quantity limitations, vessel stowage requirements, and designations for whether the requirements are intended for only domestic transport, only international, or both.

The proper shipping name is shown in roman type on the table and must appear on shipping papers that accompany the material in transit. Additional descriptive information follows the shipping name in italics and need not appear on the shipping papers.

Packaging

The entire approach to packaging hazardous materials for transportation was changed under the HM-181 provisions. The old regulations specified extensive construction requirements for each package. Today, however, the shipper and the package manufacturer have greater flexibility to design any type of package necessary for the material to be transported.

The same type of packages are authorized as under the old rules, but now they are described generically using U.N. codes. Types of packages that may carry hazardous materials include steel, aluminum, metal, plywood, fiber, and plastic drums and jerricans, with open or sealed tops; wooden barrels; aluminum, wood, plywood, fiberboard, and plastic boxes; plastic, film, textile, and paper bags. Composite and combination packagings are also authorized.

The major requirements nonbulk packagings must meet are certain performance tests spelled out in 49 CFR 178 to ensure that the packaging can withstand conditions of transportation. The packaging must be made and assembled so that it successfully passes the following tests while in transportation: drop, leakproofness, hydrostatic pressure, stacking, and cooperage. Documentation of each test must be maintained.

A package manufacturer is responsible for testing its products or having them certified by a third-party laboratory. Either is acceptable in the United States, though in other countries either the government tests them or a third party only.

The shipper is also responsible for the package performance in that the shipper must perform assembly functions—such as closure—correctly, as described by the package maker.

A package maker tests only design-type packages, which are models for each different type of package. Each package manufactured does not need to be tested. Certain variations in the design type may occur without retesting. Those selective testing variations are described in RSPA's Competent Authority notice 91-A.

A contentious provision in the U.S. regulations, which is not found in requirements in other countries, is a capability test for vibration. While the test does not actually have to be performed, DOT requires that packages must be able to withstand the vibration that occurs during transportation, especially by highway and rail.

DOT, following the U.N. system, has adopted a Packing Group system, in which packages can meet varying results of each test, depending on the hazard of the material intended to be transported in the package. Specifically, packing Group I is the strictest packaging group, and packages that carry the most dangerous materials must meet the most stringent results of the performance tests. Packing Group II is intended for packages that are designed to carry materials that present a medium danger when in transport. Therefore, Packing Group II packages must pass more stringent criteria than Packing Group III, but do not have to perform as well as Packing Group I. Packing Group III packages are intended to transport materials that pose a modest danger, and must meet the least stringent performance test requirements.

The regulations specify the packing groups of certain materials, giving shippers guidance about which packing group their materials might fall under, and what type of package is appropriate for a material in each packing group.

Some limited quantities of hazardous materials, and consumer commodities, do not have to be transported in performance packages. See 49 CFR 173.4.

Package Markings

The packages of all regulated materials must be marked to identify the package, the material, the package manufacturer, and other information listed in 49 CFR 178.3 and 178.503. The package maker is responsible for marking the package with a U.N. symbol, a code identifying the package type, construction material, a letter identifying the packing group, the gravity or mass for which the package has been tested, the test pressure for liquids, and the year the package was made. These marks, if they appear on packages that may be reconditioned, must be embossed—marked permanently—on the package to withstand the reconditioning process.

Other marks that are required on the package in durable—not necessarily permanent—form are the letters "USA;" the name and address or symbol of the package maker; and the minimum thickness of metal or plastic drums or jerricans intended for reuse.

Labeling

A label is a hazard warning that must be placed on the packages. Most hazardous materials packages must bear a label denoting one of the nine hazard classes. If more than one hazard exists for a material in a package, subsidiary risk labels also must be attached. For specific requirements on subsidiary risks, see 49 CFR 172.402.

The labels, which can be obtained from label manufacturers, usually contain a pictogram representing the type of hazard presented from the material corresponding with the hazard class. For instance, the label describing Class 3—flammable liquids—displays a flame symbol above the word "flammable liquid." Below the words appears the number 3, denoting hazard Class 3.

Shipping Papers

Each shipment of hazardous materials must be accompanied by documentation that identifies the substance being shipped. In most cases, the shipper prepares the shipping papers and gives them to the carrier. In cases where the shipper is re-shipping, the original source must provide the information. The carrier (in many cases a freight forwarder or agent) may copy the information onto other documentation but must comply with the same content and order requirements imposed on shipper-originated shipping papers. In most cases, the shipping papers are combined with the bill of lading or other document that accompanies any package shipped by a carrier.

If the hazardous materials are shipped by highway, the shipping papers must be kept next to the driver, either on the seat or in a pocket in the door. If the driver leaves the truck, the papers must be placed on the driver's seat or in the door pocket or pouch where they can be found in case of emergency. Railroad crews keep the hazardous materials shipping papers for shipments by rail. Aircraft pilots carry both the shipping papers and a notification that hazardous materials are aboard. For shipments by water, the master of the vessel carries the shipping papers with the vessel manifest.

Information Required

The information that must appear on shipping papers, specified in 49 CFR 172, must appear in a particular order. The hazardous materials must be described in terms of quantity, proper shipping name from the hazardous materials table, hazard class, and United Nations (U.N.) or North America (N.A.) identification number (also from the DOT table). The identification numbers are keyed to emergency response information contained in the DOT *Emergency Response Guidebook*. The *Guidebook* classifies materials by hazard and proper method of emergency handling, and informs those who respond to an emergency of the proper actions to take.

Hazardous materials contained in mixed shipments of hazardous and nonhazardous materials must be highlighted on shipping papers, and must appear first on the papers or be specially marked so that they are easily recognizable.

New requirements, recently adopted by DOT, require that the shipper place on the shipping paper a phone number of a person familiar with the shipment who is able to give emergency response information in case of an incident. The telephone number must be someone's direct number, so that an emergency response official can reach the person in one attempt. The designated person must be available at the number when the shipment is in transport. This requirement is watered down from the original RSPA proposal that the person be available 24 hours a day.

If a shipper is registered with the Chemical Manufacturers Association (CMA) it may use the telephone number to CMA's CHEMTREC program, a national data base system listing materials and their hazards, and emergency response information.

Shipper Certification

Most shipping papers must also contain a statement signed by the shipper that the shipment meets all DOT hazardous materials requirements. Specific wording for the certification is contained in the hazardous materials rules (49 CFR 173).

Hazardous Wastes

When shipped, all hazardous wastes that are regulated by EPA must be accompanied by a uniform hazardous waste manifest. The shipper provides this manifest to the carrier. The manifest must accompany the waste while in transit; a copy of it is returned to the shipper by the person to whom the waste is shipped.

The manifest form is published at 40 CFR 263. Its content is explained in the chapter on the Resource Conservation and Recovery Act.

Placarding

DOT requires that placards be placed on each end and on each side of trucks, railroad cars, portable tanks, and intermodal containers carrying hazardous materials. A placard is a color-coded, diamond-shaped sign that identifies by word and/or by pictograph the hazard posed by the hazardous materials shipment. The symbols on the placards are the result of international standardization of such warnings. As exceptions, shipments of limited quantities of materials, ORM-classified materials, and etiologic agents need not be placarded. Highway shipments that contain less than 1,000 pounds of hazardous materials also do not require placards; aircraft are never placarded.

The shipper and carrier share the responsibility for proper placarding. The shipper provides the proper placard to the carrier. If the carrier is combining the shipment with others, the carrier must determine the proper placard to apply to the vehicle.

DOT specifies what each placard must look like. Most placards contain a picture representing the hazard. Under HM-181 changes, the hazard class name is optional for every hazard class except radioactive materials—Class 7. The class or division number is required on the bottom corner of each placard. Carriers may use placards that meet the U.N. recommendations or the International Civil Aviation Organizations regulations codified in the Transport of Dangerous Goods.

Certain hazard classes and certain vehicles have special placarding requirements. Refer to the placarding regulations in 49 CFR 172.519.

Carrier Requirements

Carriers may be private, common, or contract haulers of hazardous materials shipments. The carrier may not accept hazardous materials that are not in proper condition for shipment. The carrier must check to make sure that none of the packages accepted are leaking or damaged, and must verify that shipping papers, labeling, and marking are consistent.

Carriers also are responsible for seeing that their vehicle is properly placarded, that labels are not obliterated in transit, and that cargo is loaded properly. Some hazardous materials must be segregated from other cargo or may not be carried next to, on top of, or with certain other hazardous or nonhazardous materials. For example, some hazardous materials cannot be carried in a vehicle that contains food shipments.

The separation and segregation requirements are codified in 48 CFR 174.81.

Under the rule changes in HM-181, more strict requirements are placed on keeping poisons away from foodstuffs. Those separation requirements will be expanded when RSPA issues a final rule mandated under the Sanitary Food Transportation Act (Pub. L. No. 101-500). Concern about carriers loading solid and hazardous wastes and hazardous materials into the same vehicle that carried edibles on alternate trips led Congress to enact legislation on food transportation.

RSPA was delegated the lead authority on developing the rules, which will list the foods that are and are not compatible with transport in the same vehicle as other materials. The agency issued an advance notice of proposed rulemaking in February 1991 (56 FR 6934), and as of mid-1992 was still analyzing public comments.

The RSPA administrator asked the Food and Drug Administration commissioner in December 1991 to consider taking the lead on the rulemaking, but RSPA continued to move ahead with the rule assuming the negotiations with FDA will not change the current status.

Spills and Emergencies

Carriers of hazardous materials are responsible for filing an incident report with DOT within 15 days if *any* quantity of hazardous materials is spilled or discharged in transit. The report must be sent to DOT on the agency's "Incident Report" form. Spills of consumer commodities in the ORM-D class, of electric storage batteries, and of certain paints and related materials are exempt from this reporting requirement.

Accidents that result in death, severe injury, property damage in excess of $50,000, or severe environmental impact must be reported immediately to the National Response Center. The center operates 24 hours a day and may be reached by calling (800) 424-8802. Releases of reportable quantities (as defined under CERCLA) of hazardous substances into the environment and discharges of oil into navigable waters also must be reported immediately to the National Response Center. The center will coordinate emergency response to the discharge. More information on the center and on spill response procedures is contained in the chapter on CERCLA.

Emergency Assistance

Information necessary for immediate handling of spills, such as how to identify the contents of leaking packages and how to contact the owner of the shipment, is available toll-free from CHEMTREC, a service of the Chemical Manufacturers Association (CMA), by calling (800) 424-9300.

CMA operates a two-part voluntary initiative to improve emergency response planning and training at the local level and to expand industry's capability to provide direct assistance to fire, police, and medical personnel responding to chemical emergencies. The two parts of the program are as follows:

- The Community Awareness and Emergency Response (CAER) program reviews and establishes emergency response plans and involves private citizens in meshing an industrial facility's emergency plans with similar emergency preparedness already established in the surrounding area.
- The National Chemical Response and Information Center is intended to provide "hands on" assistance in response to chemical emergencies, a chemical hazard information referral service, and training for those first on the scene of a chemical emergency. Basically the center is expanding CHEMTREC to enable it to respond to nontransportation emergencies, to provide first aid advice, and to provide data on specific chemicals.

Under DOT regulations, carriers are only required to report the spill. EPA, however, makes the carrier responsible for the cost of damage and cleanup in cases of spilled hazardous substances or hazardous wastes (see chapter on CERCLA).

All motor vehicle carriers, including those transporting hazardous materials, must comply with DOT requirements concerning motor vehicle operation, driver qualification and hours of service, parking, and actions to be taken in emergencies. These rules are promulgated by the Bureau of Motor Carrier Safety and are published at 49 CFR 390–399.

Enforcement

The HMTA allows DOT to impose civil and criminal penalties, compliance orders, and imminent-hazard orders, as explained below, to force compliance with hazardous materials regulations.

- *Civil penalties* are the most common enforcement tool. Fines of up to $25,000 per violation are authorized, with shippers and carriers liable for fines of up to $25,000 per day for continuing violations. A minimum penalty of $250 was established under the HMTUSA.
- *Compliance orders* are used to require the violator to take specific actions to halt a violation of the hazardous materials rules.
- *Imminent-hazard orders* are issued in cases where an imminent public hazard exists and immediate corrective action is necessary.

In most cases, penalties are negotiated after the agency takes into account the nature of the violation, the degree of culpability, ability to pay, and history of prior offenses. Penalties assessed often are a few hundred dollars and involve such violations as transporting a hazardous material without proper shipping papers or packaging or placarding a hazardous material incorrectly.

As mentioned earlier, the DOT rail, highway, and aviation administrations and the Coast Guard carry out enforcement of the hazardous materials regulations for shipments involving their specific transport mode, while RSPA enforces rules applicable to multimodal transport. RSPA's enforcement thus is focused on container manufacturers, testers, and reconditioners and on rules that apply to shipments traveling by more than one transport mode. Enforcement actions usually begin with an inspection of a hazardous materials shipment or facility. The inspection of shipments frequently is carried out by state officials, often the state police.

Conflicts With State or Local Requirements

Under the HMTUSA, RPSA's role in state and local regulations increased dramatically. The inconsistency ruling procedures the agency developed after the 1975 act were bolstered to implement Congress' goal of national uniformity.

RSPA's inconsistency rulings formerly were advisory. In the HMTUSA, Congress included a preemption determination process that makes those decisions binding. Also, state and local governments, as well as American Indian tribes, must issue regulations in five areas that do not substantially differ from the federal rules:

- Classification of hazardous materials
- Hazardous materials packing, handling, and communication
- Shipping documents
- Written notification of releases
- Packaging

These are the five areas of exclusive federal jurisdiction. State and local governments and Indian tribes may issue regulations in other areas that are not substantively the same as the federal rules, but these regulations must meet the dual compliance and obstacle tests DOT used under the 1975 act to make inconsistency rulings.

The implementation of the beefed up preemption determination process has affected pending inconsistency rulings and appeals. Parties who had applications or appeals pending when the reauthorization was enacted were notified by the agency and given the chance to refile under the new system or withdraw their applications or appeals.

Already the agency has received new applications for preemption determinations, and at least one is a challenge of a state's highway routing designation, which the Federal Highway Administration will handle for the first time.

The tougher preemption standards have helped the agency in court actions. A long-running suit between the Department of Energy (DOE) and Colorado's Public Utilities Commission (*Colorado Public Utilities Commission v. Department of Energy* (10th Cir. 1989)) was settled in December 1991. DOE was fighting for the right to make shipments to and from its Rocky Flats plant, where it produced plutonium triggers, without the constraints of restrictive state hazardous materials transportation requirements. In several areas, according to DOT and DOE, the state rules went beyond the federal rules. The court ruled in favor of DOE, saying that national uniformity is the key to safe transportation of hazardous materials. Much of the decision was based on Congress' goal embodied in HMTUSA of a uniform set of rules in the United States.

FUTURE UNITED NATIONS ACTIVITY

Performance-oriented packaging standards were developed by the United Nations in the early 1980s, but they did not take effect until January 1, 1991. The United States changed its hazardous materials transportation rules to accommodate the U.N. system in the interest of safety and international commerce.

The United States is active in the United Nations' ongoing efforts to improve its recommendations. The performance packaging standards are only one chapter of a 17-chapter book of recommendations on hazardous materials transportation.

DOT plans to change domestic regulations to incorporate U.N. recommendations as appropriate. Future topics include criteria for the corrosives hazard class, emergency response information requirements, and rules on intermediate bulk containers.

Although the DOT officials do not promise that the domestic regulations will mirror the U.N. recommendations, they are quite similar. In the areas that differ from the U.N. recommendations, DOT usually claims a more stringent safety standard.

The U.N. recommendations are updated every two years. The international modal agencies for air and water, and for road and rail in Europe, adopt the recommendations as law in international commerce. Many of those regulations are acceptable for transport in the United States.

Part V

Other Laws Affecting Chemicals

Consumer Product Safety Act
(CPSA)

Public Law Number: Pub. L. No. 92-573

U.S. Code citation: 15 USC 201 *et seq.*

Enacted: October 27, 1972
> *Amended:* 1976, 1978, 1980, 1981, 1983, 1990 (reauthorization Pub. L. No. 101-608)

Regulations at: 16 CFR 1000–1406

Federal agency with jurisdiction: Consumer Product Safety Commission (CPSC)

Congressional committees/subcommittees with jurisdiction:
> *House of Representatives:* Commerce, Consumer Protection, and Competitiveness Subcommittee of the Energy and Commerce Committee
> *Senate:* Consumer Subcommittee of the Commerce, Science, and Transportation Committee

BNA reporting service: *Product Safety and Liability Reporter*
Text of law appears in Reference File at 21:0101 *et seq.*
Text of regulations appears in Reference File

What the CPSA regulates and why: The goals of the act are to assist consumers in evaluating the safety of consumer products, to protect the public against unreasonable risks associated with consumer products, to develop uniform safety standards for consumer products, and to research and prevent product-related deaths, illnesses, and injuries.

Consumer Product Safety Act—Contd.

Under the act, the CPSC maintains product safety information, promulgates safety standards, bans unsafe products, and requires recalls or corrective action for unsafe products.

Standards promulgated under the act may require specific labeling, design, packaging, or composition of products intended for sale to the public.

Chemical regulations include rules on consumer uses of asbestos and formaldehyde and on labeling of hazardous substances such as paints and cleaning compounds.

The act also requires manufacturers, importers, distributors, and retailers to notify the commission immediately if they receive information that one of their products fails to comply with a product safety rule or may contain a defect that could create a substantial product hazard.

Latest developments: The CPSA was reauthorized in 1990, the first time in nine years that the statute had undergone extensive changes. As with any major reauthorization, the passage through Congress was not without its controversies.

The significant changes to the statute are aimed at allowing the Consumer Product Safety Commission to run more effectively, resulting in safer products for the public. Before the reauthorization, the commission was fraught with financial shortfalls and was forced to reduce its force from five to three. When the chairman resigned, the commission comprised only two members, not enough for a quorum. Congress changed the quorum rules so that when there are only three commissioners, a quorum is two. When there are only two commissioners, a temporary quorum of two can be used for six months so the agency can function when there are vacancies.

One of the major differences between the House and Senate versions of the legislation was a reporting requirement for any product manufacturer who has been sued for product liability. The differences were ironed out in conference, and the final legislation established a new requirement for any firm to file a report with the agency if its product has been the subject of three product liability suits within a two-year period.

The commission's regulatory process should function more quickly under a new requirement that the commission issue a proposed consumer product safety rule within a year after an advance notice of the rulemaking has been issued. The CPSC also was charged with studying the feasibility of requiring industry to pay user fees for the commission's services.

The 12-month deadline to issue proposed rules should improve the role of voluntary standards by giving industry an incentive to develop voluntary standards more rapidly. Also, the commission has the flexibility to extend a rulemaking deadline if the development of a voluntary standard is proceeding efficiently and in good faith. The amendments require the commission to consider public comments on voluntary standards and to develop procedures to monitor compliance with voluntary standards.

Civil penalties were increased for the first time since 1972. The maximum fine for each violation jumped from $2,000 to $5,000, and the maximum penalty for aggregate violations increased from $500,000 to $1.25 million. The amendments provide for automatic adjustments for inflation every five years. The same civil penalty changes were made to the Federal Hazardous Substances Act and the Flammable Fabrics Act.

Enforcement powers for state attorneys general were extended to apply to the rules under the Federal Hazardous Substances Act and the Flammable Fabrics Act, with a 30-day advance notice to the commission, the U.S. Attorney General, and potential defendants. The state attorneys general already can seek injunctive relief for violations of CPSA.

The statute also addressed certain individual products. For example, the commission must establish a safety standard for cigarette lighters considering the need to protect children from harm. In addition, the commission is required to study exposure to indoor air pollutants, and must set standards for automatic garage door openers.

The study was to be completed in 1992.

Federal Hazardous Substances Act
(FHSA)

Public Law Number: Pub. L. No. 86-613

U.S. Code citation: 15 USC 1261 *et seq.*

Enacted: July 12, 1960; effective when enacted
  Amended: 1966, 1969, 1970, 1972, 1976, 1978, 1981, 1983, 1984, 1990

Regulations at: 16 CFR 1500–1512

Federal agency with jurisdiction: Consumer Product Safety Commission (CPSC)

Congressional committees/subcommittees with jurisdiction:
  House of Representatives: Commerce, Consumer Protection, and Competitiveness Subcommittee of the Energy and Commerce Committee
  Senate: Consumer Subcommittee of the Commerce, Science, and Transportation Committee

BNA reporting service: *Product Safety and Liability Reporter*
  Text of law appears in Reference File at 91:0101 *et seq.*
  Text of regulations appears in Reference File

What the FHSA regulates and why: The act, which began as a cautionary labeling law, allows the CPSC to ban or regulate hazardous substances produced for use by consumers. Under the law, the commission has labeling authority over consumer products that meet established definitions as being toxic, corrosive, flammable, irritant, or radioactive.
  Under the law, the CPSC may require special labeling for hazardous household substances, require removal of substances from

248

Federal Hazardous Substances Act—Contd.

the consumer market, or ban substances deemed to be too hazardous for consumer use. Among the substances covered are turpentine, charcoal, cleaning fluids, alcohols, fireworks, fire extinguishers, anti-freeze, toys, bicycles, and infant cribs.

Flammable Fabrics Act
(FFA)

Public Law Number: 88, Chapter 164 (83rd Congress)

U.S. Code citation: 15 USC 1191 *et seq.*

Enacted: June 30, 1953
  Amended: 1954, 1967, 1972, 1976, 1978, 1980, 1981, 1990

Regulations at: 16 CFR 1602–1632

Federal agency with jurisdiction: Consumer Product Safety Commission (CPSC)

Congressional committees/subcommittees with jurisdiction:
  House of Representatives: Commerce, Consumer Protection, and Competitiveness Subcommittee of the Energy and Commerce Committee
  Senate: Consumer Subcommittee of the Commerce, Science, and Transportation Committee

BNA reporting service: *Product Safety and Liability Reporter*
  Text of law appears in reference File at 91:1101 *et seq.*
  Text of regulations appears in Reference File

What the FFA regulates and why: The act provides the regulatory vehicle for regulating the flammability of fabrics used in clothing, children's sleepwear, mattresses, carpets and rugs, and vinyl plastic film.
  Under the act, the CPSC sets flammability standards and provides guidelines for testing and rating fabrics to certify that the fabrics burn at a rate less than or equal to that specified in the applicable standard.

Poison Prevention Packaging Act
(PPPA)

AT A GLANCE

Public Law Number: Pub. L. No. 91-601

U.S. Code citation: 15 USC 1471–1476

Enacted: December 30, 1970; effective when enacted
  Amended: 1972, 1976, 1981, 1983

Regulations at: 16 CFR 1700–1704

Federal agency with jurisdiction: Consumer Product Safety Commission
  (CPSC)

Congressional committees/subcommittees with jurisdiction:
  House of Representatives: Commerce, Consumer Protection, and Competitiveness Subcommittee of the Energy and Commerce Committee
  Senate: Consumer Subcommittee of the Commerce, Science, and Transportation Committee

BNA reporting service: *Product Safety and Liability Reporter*
  Text of law appears in Reference File at 91:2101 *et seq.*
  Text of regulations appears in Reference File

What the PPPA regulates and why: The act authorizes the CPSC to establish special packaging standards for household substances in order to discourage children from handling, using, or ingesting hazardous substances. Among substances that must be packaged in child-resistant containers are turpentine, most prescription drugs, methanol, antifreeze and other products containing ethylene glycol, sulfuric acid, aspirin and certain other nonprescription drugs, furniture polish, and kindling/illuminating preparations such as charcoal and cigarette lighter fluids.

Ports and Waterways Safety Act
(PWSA)

Public Law Number: Pub. L. No. 92-340

U.S. Code citation: 33 USC 1221 *et seq.*

Enacted: July 10, 1972
    Amended: 1978 (Pub. L. No. 95-474, Port and Tanker Safety Act),
    1990 (Pub. L. No. 101-380)

Regulations at: 33 CFR 160–165, 46 CFR 71, 91

Federal agency with jurisdiction: Coast Guard, Department of Transportation (DOT)

Congressional committees/subcommittees with jurisdiction:
    House of Representatives: Coast Guard and Navigation Subcommittee
    and Merchant Marine Subcommittee of the Merchant Marine
    and Fisheries Committee
    Senate: Commerce, Science, and Transportation Committee and Environment and Public Works Committee

BNA reporting services: *Environment Reporter* and *Chemical Regulation Reporter*
    Text of law appears in *Environment Reporter* Federal Laws at 71:5941
    et seq.
    Text of regulations appears in *Chemical Regulation Reporter* Hazardous Materials Transportation binders

What the PWSA regulates and why: The act provides authority for the Coast Guard to regulate the movement, operation, and maintenance of ships and similar vessels operating in the navigable waters of the United States. The goal of the act is to protect human health, property, and the marine environment from operational accidents and hazardous substances transported by water. The act provides for notification before entering a U.S. port, forbids carriage of certain substances, and prescribes safety equipment and inspection procedures.

Latest developments: After the *Exxon Valdez* spill, in which a tanker spilled thousands of gallons of oil in Alaska's Prince William Sound, Congress enacted the Oil Pollution Act in August 1990. The law is designed to help prevent similar accidents, to provide for federal response, and to establish liability standards.

The act has 10 titles. The Ports and Waterways Safety Act was one statute of several amended by title II of the massive Oil Pollution Act.

Under the amendments the Secretary of Transportation was given more authority to regulate vessel operating requirements, including vessel equipment, communications systems, and routing systems.

The conditions for entry to ports also were amended. Entry to U.S. ports is forbidden under the amendments unless a vessel is staffed by one or more officers licensed by a government with licensing and certification standards that are comparable to or more stringent than those of the United States.

Criminal penalties under the act are considered Class D felonies. Willfull and knowing violation of the rules by using a dangerous weapon, or engaging in conduct that causes bodily harm or fear of imminent bodily injury to any officer is considered a Class C felony.

Natural Gas Pipeline Safety Act
Hazardous Liquid Pipeline Safety Act
(NGPSA, HLPSA)

AT A GLANCE

Public Law Number: Pub. L. No. 90-481, Natural Gas; Pub. L. No. 96-129, Hazardous Liquid

U.S. Code citation: 49 USC 1671, 49 USC 2001

Enacted: August 12, 1968
Amended: 1972, 1974, 1976, 1979 (Pub. L. No. 96-129, adding title II regulating pipelines carrying hazardous liquid to the act's original provisions on pipelines carrying natural gas), 1988 (Pub. L. No. 100-561, imposing more stringent controls)

Regulations at: 49 CFR 190–195

Federal agency with jurisdiction: Department of Transportation (DOT)

Congressional committees/subcommittees with jurisdiction:
House of Representatives: Surface Transportation Subcommittee of the Public Works and Transportation Committee, Energy and Power Subcommittee of the House Energy and Commerce Committee
Senate: Surface Transportation Subcommittee of the Commerce, Science, and Transportation Committee

BNA reporting service: *Chemical Regulation Reporter*
Text of law appears in Hazardous Materials Transportation binders at 215:1201 *et seq.* (natural gas) and 215:1251 *et seq.* (hazardous liquids)
Text of regulations appears in Hazardous Materials Transportation binders

What the NGPSA and the HLPSA regulate and why: The acts provide the regulatory vehicle for DOT to set minimum safety standards for pipelines carrying natural gas, liquefied natural gas, or hazardous liquids. Included are design, welding, operating inspection, and repair requirements and reporting requirements for accidents and leaks.

Regulations under the law are drafted and enforced by the Office of Pipeline Safety (OPS), Research and Special Programs Administration, DOT.

Latest developments: Congress was considering major amendments to the NGPSA and the HLPSA in the 102d Congress, even though DOT was working to complete studies and rules mandated under the 1988 amendments.

The full Senate passed the legislation, as did the House Energy and Commerce Committee. The House Public Works Committee marked up the bill in June 1992, and made major changes to the proposed legislation. Staff members from both committees were working out the differences as of mid-1992.

As the bills read at press time, the Office of Pipeline Safety (OPS) in DOT's Research and Special programs Administration would have to consider environmental protection—not just public safety—in developing rules. Both bills call for identification of environmentally sensitive areas where pipelines operate, and impose various environmental requirements for those pipelines.

Several safety standards would be developed, such as requiring gas pipelines to be installed with excess flow valves that automatically shut off flow of gas when a surge occurs. So-called "smart pigs"—instrumented internal inspection devices—also would have to be installed in some pipelines to detect corrosion that leads to leaks. While the pipeline safety office has spent years studying these two safety devices, neither has yet been proven to provide reliable benefit without an exorbitant cost to industry if required in all pipelines.

Pipelines that operate at 20 percent or less of their specified minimum yield strength would be subject to the federal pipeline safety rules, from which they are now exempt, if the legislation is passed. DOT was considering the elimination of this exemption.

Abandoned pipelines would be subject to OPS's jurisdiction if either the Senate or House version is passed. Louisiana lawmakers are concerned that the abandoned lines—which are purged of natural gas or hazardous liquid, filled with water, and sealed shut—create an obstacle to navigation in the Gulf of Mexico. OPS is studying the issue in conjunction with other relevant federal agencies.

White House Chief of Staff and former Secretary of Transportation Samuel Skinner warned Congress that if the legislation passes as it was proposed, he would recommend that President Bush veto it.

In 1990 Congress enacted legislation requiring underwater pipelines to be buried properly to prevent exposed pipelines from becoming a hazard to navigation. The legislation was prompted by an accident in which a fishing vessel collided with an exposed underwater pipeline in the Gulf. The explosion killed all 11 crew members on board.

The 1990 legislation applies only to those pipelines in the hurricane-prone Gulf of Mexico, which often become exposed from the seabed and cause a hazard to navigation. OPS issued the final rules in December 1991 implementing Congress' mandate to require the proper inspection and burial of underwater pipelines (56 FR 63764).

The reauthorization bills pending in the 102nd Congress would expand the requirements to the remaining 5 percent of the pipelines in other U.S. waters.

Glossary

As in any specialized subject matter, a specialized vocabulary has evolved in the fields of environmental and chemical regulation. In addition, abbreviations or acronyms are often used. The definitions that follow are intended to provide a guide to these terms and abbreviations.

ACGIH   American Conference of Government Industrial Hygienists.

Ambient air quality standard   A basic standard for concentration of a particular air pollutant.

Best Available Demonstrated Control Technology (BADCT)   Used for new industrial sources of pollution, essentially a zero-discharge requirement.

Best Available Technology (BAT)   Most stringent level of control technology for existing dischargers.

Best Conventional Technology (BCT)   More stringent level of control technology than BPT.

Best Engineering Judgment (BEJ)   Best professional judgment used to set permit limits on effluents not covered by regulations.

Best Practicable Technology (BPT)   Minimum acceptable effluent treatment for discharge of water pollutants.

CAA   Clean Air Act.

Carcinogen   A substance that causes cancer.

CEPP   Chemical Emergency Preparedness Program.

CERCLA   Comprehensive Environmental Response, Compensation, and Liability Act (superfund law).

CFCs   Chlorofluorocarbons.

CFR   Code of Federal Regulations.

CHIP   Chemical Hazard Information Profile.

CPSA   Consumer Product Safety Act.

CPSC   Consumer Product Safety Commission.

CWA   Clean Water Act.

Delaney Clause   A provision of the Federal Food, Drug, and Cosmetic Act banning the intentional addition to food of substances known to cause cancer in animals.

DOT   U.S. Department of Transportation.

Effluent guidelines   Minimum standards for pollutant discharges into water by specific categories of industry.

EPA   U.S. Environmental Protection Agency.

ER Cases   Environmental Reporter Cases (published by BNA).

FDA   Food and Drug Administration.

FFA   Flammable Fabrics Act.

FFDCA   Federal Food, Drug, and Cosmetic Act.

FHSA   Federal Hazardous Substances Act.

FIFRA   Federal Insecticide, Fungicide, and Rodenticide Act.

FR   Federal Register.

FWPCA   Federal Water Pollution Control Act (Clean Water Act).

Greenhouse effect   Retention of heat by the earth because of absorption by atmospheric gases.

Hazard communication standard   A right-to-know regulation that requires industrial users and processors of chemicals to warn their workers of hazards, to conduct training in the safe use of the materials, and to make available information on the chemicals contained in material safety data sheets.

Hazardous Materials Table   A table (at 49 CFR 172.101) summarizing regulatory requirements for shipping hazardous materials.

Health standards   Specific limits and conditions set by the Occupational Safety and Health Administration for use and exposure to certain chemicals in the workplace.

HLPSA   Hazardous Liquid Pipeline Safety Act.

HM-181   A 1990 DOT final rule issued under the Hazardous Materials Transportation Act that adopted the United Nations hazard classification system and performance packaging requirements for containers carrying hazardous materials.

HMTA   Hazardous Materials Transportation Act.

HMTUSA   Hazardous Materials Transportation Uniform Safety Act, the 1990 amendments to the HMTA.

IARC   The International Agency for Research on Cancer, based in Paris.

Interagency Testing Committee   A committee representing eight federal agencies set up under the Toxic Substances Control Act to set priorities for testing chemicals.

ITC   Interagency Testing Committee.

Lender Liability   Legal liability imposed on financial institutions that lend money for the purchase of real estate and thus hold a security interest in a property.

LUST   Leaking underground storage tank, regulated under the Resource Conservation and Recovery Act.

MACT   Maximum achievable control technology.

Material safety data sheets   Written information on chemicals, including identity, physical and chemical characteristics, health hazards, symptoms of exposure, precautions for safe handling, and emergency and first aid procedures.

MSDS   Material safety data sheets.

Mutagen   A substance that causes gene mutation.

NAS   National Academy of Sciences.

National Pollutant Discharge Elimination System   A procedure under the Clean Water Act for issuing permits that specify control equipment and discharge limits for facilities, taking into account water quality of the receiving waters.

NEPA   National Environmental Policy Act.

New source performance standard   An air quality standard set for new industrial sources of pollution to assure that ambient air pollution will not increase.

NGPSA   Natural Gas Pipeline Safety Act.

NIOSH   National Institute for Occupational Safety and Health.

NOx   Nitrogen oxides.

NPDES   National Pollutant Discharge Elimination System.

NSPS   New source performance standard.

NTP   The National Toxicology Program.

OMB   The White House Office of Management and Budget.

OPS   Office of Pipeline Safety, part of DOT's Research and Special Programs Administration.

ORM   Other Regulated Material, used to describe categories of hazardous substances under the Hazardous Materials Transportation Act.

OSHA   Occupational Safety and Health Administration.

OSH Act   Occupational Safety and Health Act.

OSH Cases   Occupational Safety and Health Cases (published by BNA).

PCBs   Polychlorinated biphenyls.

Performance packaging   Packages for which exact manufacturing instructions are not specified. Instead, they must meet certain tests that correspond to the degree of hazard of the materials to be shipped in them.

Pesticide residue tolerance   An allowable concentration of pesticide residue concentration, set by the Food and Drug Administration for processed foods and the Department of Agriculture for unprocessed meat and agricultural products.

Pheromone   A sex attractant; its action may be exploited in pesticides.

PMN   Premanufacture notice under the Toxic Substances Control Act.

Point source   A well-defined source of water pollution, such as a discharge pipe at a particular facility.

POTW   Publicly owned treatment works.

PPPA Poison Prevention Packaging Act.

Premanufacture notice A requirement under the Toxic Substances Control Act to notify EPA before introducing a new chemical into commerce.

Pretreatment standards Required treatment of industrial wastewater before it can be sent to a publicly owned treatment works.

Primary air quality standard An air quality standard necessary to protect public health.

Primary drinking water standard A drinking water quality standard required to protect health.

Primary treatment Wastewater treatment removing 35 percent of oxygen-demanding pollutants.

Proper shipping name The name used for a substance in the Hazardous Materials Table, which must be used in that form on shipping papers and labels.

PRP Potentially responsible party [for cleanup under the Comprehensive Environmental Response, Compensation, and Liability Act].

Publicly owned treatment works Municipal wastewater treatment plants as regulated by the Clean Water Act.

PWSA Ports and Waterways Safety Act.

RACT Reasonably available control technology.

RCRA Resource Conservation and Recovery Act.

Rebuttable presumption against registration A process for reviewing pesticide registration in which EPA announces its intent to begin a special review. Registrants have 30 days to dispute the agency's evidence of unreasonable risk.

Registration Pesticide products must be registered with EPA, which must determine their efficacy and safety.

Reportable quantity The quantity of a hazardous substance for which reporting of a spill or discharge is required.

Reregistration A review of older pesticide products to ensure that they meet current, more stringent health and safety testing requirements.

Research and Special Programs Administration The authority in the Department of Transportation that drafts and issues hazardous materials regulations.

Restricted use Pesticide use may be restricted to application by certified applicators.

RPAR Rebuttable presumption against registration (see above).

RQ Reportable quantity.

RSPA Research and Special Programs Administration.

SARA Superfund Amendments and Reauthorization Act, major amendments to the Comprehensive Environmental Response, Compensation, and Liability Act (1986).

SDWA Safe Drinking Water Act.

Secondary air quality standard An air quality standard, more stringent than a primary standard, which protects the public welfare.

Secondary drinking water standard A drinking water quality standard required to assure acceptable color, taste, odor.

Secondary treatment Wastewater treatment removing at least 85 percent of pollutants.

Significant new use rule EPA, under the Toxic Substances Control Act, must be notified of any significant new use of a chemical. EPA may as a result require restrictions on production volume, worker exposure, or uses.

SIP State Implementation Plan under the Clean Air Act.

Small-quantity generator A category of waste generators defined under the Resource Conservation and Recovery Act made up of generators of hazardous wastes in quantities between 100 kilograms and 1,000 kilograms per month.

SNUR Significant new use rule.

Special pesticide registration Conditional registration may be issued pending reregistration; special local need and experimental-use permits are also issued.

Stage II Systems Devices installed on gasoline pumps designed to collect vapors when vehicles are refueled.

State Implementation Plan An EPA-approved plan for a state to conduct enforcement and issuing of permits of sources of air pollution.

Substantial risk Section 8(e) of the Toxic Substances Control Act requires that EPA be notified whenever a study or event indicates that a chemical may cause a health or environmental problem.

Superfund A federal trust fund established to pay for cleaning up hazardous waste sites. The Comprehensive Environmental Response, Compensation, and Liability Act is also referred to as the superfund act.

Teratogen A substance that causes birth defects.

Test rule A regulation issued under the Toxic Substances Control Act to require testing of a chemical substance for long-term health or environmental effects.

Toxic The use of the word is specialized in the Toxic Substances Control Act to refer to substances that may present a long-term threat to human health or the environment: carcinogens, mutagens, and teratogens.

TSCA Toxic Substances Control Act.

TSP Total suspended particulates; a measurement used in water quality standards.

UIC   Underground Injection Control.

Underground Injection Control   A program under the Safe Drinking Water Act, state enforced, controlling subsurface discharge of pollutants that may contaminate groundwater.

U.N.   United Nations.

USC   United States Code.

VOCs   Volatile organic compounds.